A BIRDWATCHING GUIDE TO DOÑANA

(The hidden Doñana)

John Butler

Trafford
PUBLISHING™

A BIRDWATCHING GUIDE TO DOÑANA
(The hidden Doñana)

Is published by Trafford Publishing

Order this book online at www.trafford.com/07-0594
or email orders@trafford.com

Most Trafford titles are also available at major online book retailers.

© Copyright 2007 John Butler
Maps by John Butler
Map enhancement and graphics by Oliver Seville. www.outworldvisions.com
Cover illustration by Rebecca Butler

Note for Librarians: A cataloguing record for this book is available from Library and Archives Canada at www.collectionscanada.ca/amicus/index-e.html

Printed in Victoria, BC, Canada.

ISBN: 978-1-4251-2192-1

We at Trafford believe that it is the responsibility of us all, as both individuals and corporations, to make choices that are environmentally and socially sound. You, in turn, are supporting this responsible conduct each time you purchase a Trafford book, or make use of our publishing services. To find out how you are helping, please visit www.trafford.com/responsiblepublishing.html

Our mission is to efficiently provide the world's finest, most comprehensive book publishing service, enabling every author to experience success. To find out how to publish your book, your way, and have it available worldwide, visit us online at www.trafford.com/10510

⌁ Trafford
PUBLISHING™ www.trafford.com

North America & international
toll-free: 1 888 232 4444 (USA & Canada)
phone: 250 383 6864 ♦ fax: 250 383 6804 ♦ email: info@trafford.com

The United Kingdom & Europe
phone: +44 (0)1865 722 113 ♦ local rate: 0845 230 9601
facsimile: +44 (0)1865 722 868 ♦ email: info.uk@trafford.com

10 9 8 7 6 5 4 3 2

Contents

Author's Note   5

Introduction   7

The Northern Sector   36

Centro De Visitantes Dehesa Boyal 37
Laguna San Lázaro 41
Laguna De Mancho Zurillo, Laguna De Quema
and The Corredor Verde De Guadiamar 43
The Dehesa de Pilas And The Dehesa De Banco 49
Arroyo De Las Cigüeñas / Los Labrados 53
The Entremuros... 54
The Isla Mayor Rice Fields 57
The Reedbeds 60
Dehesa De Abajo / Cañada De Rianzuela................... 63
The Gravel Pits 66
Cantarita Ricefields...................................... 69
Cortijo De Los Madrigales and The Puente de Vaqueros 72
Casa De Bombas (The pump house)........................74
Huerta Tejada 77
Lucio Del Lobo (Pool of the wolf)......................... 80
Centro De Visitantes "José Antonio Valverde" (Cerrado Garrido)... 82
Caño De Rosalimán (Marismas de Hinojos) 85
Caño De Guadiamar 88
Hato Ratón Rice Fields and Partido De Resina................ 91

The Eastern Sector   94

Isla De Los Olivillos..................................... 95
Brazo Del Este 98
El Lago De Diego Puerta 104
Salinas De Bonanza 106
Laguna Tarelo 108
Pinar De La Algaida.....................................110
Salinas De Monte Algaida 112
El Puntal, The East Bank Of The Río Guadalquivir 115

The Southern Sector 118

La Madre De Las Marismas Del Rocío 119
Boca Del Lobo 122
Puente De Canaliega 122
Puente De Ajolí / Arroyo De Las Cañadas 123
Camino De Moguer 125
Centro De Visitantes La Rocina 126
Palacio Del Acebrón 130
Centro De Visitantes "El Acebuche" 133
Matalascañas 136
Los Guayules 139
Arroyo De Santa Maria 144
The Villamanrique De La Condesa Road 146

The Western Sector 149

Niebla Castle 149
Laguna Balestrera 151
Paraje Natural Marismas Del Odiel 154
Lagunas De Palos Y Las Madres 160
Estero De Domingo Rubio 164
The Río Tinto At La Rábida 167
Laguna El Portil 170
El Rompido and The Marismas de Río Piedras 173
La Ribera 176

Other Sites of Interest 180

The Doñana Bird List 189

Rare Birds List 223

Author's Note

For many years, Doñana has acted like a magnet, attracting birders from all over the world to what is surely one of Europe's most famous and productive wetland areas.

Although much has been written about birdwatching in Doñana, with some books containing information on several of the lesser-known birding sites in this bird-rich region, there has never been a fully comprehensive and in-depth book that has given visiting birders to Doñana the opportunity to explore the endless possibilities that exist here. The main purpose of this book is to make information available and to guide you to some of the finest and most productive birding sites in Europe. All of the information contained herein is based on my extensive knowledge and experience, gained after several years of living and working as a bird tour guide in this region, conducting hundreds of tours and guiding thousands of birders, with my own birding company, "Doñana Bird Tours". I believe that my intimate knowledge of the region, the birds, their migration patterns, their breeding grounds and their feeding habits, together with the effects of local climate changes, makes me suitably qualified to write the most comprehensive guide book to this region that has ever been produced.

Unfortunately, most visitors to Doñana only ever get to see the birding sites of El Rocío marshes and the well advertised visitors centres at La Rocina and El Acebuche, in the southern area of the region. As good as these sites may be, many birders leave Doñana with the feeling that it hasn't really lived up to their expectations. This is a vast area and there are dozens of excellent little-known areas where the full birding potential of the region can be realized. The majority of these are in the northern and eastern areas of the natural park, generally referred to by me as "the northern marshes". However, due to the lack of decent up-to-date maps and information leaflets, these sites are rarely found by the average visiting birder.

This book gives detailed information on almost 50 sites within the Doñana region, and although a few of these have been mentioned in other publications, most are new and are seldom found by visitors to the area. The precise directions and descriptions contained within will lead you right into the heart of this birdwatching wonderland and open up a treasure chest of previously un-recorded areas, where geese, ducks, flamingos, cranes, ibis, herons, egrets and waders gather to feed, roost and breed in their thousands. You will also find areas with high raptor densities and the breeding grounds of some of Europe's scarcest and most endangered species, such as the Red-knobbed Coot, the Marbled Duck and the Spanish Imperial Eagle. You will be able to discover for yourself the sites that I refer to as "the hidden Doñana".

Also contained within this book are a few sites, that although technically not a part of the Doñana region, are close enough and important enough to warrant their inclusion.

The vast majority of people who visit this region do so to see the birds and other wildlife. For this reason I am confining this book to those subjects. For those who wish to investigate the long history of the area, there are hundreds of alternative resources available.

In an effort to produce this book so that it can be sold at the most economical price, I have not included pictures of birds or any other superfluous images. The book is all about guiding you to the sites and helping you find the birds.

I sincerely hope you find this book both interesting and helpful in your quest for birds in one of the most ornithologically important wetlands reserves in Europe.

Good birdwatching!

John Butler.
Doñana Bird Tours.
Villamanrique.
41850 Sevilla.
Spain.

2007

Introduction

This book deals almost exclusively with the Doñana region of Andalucia, in southwestern Spain, and the wealth of birding sites that exist there. The vast wetland and dune systems, for which Doñana is famous, stretch through three provinces, Sevilla, Huelva and Cádiz. The Parque Nacional de Doñana is situated exclusively in the former two provinces, which also contains the largest area of the natural park. The natural park area in Cádiz province is relatively small in comparison, but holds some excellent birding sites, which should not be missed.

The Atlantic coastline *(Costa de la Luz)* stretches for over 100 kms between the estuaries of the Río Guadalquivir to the east and the Río Guadiana, which forms the Spanish/Portuguese border, to the west and forms the southernmost boundary to the region. The coastline is mainly un-developed, although there are several Spanish resort towns, such as Matalascañas, Mazagón, El Portil and El Rompido. They are usually very quiet during most of the year and only really come alive during the summer period between June and September.

The beautiful beaches are typical of the Atlantic coast, long, wide and with fine golden sand. The mainly deserted beaches, cliff tops and several estuaries and salt marshes offer good opportunities for sea-watching and discovering large flocks of resting gulls, terns and waders.

The human population of this extensive area is very low, with only about 200,000 inhabitants. The majority of these live in the city of Huelva and in numerous small towns and villages that are spread throughout the region. The main local economy comes from agriculture and vast areas are dedicated to the growing of oranges, strawberries, melons, potatoes, olives, beans, plums, peppers, sunflowers, avocados, grapes, rice and cotton. Much of the labour-intensive work on the farms is carried out by itinerant workers from the African continent and from eastern Europe.

As the economy does not rely on tourism, as it does in the other more popular resort areas along the Costa del Sol, the Costa Brava and Costa Blanca, the average income is a lot lower than in those areas. This is reflected in the fact that the cost of living is also much cheaper and you will find yourself paying a fraction of the price, for similar goods and services, that you would do in the tourism-minded regions.

Spanish is very much the language of the locals and outside of the cities you will find very few people who will speak English and even fewer who can converse in German, Dutch, French, etc. This should not necessarily cause major problems, as the Andalusians are among the most patient and friendliest people I have ever met and are always willing to go to great lengths to help strangers.

Introduction To Doñana

The Doñana National Park and the surrounding areas of the natural park of Doñana consist of almost 139,000 hectares (343,500 acres) of protected and semi-protected land and are situated in the southwestern region of Andalucia. The great diversity of habitats that exist hold significant numbers of mammals, rodents, amphibians, reptiles and fish species, along with about 750 plant species and vast numbers of moths, dragonflies and butterflies. The full list of bird species that have been recorded in the area is now over 360, although many of these have been vagrants and the true number of species that are regularly recorded is nearer to 275. The geographical position means that the area is likely to attract any vagrants or accidentals that may wander, or be storm-blown, into the region and many Spanish and European rarities have been recorded.

The importance of the entire Doñana region as a conservation site cannot be overstressed. Millions of wintering birds, mainly waterfowl and waders from the north, flock to this area each year, attracted by the mild climate and the abundant food supply. The region is also on a major migratory route for birds travelling from and to north and west Africa during the spring and autumn migration periods. It is estimated that up to six million birds pass through this region each year. It is also of major importance as a breeding ground for some of the scarcest and most endangered bird species in Europe, such as Marbled Ducks, Red-knobbed Coots and Spanish Imperial Eagles.

Parque Nacional de Doñana
The National Park

The national park of Doñana is situated in the south-eastern corner of the province of Huelva and the south-western area of the province of Seville. The terrain is mostly flat, with the highest point being only 47 metres above sea level. Land borders exist to the north and west of the park, whilst the Río Guadalquivir, to the east, and the Atlantic Ocean, to the south, form the other borders.

Following recent land purchases, the national park consists of 54,252 hectares (136,000 acres) of protected land, in which there are dune systems, forests of stone pine and cork-oaks, open scrubland and a vast area of seasonal marsh-land and lagoons, considered by many to be amongst the finest and most important wetland systems in Europe. For hundreds of years it was the royal hunting grounds (cotos), where kings, queens and other notable dignitaries would come to enjoy their sport. Then, in 1963, an area of 6,794 hectares of the land was purchased by the World Wildlife Fund to aid conservation and set up a scientific research station. It was declared a national park in 1969 and in 1978 more land was added. In 1981, certain areas of the park were turned into Biospheric Reserves and in 1982 it became a RAMSAR site. Then, in 1988, it achieved the status of a Special Protection Area for birds and finally, the park was declared a World Heritage Site in 1994.

The park management is now the responsibility of the Consejería de Medio Ambiente, the environmental agency of the Andalusian government and is a part of "Red Espacios Naturales Protegidos de Andalucía" (RENPA), the network of protected natural areas of Andalucía and entry into the park is restricted to tours operated by a licensed company, the "Co-operativa de Marismas del Rocío", using 21-seater safari vehicles. These tours last for approximately four hours and cover some 70 kilometres of trails along the Atlantic coast, the sand dunes and inside the park proper. Unfortunately, as interesting as these tours may be, they are not an ideal way to watch birds, insects or to study flowers, as the drivers, who mostly only speak Spanish, are on a schedule and cannot stop just because you have caught a fleeting glimpse of a "lifer" and would like to investigate it further. The main objective of these tours is to allow you to experience for yourself all of the various eco-systems that exist within the park

There are four visitors centres within the park that are open to the public and three of these should form a part of any visit to Doñana . The fourth, the José Antonio Valverde Visitors Centre, is many kilometres out into the Marismas del Guadalquivir and access can be difficult, unless you know the way. However, in recent years this has become a major breeding ground for Glossy Ibis, Squacco, Purple and Black-crowned Night Herons, Little and Cattle Egrets, Little Bitterns, Purple Swamphens and Red-knobbed Coots and any serious birder should make the effort to visit this site. Without doubt, in the spring, this centre and the surrounding marsh-land is one of the finest birdingwatching areas in Europe and is one of the regular highlights of my guided tours.

Parque Natural de Doñana
The Natural Park

The national park is further protected by some 84,200 hectares (208,000 acres) of surrounding natural parkland and by the Atlantic Ocean to the south, where over 30 kilometres of deserted sandy coastline forms the boundary. This buffer zone, the Parque Natural de Doñana, also benefits from protected status, but not to the same strict degree as the national park. Much of the protection and management of the natural park also comes under the umbrella of the "*Consejeria de Agencia de Medio Ambiente*" (AMA).

There is a great diversity of habitats within the natural park and these include streams, rivers, lagoons, beaches, saltmarshes, estuaries, forests, ricefields, pastureland, agricultural land and open heathland, all of which hold a wide range of bird species and other wildlife. Entry into these areas is largely un-restricted and there are various visitors centres with nature trails, where the general public are welcomed. All of the birds and other animals that exist within the boundaries of the park can generally be found at these sites, usually in greater numbers and at closer range.

Protected Areas

Throughout the areas covered by this book there are numerous sites that have been given varying levels of protection by the environmental agency of the Andalusian Government (AMA). The sites in question are usually well marked with cream and green signs every 100 metres or so, indicating the status of the protected area. The three levels of protection you are likely to encounter are:

The Parque Nacional de Doñana. The national park obviously receives the highest level of protection and entry into the park is strictly controlled and limited to organized conducted tours. Only a handful of local people are still permitted to work in the park, using traditional methods of collecting pine nuts, harvesting shellfish and burning charcoal.

Parque Natural. These are generally very large areas or nature parks which are open to the public. In this region they are mostly marshes, rivers, lagoons, forests and estuaries and form part of the pre-parque, or buffer zone, to the national park. In some cases there are information centres at these sites that offer leaflets and guides to the area. You may also find recreational facilities and signposted or colour-coded walking trails. Certain activities may be restricted and only selected planning permission for building is granted.

Paraje Natural. These are natural areas that can vary greatly in size and include similar sites to those mentioned above. Some may be fenced off and others may be open to the public, although certain activities may be restricted or prohibited.

Reserva Natural. This translates as a nature reserve and some of the sites may be fenced off to conserve the natural surroundings and wildlife, but all usually offer good opportunities for birdwatching.

The Birds

The current bird list for Doñana stands at over 360 recorded species of resident, summer and winter visitors, passage migrants and vagrants. The area is mainly a wetland site and the largest number of birds are usually present during the winter, when millions of ducks, geese, waders, herons, egrets and raptors arrive to escape the colder climates of the north to take advantage of the milder temperatures and the abundant food supply.

Most field guides inform you that many birds are only migratory summer visitors to Europe and will not be seen during the winter. This information is very outdated as, in fact, many species spend the winter in the Doñana region. These include Purple, Squacco and Black-crowned Night Herons, Little Bitterns, Black Storks, Short-toed and Booted Eagles, Black Kites, Egyptian Vultures, Sand and House Martins, Barn and Red-rumped Swallows and Reed Warblers.

The spring migration and the breeding seasons offer birders the chance to see many species of birds that have not been recorded, or are extreme rarities, in Britain and many other European countries. Amongst these I include Iberian (Azure-winged) Magpies, Squacco Herons, Little Bitterns, Cattle Egrets, Spoonbills, Glossy Ibis, Black Storks, Greater Flamingos, Ruddy Shelducks, Red-crested Pochards, Marbled and White-headed Ducks, Black-shouldered Kites, Spanish Imperial Eagles, Lesser Kestrels, Red-knobbed Coots, Purple Swamp-hens, Great and Little Bustards, Collared Pratincoles, Black-winged Stilts, Temminck's Stints, Slender-billed and Audouin's Gulls, Pin-tailed Sandgrouse, Great Spotted Cuckoos,

Red-necked Nightjars, White-rumped Swifts, Little Swifts, Bee-eaters, Rollers, Golden Orioles and a whole host of passerine species.

The Use of Bird Names

Over the last few years there has been a great increase in the use of pre-fixes before the names of some of the more common birds, such as the "European" Bee-eater, "Eurasian" Tree Sparrow, "Common" Kingfisher, "Northern" Gannet and "Western" Bonelli's Warbler. In the general text I have ignored these prefixes, but for the purists, and to avoid any confusion, in the "Birds of Doñana" and the "Doñana Rare Birds" sections at the back of this book, I have used the names officially used by the British Ornithologists' Union.

One grey area exists with the formerly named Azure-winged Magpie. Until recently, this bird was assumed to be the same species that exists in southeast Asia, but several years ago the fossilized remains of one of these birds was discovered near Los Barrios in Cádiz province. The fossil was given to the Gibraltar Ornithological and Natural History Society (GONHS) to perform tests on. The original theory as to why this bird only existed in two different geographical regions of the world, Asia and Iberia, supported the idea that the birds had been transported from Asia by Iberian seafarers some centuries ago and the birds had either been released, or had escaped, and formed a population in Spain and Portugal. A carbon dating test carried out by GOHNS showed the fossil to be about 44,000 years old and this immediately disproved the theory. So, could it have been that the birds originally existed here and were transported to Asia by the seafarers? To try to prove or disprove this line of investigation, researchers carried out DNA tests on Iberian birds and similar tests were performed on Asian birds. The DNA results showed that although the two magpies were almost identical in every aspect, ie. size, colour, feeding, breeding, habits, etc. they were so different genetically that they could not have come from the same stock.

The two birds have now been classed as separate species and as far as I know, the Asian birds will retain the nominate name of Azure-winged Magpie *(Cyanopica cyana)* and the Iberian species will take the Latin name of *Cyanopica cooki* and will be called either the Iberian Azure-winged Magpie or just the Iberian Magpie. It seems that the jury is still out on that one and the name has yet to be formally incorporated into the official European list, so I have used journalistic licence and referred to the birds by the shorter name of "Iberian Magpie".

Other Wildlife

Mammals. There are about 35 mammals that are recorded in Doñana and these include Red and Fallow Deer, Wild Boar, Badger, Hedgehog, Red Fox, Otter, Egyptian Mongoose, Genet, Wild Cat, Hare, Rabbit, Weasel and numerous species of rats, mice, voles and bats. The Iberian Lynx, of which there is now only an estimated world population of 130 (25 - 30 in the Doñana region), is in serious danger of extinction. The Lynx preys almost exclusively on rabbits and recent shortage of rabbits, due to outbreaks of myxomatosis, has had a drastic effect on the breeding success of this animal.

However, the greatest threat to the lynx is the automobile and 20 have been killed in road accidents in the last 6 years. Various traffic-calming measures have recently been introduced in an effort to try to stop the carnage, but even on roads, like the one between El Rocío and Villamanrique, where speed bumps, rumble strips, underpasses and fences have been introduced, the traffic still continues to flow at dangerous speeds, threatening the existence of the Lynx. Please drive carefully and at a reasonable speed at all times whilst in this region. By doing so, you may lose a few minutes of your birdwatching day, but by not doing so you may contribute to the extinction of a beautiful animal.

Reptiles. A good selection of reptiles can be found in the region and these include Lataste's Viper (venomous), Montpellier Snake, Grass Snake, Ladder Snake, Horseshoe Whip Snake, Mediterranean Spur-thigh Tortoise, Mediterranean Chameleon and European and Mediterranean pond Terrapins. Lizards and geckos abound and are perhaps the most common reptiles seen. Amongst these are the Spiney-footed and Ocelated Lizards, the latter growing up to one metre in length.

Amphibians. Numerous frogs and toads are present in the area and amongst these are Iberian Green, Common Tree and Marsh Frogs and Common and Natterjack Toads. Several species of newts and salamanders also live within the region.

Insects. There are thousands of different kinds of insects to be found in the Doñana region. These range from the unpleasant (to some), such as mosquitos, spiders, wasps, hornets, bees, centipedes, ants and scorpions, to the more attractive species which include butterflies, lacewings, dragonflies, cicadas, grasshoppers, crickets, moths, beetles and praying mantises.

Fish. About 20 species exist here and include Carp, Catfish, Chub,

Trout, Pike, Roach, Barbel and eels. Also present are crabs, shrimps and crayfish.

Travelling To The Doñana Region

The national park of Doñana is situated in the two provinces of Sevilla and Huelva, in the southwestern area of Spain. The nearest airports are Sevilla, Jerez de la Frontera (Cádiz) and Faro (Portugal). Numerous low-cost airlines operate flights to each of these and bargain seats for just a few euros have been found in the past.

The region is serviced by an excellent road system, regardless of which direction you approach it from. Assuming, that like most visitors to Doñana, you will be heading for El Rocío, the following directions will lead you to that town.

From the north, east or south of the country, or from Sevilla airport, you should head for Sevilla and as you approach the city, look out for and follow signs for the A-49 to Huelva. Continue along the A-49 until you reach junction 48 (at km 48), which is signed for Almonte and P.N. Doñana. Turn off here and then follow the A-483, which will lead you directly to El Rocío.

Travelling from the west of the region, or from Portugal, you should take the main Huelva to Sevilla road, the A-49, and turn off at junction 50. You then join the A-483 to Almonte and El Rocío.

Driving In Doñana

The road system in the Doñana region is generally first class and the traffic densities are usually low. Most of the main roads have a distance marking system, with signs bearing the road number and the kilometre number at each kilometre along the road. In many places you will see smaller white posts at regular intervals alongside the road with a single number. These signify the tenths of a kilometre between the km markers.

On the main motorways and auto routes, the junctions are numbered to coincide with the next kilometre marker. Therefore, junction 21 would be at, or just before, kilometre 21. These are generally signed on large information boards beside or above the road and show the names of the town/s that the junction leads to and the junction number, usually displayed in the top right-hand corner of the boards.

If you have older maps, you may find that the junctions are shown in numerical order, ie. 1, 2, 3, etc. All this changed a few years ago when numerous new junctions onto the main roads were created. The Spanish authorities decided, sensibly, that it would be more economic and less confusing to use the km numbering system. This enabled them to add more junctions, when needed, without having to re-number every junction beyond the new ones.

The road between El Rocío and Matalascañas, which most visitors to the region will use at some time, is usually quiet, but at weekends, national/local holidays and during the main summer holiday period it can become very congested. Most Spanish families prefer to eat out on Sunday afternoons and both El Rocío and Matalascañas are very popular destinations at this time. For some reason, everybody seems to leave both of these locations at about the same time, usually between 18.00 and 19.00hrs. This can result in long tailbacks of up to 10 kms and can take an hour or more to drive between the two towns. If you plan to visit Matalascañas, or to travel back from Huelva, or some other location to the west of El Rocío at this time on a Sunday evening, I would strongly suggest that you find an alternative route.

Many of the roads that serve the area have solid white lines painted along the edges. This indicates that you are not allowed to stop, or park your vehicle with any part of your car encroaching over the white line and onto the road. Although this can be extremely frustrating for birders, it is a sensible safety measure and can result in a hefty fine if you are caught infringing this law, by the Guardia Civil.

A law was introduced in Spain in June 2005, whereby every vehicle must contain a florescent coloured jacket/waistcoat which should be put on by the driver whenever he/she parks alongside a road in a rural area and exits the vehicle. This is hardly conducive to inconspicuous birdwatching, but it is a law and, although generally ignored by 99% of drivers, should be borne in mind. This law does not include, cities, towns and other built-up areas, nor farm tracks or dirt roads.

During the massive annual pilgrimage and religious festival that is held in El Rocío every year, when up to one and a half million people descend on the town, many of the roads and dirt tracks will often be used by thousands of slow-moving tractors, trailers, caravans (motorized and horse-drawn), ox-carts, horse riders and pedestrians, as they make their way to the festival. The pilgrims (peregrinos) will be singing and dancing along the roads and are not greatly disposed to giving way to other road users, so a great deal of caution is required if you happen to encounter such a procession.

The culmination of the festival takes place on the 7th Sunday after Easter Sunday.

The five days leading up to the final night are the main times that you will possibly encounter difficulties, but there will also be heavy movement on the local roads for the four days afterwards. During the week of the festival it will be almost impossible to find any form of accommodation in the immediate area. If there are any rooms available, you will most likely find that the charges will be about four times higher than normal. The safari tours into the national park will not operate during the festival and all of the park's visitors centres will be closed for the week.

To reach many of the best birding sites in the area, you need to go "off-road" along dirt, gravel and sandy tracks. Most of these can be negotiated safely in a normal car, under normal conditions, but some will be totally impassable in wet conditions and others will be covered in deep sand in the drier months and present the threat of your car becoming stuck. I have indicated in the "General Information" section for each of the described sites in this book where care needs to be taken.

Perhaps one of the strangest experiences will be driving in the town of El Rocío. The streets are very wide and are all of sand. There are no tarmacked roads, traffic lights or road signs and there seems to be no priority at any road junction. The locals know the streets intimately and will drive wherever the sand is shallow and the risk of getting stuck is minimal. If this means driving in the middle, or on the wrong side of the road, so be it. The simple rule I apply for driving in the town is to go slowly and be prepared to give way at every junction.

Please remember that drink driving, speeding, failing to wear a seat belt and using a mobile phone whilst driving are all offences and can, along with most other driving offences, be met by heavy on-the-spot fines. You should ensure that you obey any parking restrictions that are in force as contravention can also result in a fine, or even worse, your car being transported away to the municipal car pound by the dreaded *grua* (tow-truck), where a lot of money and time will need to be spent to get your car back.

Although car crime is not a major problem in this area, common sense dictates that you should never leave anything on display in a parked car, especially in isolated areas and if it has a car hire company sticker on it.

Maps

You would think that an important area like Doñana would be very well mapped, but unfortunately this is not the case and most maps of the region are sadly lacking in the details that are needed to guide you around the tracks and trails in the marshlands. The best map I have seen is, in fact, a free leaflet that is available from the national park's visitors centres and from the Tourist Information Office in El Rocío. Although far from perfect, it does give a good idea of the routes leading in and out of the marshes. However, I am confident, that if followed correctly, the precise directions that I have produced will get you to all of the sites mentioned.

Disabled Access

I have noticed that in many other guide books the subject of disabled and wheelchair access is generally overlooked. This is a great shame as many people with mobility problems are very keen birders. Amongst the sites I have included in this book there are a few that will not suit people who are not fully mobile. However, most of the sites have at least some degree of access to part, if not all, of the described area, whilst others can be adequately viewed from a car, road, riverside, or from some other vantage point. I have made notes with references to wheelchair accessibility under the General Information heading for each of the sites. Hopefully, this information will be helpful to anyone with mobility problems and will prevent them from wasting their time by travelling long distances to sites that are totally unsuitable for them.

General Information

When you are planning your birding holiday in the Doñana region it would be an advantage for you to know something about the seasonal variations of the bird populations, the migration times and the weather conditions you can expect to experience. Hopefully, the following information will help you in each of these cases.

The winter period, which I loosely class as being from November to mid-March, can be very changeable as far as weather conditions are concerned. In each of these months there have been times when the daytime temperatures have reached 25°C and birding has been possible in T-shirts, shorts and sandals. At other times we have experienced cold spells where the night time temperature has dropped to below 0°C and frost has been evident in the mornings. In late February 2005, many parts of Spain suffered their coldest winter on record and night time temperatures in Doñana dropped to as low as -10°C. However, both extremes usually only last for a few days at a time. Although this is the rainy season in Spain, the rains are not reliable and sometimes many months pass between wet periods. The winter period of 2004/05 was the driest winter since records began in 1947 and we were officially in a drought situation. It would be wise, if you plan to come during this period, to bring clothing that will cover all the possibilities.

Despite the vagaries of the weather, the birding is very good at this time and although the summer visitors have left, they are replaced by hundreds of thousands of wintering birds such as Common Cranes, Reed Buntings, Bluethroats, Penduline Tits, Black-shouldered Kites, Hen Harriers, Merlins, Hobbys, Great Bitterns, White-headed and Ferruginous Ducks, Black Storks, Great White Egrets and other ducks, geese, waders and raptors. Many of the resident species have their numbers greatly increased by migrant birds that arrive here to escape the freezing temperatures of the northern European winters and huge flocks of Avocets, Greater Flamingos, Corn Buntings, Calandra Larks, Spanish Sparrows, Stone Curlews and mixed finches can be seen. Offshore seabirds such as Great and Arctic Skuas, Gannets, Razorbills, Red-breasted Mergansers, Common Scoters, shearwaters and petrels can be seen. Large numbers of two of Europe's scarcest gulls, the Audouin's and Slender-billed are also present along the coastline and at several inland marsh areas, along with Sandwich and Caspian Terns.

March and April are normally much warmer than the preceding months and average daytime temperatures of between 15 - 20°C can be anticipated. This is still the rainy season, which can extend through to the end of May, so some protective clothing for the daytime and warm clothing for the evenings would be a wise choice.

This is a very productive time in the birding calendar as the main northward migration is in full swing. Many of the wintering species are returning north, joining the passage migrants and are being replaced by the summer visitors.

As the migration progresses we see the arrival of some of our most colourful birds, such as Golden Orioles, Bee-eaters, Woodchat Shrikes, Black-eared Wheatears and Rollers. These are joined by Black Kites, Montagu's Harriers, Booted and Short-toed Eagles, Marbled Ducks, Red-knobbed Coots, Little Bitterns, Squacco and Purple Herons, Savi's, Subalpine, Orphean, Olivaceous and Great Reed Warblers, Whinchats,

Turtle Doves, swifts, swallows, martins and many other passerine species that flood into the region to establish their territories and to begin their courtship and breeding rituals.

The rice fields of the Isla Mayor, the Brazo del Este and the Hato Ratón areas are usually flooded and seeded from mid-April onwards and this adds a new wetland dimension to the region and offers alternative feeding options for many species of birds.

During May and June the days are longer and the weather is starting to warm up and temperatures can reach 38°C (100°F). Comfortable loose clothing is generally the order of the day, backed up with a light hat for protection and a good sun cream.

The breeding season predominates the bird activity, offering wonderful viewing opportunities to birdwatchers at some of the large, mixed breeding colonies that exist here. This can also prove to be a very confusing part of birding, as you try to identify the juveniles and the differences between young birds of similar species, such as Woodchat and Southern Grey Shrikes and House and Spanish Sparrows.

July and August are the hottest times of the year in Doñana, with all-day sunshine and temperatures reaching up to 50°C (120°F). The heat can make birding an uncomfortable business, but there is still plenty of bird activity if you know where to look. Many of the smaller lagoons, streams, rivers and wetlands will dry out in the summer heat and birding is best achieved in the few permanent marshlands, several of the larger lagoons and rivers, the tidal saltmarshes at the Marismas del Odiel and the Río Piedras and the constantly irrigated rice fields.

September and October is generally regarded as the autumn, when the oppressive heat of the summer starts to ease off. The latter part of this period usually heralds the start of the wet season and although the weather may be warm, there is always the risk of sudden thunderstorms and prolonged periods of rain.

This is the time of the southward migration and once again birds are present in great numbers as they pass through on their way back to the African continent. Large numbers of wintering visitors again start to arrive as the summer visitors depart. The rice harvesting begins in late September and continues through to late November/early December, attracting thousands of birds to the fields. If rain has not fallen and the marshes are still dry, the harvested and ploughed rice fields of Isla Mayor, Hato Raton and Brazo del Este, along with the main rivers and coastal sites will offer the best birding opportunities.

How To Use This Book

All of the sites that are included in this book have been visited by me on hundreds of occasions on my guided bird tours and have been chosen for the quality of birding that exists at each site. I have always found them to be very reliable sites in which to see a wide variety of birds at any time of the year. To assist you in planning your day trips I have entered all of the sites into four geographical sections, ie. north, east, south and west. The sites are varied and include freshwater and salt marshes, lagoons, rivers, estuaries, beaches, saltpans, forests, open scrubland, rice fields and other agricultural areas. Most benefit from having more than one type of habitat in the immediate area, thereby increasing the number of bird species that can be found.

Site descriptions.

Most site descriptions will include the following information to assist you:

1. A detailed map of the site, highlighting the main features of the area, points of interest and all access roads, tracks and footpaths.

Legend

	Urban Areas, Pastures, Marshland
	Rivers, Lagoons, Ocean
	Footpaths, Dirt Tracks
	Roads, Roundabout
	Bird Hides
	Buildings
℗	Parking Spot
	Woodland (Coniferous)
	Woodland (Deciduous)
	Reedbeds
	Railway Tracks
	Quarry, Gravel Pits

2. Precise directions on how to reach the site. The text will guide you around the area, tell you what you can expect to find in any particular spot, point out the feeding, roosting and, where appropriate, the current breeding sites of certain birds. I will also give you any other pieces of

information and local knowledge that will hopefully make your visit to the site more rewarding and enjoyable.

3. The times of year that are likely to be the most productive for the described site, the best times of the day to visit and the times to avoid visiting, for example, at weekends and public holidays when the site may be very busy with picnickers, or very noisy.

4. A list of the main bird species that can be expected at the site. These will be based upon my own personal observations. I will make no claim for any species that have supposedly been seen by other persons unless there is documented evidence to support the sighting. This will normally include all rarities that have been reported to and accepted by the rarities committee of the Spanish Ornithological Society (SEO).

5. The accessibility of the site for wheelchair users and birders with other mobility problems, so that valuable time can be saved by not travelling to a site that is totally unsuitable for them.

Useful Words, Terms And Abbreviations

Below, I have produced a list of Spanish words and terms that are either used in this book or could be useful on your travels. As you are driving around the region, you will certainly see many square metal plates stuck on fenceposts which are painted with a diagonal black and white motif. These indicate the boundaries of private hunting areas.

Algaida	Densely vegetated stream
AMA	Agencia de Medio Ambiente
Arena	Sand
Arroyo	Stream
Arrozales	Rice fields
Autopista	Motorway
Cambio de Sentido	Turning place / change of direction
Camino	Lane / track
Camino Particular	Private road
Campo	Countryside
Cañada	Reedbed
Carretera	Road / highway
Carretera Cortado	Road closed
Casa	House
Choza	Traditional hut

Cortijo	Country house
Coto Privado de Caza	Private hunting ground
Dehesa	Meadow
Duna / s	Dune / dunes
Entrada Prohibido	No entry
Estuario	Estuary
Finca	Farm
Ganado Bravo	Fighting bulls (keep out)
Hostal / hostales	Small hotel / s
Incendio Prohibido	No fires to be lit
Isla	Island
Laguna	Lagoon
Lucio	Pool
Marismas	Marshes
No Pasa	Do not pass
Peligro / Peligroso	Danger / Dangerous
Pensión	Guest house
Peregrino	Pilgrim
Playa	Beach
Privado	Private
Puente	Bridge
Puerto	Port
Río	River
Salinas	Salt pans
Sendero	Walking route / path
SEO	Sociedad Ornitología de Española
Vado	Ford / crossing
Venta	Wayside bar / restaurant
Veta	Small island

Rice Production In The Doñana Region

The main rice producing area within the Doñana region is in the Isla Mayor (the big island), an area that was previously marshland but is now almost exclusively rice fields. A large town has grown up in the centre of the area and goes under two names. Originally, the town was called Villafranco del Guadalquivir, but many people were unhappy with the former dictator's name being ascribed to the town and they prefer to call it simply Isla Mayor. Nowadays, you can buy maps and obtain information leaflets which will give it one name or the other. There does not seem to be a standard name that is currently in use. My own preference is to use the much shorter and easier to pronounce name of Isla Mayor.

Rice was first introduced to the Doñana region in 1970, when local farmers decided to drain and level a small part of the natural marsh and attempt to grow the crop. The idea proved successful and more and more marshland was reclaimed and converted into rice fields. At that time, there was great concern shown by some conservationists that the draining of the marshes would have an adverse effect on the birds and other wildlife, but in fact, the outcome was completely different to that which was forecast. Successful rice growing relies on the roots being permanently submerged under a few centimetres of water throughout the growing process. The rice growing created new "wetlands" and the birds, which beforehand were forced to leave the Doñana region during the dry, hot summer in search of suitable wetland feeding areas, now moved in to the rice fields, attracted not only by the grain, but also by the rich and abundant food supply of frogs, fish, eels, insects, grubs and larvae that lived in the fields.

In 1974, in an effort to maximize the profit he could gain from his land, a local rice farmer imported 200 kilograms of Red Swamp Cray-fish *(Procambarus clarkii)* from America and introduced them into the rice fields. Some people say that his main idea was that he would have a constant supply of the basic ingredients for "*paella*", ie. rice and shell-fish. Others subscribe to the idea that he was a shrewd businessman and was supplying local bars and restaurants with constantly fresh crayfish.

Whatever the reason, this was also a great success and nowadays thousands of tonnes of crayfish are harvested annually. However, there is always a price to pay for introducing "foreigners" into any area and these larger, more aggressive creatures resulted in the loss of the indig-enous crayfish species *(Austropotamobius pallipes)*.

Apart from the commercial harvesting of the crayfish, many more tonnes are consumed annually by birds and other wildlife. It is now possible that this food variety can account for up to 50% of some birds' summer food intake. Most certainly, White Storks, Glossy Ibis, Little and Cattle Egrets, Grey, Squacco and Purple Herons, Whimbrels and even Marsh Harriers now see crayfish as an important and convenient part of their diet.

A recent study of the Glossy Ibis eating behaviour in the Doñana region showed that, although primarily eaters of invertebrates such as salamanders, newts, dragonfly larvae, worms and aquatic beetles, they often supplement their diet with rice grain and I have personally witnessed them eating crayfish on many occasions. The ibis is a recent addition to Spain, having first arrived as a winter visitor in the early 1990's and started to breed here in the latter part of that decade. They are now a common resident species and their rapid colonization of the region may well be as a direct result of them changing their eating habits to include both rice and crayfish.

The rice industry is now almost completely under the control of large co-operatives and covers an ever expanding area, which is currently over 55,000 hectares of land. This is a comparable land mass to that of the national park, which is now, following recent expansion, also about 55,000 hectares.

If the rice growing season sustains the birds throughout the summer, then the harvesting time supplies them with a magnificent banquet. The harvesting, which commences in late September and can last through to early December, is carried out by combine harvesters that cut the top of the stems that hold the grain and leave about 30 cms of stalk still standing. Once the rice has been cut, the remaining stalks in the still flooded fields are then ploughed back into the mud to add nutrients to the soil for the next growing season. Specially adapted tractors perform this task and are fitted with very wide rear wheels made of slatted metal and as they carry out the ploughing process they are also churning up the fish, eels, frogs, newts, crayfish, insects, grubs and larvae by the millions. Many bird species are attracted to the fields by the rich soup that is being churned up and it is not unusual to find 10 - 15,000 birds in one field, fighting for the choicest morsels. The food is so abundant that many birds literally become earth-bound by the sheer weight of food consumed and have to wait for their digestive systems to pass the food through their bodies before they can even think of flying, or re-joining the feast.

This is truly one of the great spectacles in the Doñana birding calendar and all who have witnessed it have been utterly amazed by the sheer number of birds. What better way of spending a few hours than to get out the picnic table and chairs in a suitable location, set up your telescope, have a cold beer and watch the spectacle of storks, herons, egrets, ibis, terns, gulls, waders, ducks, larks, wagtails and raptors gorging themselves, less than 100 metres away. In my opinion, the rice harvesting season rates alongside the stork and raptor migration at Tarifa and along the Strait of Gibraltar as a "must see" spectacle for all serious birders.

Pollution In Doñana

Due to the intensive farming and mining activities that occur in many of the areas surrounding the national and natural parks, pollution is a constant threat to the flora and fauna of the region. The major pollutants are chemicals that are used by the farming community, who appear to have little regard to the damage that they are causing to the environment. The spillage of animal slurry and the intensive use of fertilizers and pesticides, which leak into the streams and rivers that feed the main marshes, are a constant danger to the fragile ecosystems that exist here.

The greatest contamination threat to Doñana came from a mining accident in April 1998, when thousands of birds, fish and other wildlife died. A Swedish/Canadian company were mining for iron pyrites near the town of Aznalcóllar, to the north of the region. The contamination (arsenic, cadmium, zinc, lead, copper, silver and other elements) occurred after a tailings dam that was holding up to 5 million cubic metres of polluted water burst following heavy rain and flowed down the already flooded Río Guadiamar. The water and the thick sludge containing the pollutants overflowed the river banks, completely wiping out thousands of hectares of prime agricultural land. A total length of 62 kms of the river and surrounding land was affected and it was only thanks to the rapid and sustained response of several agencies, who dammed and diverted the course of the river, that the contamination did not enter the national park.

Because many of the polluting elements were of heavy metal, they sank deep into the ground and are not expected to degenerate for many years, rendering the soil unsafe for agricultural purpose. Following the massive clean-up operation, all of the contaminated land was purchased by the Andalusian Government and a new wildlife reserve was created: the "Corredor Verde del Río Guadiamar".

The rice growing industry contributes to pollution in two main ways. During the growing season, pesticides are sprayed from the air over the ricefields. Unfortunately, spraying liquid pesticide from planes can be very indiscriminate, as the wind can carry the spray into nearby sensitive areas and cause many problems to wildlife. Also, the water from the fields then runs off into numerous irrigation channels, carrying some of the pesticide with it. This polluted water then runs into rivers and streams that eventually flow into the marshes.

The second pollution problem occurs after the rice has been harvested. The fields are sometimes set alight to burn off most of the cut chaff that has been expelled by the harvesting machines. It is not uncommon to drive through the main rice producing areas in October and November and be faced with a wall of dense smoke, often resulting in visibility being cut down to less than 100 metres.

Although burning chaff and stubble is supposedly against the EU farming policy, the practice is still widely employed here, although in 2005/06 it was noticed that some of the chaff was being "baled" by machines, presumably to be used as winter fodder for grazing animals.

The farming community is responsible for perhaps the most dangerous form of pollution. As you drive around the area you are likely to come upon several "official" plastic dumps. Plastic sheeting, irrigation hoses, chemical drums, bottles and crates, which are widely used on the farms, are dumped in such an indiscriminate manner that some of the tracks become completely covered and impassable by normal cars. This does not affect the farm workers, who generally drive around in 4x4 vehicles or tractors.

At the time of writing, no re-cycling policy seems to exist and the dumps are never cleared by the local authorities or the farmers, so a massive build up occurs. Occasionally, the plastic is drenched in petrol and set alight, in an attempt to clear the tracks. This releases a foul cocktail of toxic pollution into the atmosphere, a mixture of burning plastic, rubber and the dregs of the chemicals from the containers. I fail to understand how this practice, which is highly dangerous to both humans and wildlife, can be allowed to continue anywhere, never mind within a few kilometres of the most protected conservation area in Europe.

Migration

The main migration route for most soaring and gliding birds (storks and raptors) that cross between the African continent and Spain in the spring is along the Strait of Gibraltar, some 150 kms to the southeast of the Doñana region. However, as these birds are prone to drifting due to the lateral effects of the wind, we benefit greatly when there are strong easterly winds that bring the birds in our direction. Although we can never compete with the spectacle of the sheer numbers of the species that occurs annually along the Strait, we still see good numbers of Black Kites, Honey Buzzards, Lesser Kestrels, Sparrowhawks, Short-toed and Booted Eagles, Egyptian Vultures and Black Storks.

The smaller migratory birds, ie. doves, swallows, martins, swifts, larks, warblers, wagtails and chats, etc., which are much stronger fliers, tend to ignore the shorter sea-crossing preferred by the larger birds and will cross the ocean at almost any point along our 100 km coastline. This can often result in significant "falls" of migrating birds.

During the autumn migration, Doñana enjoys spectacular numbers of passerines, raptors, storks, herons, egrets and waders as they pass through on their way to Africa. Many of these remain in the region for long periods before finally moving on, sometimes until late November/early December and flocks of thousands can be seen feeding in the marsh and agricultural areas.

It should be noted that over 20 bird species that are classified in most field guides as summer visitors to Europe regularly remain in the Doñana region throughout the year, making this one of the few areas where you can see such species as Squacco, Purple and Black-crowned Night Herons, Little Bitterns, Short-toed and Booted Eagles, Black Kites, Egyptian Vultures, Black Storks, Hoopoes, Greater Short-toed Larks and Yellow Wagtails, during the winter.

The Birding Calendar

July. This is generally the quietest time for birding in the region. The breeding season has ended and the high summer temperatures mean that bird activity is at its lowest. Most of the marshes and lagoons will be dry and the main birding activity occurs in the Corredor Verde, the Isla Mayor rice fields, the Brazo del Este and at the saltmarshes of the Río Odiel and the Río Piedras.

August. White Storks, Montagu's Harriers, Honey Buzzards, Black Kites, Sand Martins and Golden Orioles start to pass through the region on their way back to Africa. Thousands of Black-tailed Godwits, Dunlins, Ruff, Ringed Plovers, Green Sandpipers and other waders start to arrive from their more northerly breeding grounds.

September. Significant numbers of Slender-billed and Audouin's Gulls arrive from the Mediterranean. Wader numbers increase and the first Black Storks, Whimbrels and Curlews arrive to spend the winter here. Squacco and Purple Herons, Little Bitterns, Bee-eaters, Woodchat Shrikes, Pied and Spotted Flycatchers, Common Redstarts, warblers and terns depart. Large numbers of raptors pass through on migration and wintering Black-shouldered Kites arrive. This is the main breeding season for Golden and Red Bishops. The rice harvesting season begins, attracting thousands of birds into the fields.

October. Wintering Black Stork numbers increase. Common Cranes, Great White Egrets, Red Kites, Hen Harriers, Short-eared Owls, Barn Owls, Hobbys, Ospreys, Greylag Geese and massive numbers of wildfowl and waders arrive. Many raptors and passerines will still be passing through on the southward migration. The rice harvesting continues.

November. The southward migration continues with increased numbers of Common Cranes, Red Kites, Peregrines, Black-necked Grebes, geese, ducks and waders arriving. Pin-tailed Sandgrouse and Stone Curlews form wintering flocks. Seabird activity increases and shearwaters move through the Strait and into the Atlantic. Common Scoters, Red-breasted Mergansers and Razorbills are present offshore. The rice harvesting continues.

December. Wintering bird numbers will now be at their highest. Great Bitterns are usually present in small numbers. Very large flocks of Calandra Larks, Spanish Sparrows and Corn Buntings form in the northern marshes area.

January. Large flocks of Greater Flamingos, White Storks, Spoonbills, Avocets and other waders are usually evident.

February. Still large numbers of wintering birds present. Barn Swallows and House Martins cross back over to Spain from Africa. White Storks begin breeding. The latter part of the month sees the early arrival of Great Spotted Cuckoos, Lesser Kestrels, Black Kites and Short-toed Eagles.

March. The northward migration begins in earnest with the arrival of Short-toed and Booted Eagles, Red-rumped Swallows, Common Cuckoos, Pallid Swifts, Bee-eaters, Woodchat Shrikes and many other passerines. Wintering wildfowl and Common Cranes start to move northwards.

Breeding begins for Purple Swamp-hens, Red-knobbed Coots and Marbled Ducks. Purple and Squacco Herons and Little Bitterns start to arrive at the end of the month.

April. The busiest time for the northward migration. Hundreds of thousands of birds arrive or pass through the region. Montagu's Harriers, Whinchats, Black-eared and Northern Wheatears, Subalpine, Willow, Melodious, Savi's and Great Reed Warblers, Red-necked Nightjars, Rufous-tailed Scrub Robins, Rollers, Common Redstarts, Spotted and Pied Flycatchers, Golden Orioles, Turtle Doves, Nightingales, Black, Whiskered and Gull-billed Terns, Slender-billed Gulls, Little Bitterns and Collared Pratincoles are particularly obvious.

Many migrating waders arrive in winter plumage and remain in the area until they have come into full breeding plumage before moving to their breeding grounds in the north. This gives you the opportunity to see Ruff, Black-tailed Godwits, Ruddy Turnstones, Dunlin, Red Knots, Grey Plovers, Spotted Redshanks and Curlew Sandpipers in their finest colours.

Large mixed breeding colonies of Purple, Squacco and Black-crowned Night Herons, Little and Cattle Egrets and Glossy Ibis can be found.

During the last few days of the month we see the start of the Honey Buzzard passage.

The flooding and seeding of the rice fields begins.

May. All of the resident birds and summer visitors are now present and the breeding season is in full swing. Honey Buzzards continue to pass through until the middle of the month.

June. Although breeding continues throughout the region the bird activity diminishes as some lagoons and marshes start to dry out and the rising temperatures drive the birds under the cover of shade. The main birding activity is now centred around the tidal marshes at the Río Odiel and the Río Piedras and the sites on the east bank of the Río Guadalquivir. Large numbers of Black-tailed Godwits arrive back from their breeding grounds in Scandinavia.

Risks And Hazards

Insects. In this region there are many species of insects (mosquitos, scorpions, spiders, bees, horseflys, wasps, ants, etc.) that are very capable of delivering quite painful bites and stings. It is a fact of life that whilst you are out in the countryside you will encounter some of these at some time. I strongly suggest that if you are susceptible to being bitten by insects, that you invest in one of the many brands of insect repellent sprays or creams that are available, before travelling to Spain.

The night time poses the major threat from mosquitos and there are several deterrents that can help you to minimize this risk. Anti-mosquito candles are an effective deterrent, giving off fumes that may be detectable to humans but will at least keep your room free of mosquitos and other insects for as long as the candle lasts. Electrical devices that plug into wall sockets give off repellent fumes throughout the night. Other electrical devices, which emit ultra-sonic sound waves are also very effective. All of these items can be purchased in supermarkets and pharmacies. The electrical devices should be bought here in Spain, not in Britain, as the British plugs will not fit into Spanish sockets.

Snakes. There are 13 species of snakes in Spain and several of these are to be found in the Doñana region, but only one, the Lataste's (Snub-nosed) Viper, is poisonous. However, it is not common and its bite should not prove fatal to a normal healthy person, but common sense dictates that any snake bite should receive immediate medical attention.

The most common snake seen by visitors to this area is the Montpellier's Snake. These can grow up to 2 metres in length and are often seen on roads and dirt tracks. These are considered to be dangerous, but as the fangs are located at the rear of the mouth, it is unlikely to be able to inflict a nasty bite on a human.

Cattle. Andalucia is the birthplace of Spanish bullfighting and is, traditionally, the breeding centre of the finest fighting bulls. These animals have been bred, through many generations, to fight and kill. Even the young, harmless-looking bulls will attack you if you offer them the chance.

Some farms may have signs on fences stating "*Ganado Bravo*" (fighting bulls), but even if there are no warning signs the simple rule is to keep out of any field or paddock where cattle are grazing. These animals are very dangerous and the pursuit of no bird, regardless of how rare it may be, is worth the risk of injury, or even death. You have been warned!

Wild animals. Generally, there is no threat from wild animals. However, although fairly scarce, Wild Boar do roam and breed in some of the surrounding forests and dehesas. These will normally hear you approaching long before you see them and will move off, posing no threat.

You are more likely to encounter stray or abandoned dogs in the countryside. Usually, these have been quite badly abused by humans in the past and are very wary. However, there are occasional reports of people being bitten and although Spain is classed as a rabies-free country, any bite should receive medical treatment as soon as possible.

Effects of the sun. Many visitors to Doñana underestimate the powerful effects of the sun, which can produce temperatures of up to 50°C (120°F) in the height of summer. Even during the milder months the sun can have an adverse effect on your body and suitable precautions should be taken. Over-exposure to the sun can result in painful sunburn, dehydration and sunstroke if care is not taken. It is advisable to bring a high-factor sun cream, a hat for head protection and light long-sleeved shirts/blouses to cover the shoulders and arms. Ensure that you drink plenty of water each day (up to two litres in very hot conditions) to counter the loss of body fluids.

Accommodation

Most birdwatching visitors to Doñana find that there is far too much to see and do in just one day and choose to spend several days here. If you do decide to stay overnight you will require some form of accommodation. Surprisingly, for such a large town, El Rocío is rather limited in its options. There is only one hotel in the town, the Toruño, which is owned and operated by the same company that has the concession to operate the 4-hour safari tours into the national park. There are a couple of "hostales", the Isidro and the Cristina, which offer reasonably cheap and basic accommodation. There are also several "Casas Rurales" in the town, offering reasonable accommodation, but these are widely used by Spanish families and groups and tend to be rather noisy.

A popular option with many birders, especially groups, is the La Aldea campsite, on the northern edge of the town and only 700 metres from the marsh. This Category 1 campsite offers 2, 4 and 6-person cabins/bungalows, which work out cheaper than the other options and offers self-catering. As the campsite is away from the town centre, it is not subjected to so much noise and, in keeping with all campsites, insists on silence between midnight and 7 o'clock in the morning.

El Rocío has now become a very popular tourist resort and features in many Spanish coach tour operators' itineraries. The hotel and "hostales" in the area have jointly realized this and have increased their prices significantly in recent years to cash-in on this new wealth of tourism. It should also be pointed out that if you do choose to stay at any of the options in El Rocío, the increased number of tourists to the town has resulted in a noticeable increase in noise levels, both during the day as well as at night, especially at weekends, when wedding ceremonies, baptisms, mini-pilgrimages and general revelry can result in sleepless nights.

In the past, I have always recommended that people should stay in the town, partly for the birding aspect, as it is central to most of the birding sites in the southern sector of Doñana, and partly because in the past there were no real alternative accommodation options. Nowadays, there are suitable alternatives in the towns and villages just a few kilometres away from El Rocío, where clean, quiet, comfortable and affordable accommodation can be found and I would suggest that these should be given serious consideration.

Accommodation in El Rocío

Hotel Toruño. Plaza Acebuchal. Tel. (0034) 959 442 323 or 959 442 626. This is the only hotel in the town and is very popular with birders as it is only 15 metres from the edge of the main marshes. Each of the rooms has a refrigrated mini-bar and many of the rooms (Nos. 219, 221, 223 and 225 in particular) have windows or small balconies that look out directly over the wetland.
Most of the staff speak English.
Current prices (2007):-
80.25 euros per night for a double room.
56.17 euros per night for a single room.
Breakfast, which is included in the price, is from 08.00 hrs onward.
All major credit cards are accepted.

Pensión Isídro. Avenida de los Ansares. Tel. (0034) 959 442 242.
This is a fairly comfortable hostal situated towards the back of the town, about 500 metres from the marsh. The rooms are basic but have heating and air-conditioning.
Only Spanish is spoken.
Current prices:- 48 euros per night for a double room and 24 euros per night for a single room.
Basic breakfast (not included in the price) is not usually available until 09.00 hrs.

Hotel Cristina. Calle Real. Tel. (0034) 959 442 413.
The cheapest in the town and very basic. Close to the marshes and ideal for those only wishing to stay for one or two nights, or are on a budget.
Only Spanish is spoken.
Current prices:- 36 euros for a double room and 30 euros for a single room.
Basic breakfast (not included in price) is not available until 09.00 hrs.
Please note than none of the hotels/hostals have tea/coffee making facilities.

Camping La Aldea. Tel. (0034) 959 442 677. www.campinglaaldea.com
This is a fairly modern category 1 campsite situated beside the A-483
on the approach to El Rocío, just 700 metres from the marsh. It has a
swimming pool and bar/restaurant and apart from the usual camping
facilities you can also rent 2, 4 and 6-person bungalows.

These bungalows are equipped with an en-suite shower/toilet and also,
with the exception of the 2-person version, there are basic cooking facilities and a refrigerator, thereby allowing self-catering.

The reception staff speak English.

Current prices (2007):-

42 euros per night for a 2-person bungalow

68 euros per night for a 4-person bungalow.

90 euros per night for a 5/6 person bungalow.

A 10% discount is offered for stays of 3 - 6 nights.

A 15% discount is offered for stays of 7 - 14 nights

Most major credit cards are accepted.

Recommended accommodation outside El Rocío.

Hostal Pino Doñana. Calle Ramon y Cajal 4. Hinojos. Tel. (0034) 959
459 413.

This is a fairly modern hostal in the town of Hinojos, just 20 minutes
from El Rocío. It has 8 double and 3 single rooms, all of which are
equipped with central heating and air-conditioning, en-suite shower/
toilet, Spanish TV and internet connections.

There is an adjoining bar/restaurant with direct access from the hostal.
and it is situated in the centre of the town and close to all facilities, including all the major birding sites.

The owner of the hostal speaks English.

Current prices (2007):-

38 euros per night for a double room.

20 euros per night for a single room.

Credit cards accepted.

Casa Doñana. Calle Lirio 15, Urbanizacion Las Animas, Hinojos. www.
casadonana.com.

This is a four bedroomed fully equipped house that can sleep up to 10
people in a very peaceful setting on the outskirts of the village of Hinojos, 20 minutes away from El Rocío. It has enclosed gardens, orange and
lemon trees and a good sized swimming pool.

This is an ideal option for groups of birders that want good value accommodation with a bit more comfort and space than the hotels or hostals
can offer. It is also perfect for family holidays, especially if non-birding

partners/families are involved, as they can enjoy the pool whilst the other is out birding.

Current prices (2007):-

700 euros per week in the low season (October to May inclusive).

750 euros per week in the mid-season (June and September plus Easter and Christmas).

800 euros per week in the high season (July and August).

Villamanrique de la Condesa. Tel. (0034) 955 755 220 or 615 422 054.

The following options exist in Villamanrique, which is 15 minutes from El Rocio, 5 minutes from the Corredor Verde and 10 - 20 minutes from most of the major birding areas in the northern marshes

Modern fully equipped self-catering apartments that sleep up to four persons in a quiet location, close to the centre of the village and all facilities. The apartments have a cooking hob, fridge/freezer, microwave oven, washing machine, dish washer, tumble dryer, Spanish TV, internet connections, air-conditioning/central heating, a full en-suite bathroom and an outside terrace. These are ideal choices for those that wish to spend more than just a couple of days in the region. The current cost (2007) is 80 euros per night, although there will be a discount for bookings of 7 days or more.

Clean, comfortable double rooms in a quiet location, close to the centre of the village and all facilities. Each of the rooms has twin beds, central heating/air-conditioning, full en suite bathrooms, tea/coffee making facilities, Spanish TV and internet connections and are ideal for those that plan to be here for only a few days. The current cost (2007) is 60 euros per night. As above, there will be discounts for longer stays.

Bed and Breakfast.

Comfortable rooms close to Villamanrique. English, Spanish, French, German and Italian spoken. Tel. (0034) 955 755 820 or 629 707 316.

Sectors

The Doñana region is a vast area of rapidly changing habitats that could easily keep a birdwatcher busy for weeks. There are so many excellent sites, spread over the entire region, that I have decided that it would be easier for the reader if I were to divide the sites into more localized sectors, ie. the north, south, east and west. This should help you to plan your itineraries without having to keep returning to the same sector to see other sites in that particular area.

The northern sector. The sites around the village of Villamanrique de la Condesa, which include the Dehesa Boyal and Laguna San Lazaro and the sites that are best accessed from the village, which include the Entremuros, Isla Mayor, the Corredor Verde, Dehesa de Pilas, Dehesa de Abajo, the Cañada de Rianzuela, the "gravel pits", Huerta Tejada, the "reedbeds", Laguna Mancho Zurillo, Laguna de Quema, Hato Raton rice fields, Partido de Resina, Lucio del Lobo, Casa de Bombas, Marismas de Hinojos, the Caño de Guadiamar and the José Antonio Valverde Centre.

The eastern sector. This includes the sites that are on the eastern side of the Río Guadalquivir, ie. The Brazo del Este, the Isla de los Olivillos, El Lago Diego Puerta, the Salinas de Bonanza, the Pinares de Algaida, Sanlucar de Barrameda, Laguna Tarelo and El Puntal. Access to these sites from the main Doñana region is either by ferry across the Río Guadalquivir at Coria del Río or via Sevilla.

The southern sector. The sites around El Rocío, which include El Acebuche, La Rocina, Puente de Canaliega, the Boca del Lobo, the Moguer road, the Raya Real, the Palacio de Acebron, Puente de Ajóli, Las Guayules, the Arroyos de las Cañadas and Santa Maria, Matalascañas and the El Rocío marshes.

The western sector. The sites in the Huelva region. These include the Marismas del Odiel, Laguna El Portil, La Rábida, Niebla, El Rompido, the Marismas de Río Piedras, Estero de Domingo Rubio, La Ribera and the Lagunas Primera de Palos.

The Northern Sector

The northern sector of the region is perhaps the most important area for birds in Doñana. There are numerous differing habitats and sites that can be found and these include pine, oak and eucalyptus forests, rivers, streams, lagoons, agricultural land, ricefields, pastures, dense reedbeds and, of course, the northern marshes themselves.

All of the sites in this sector can be accessed via the town of Villamanrique de la Condesa (see map) and all the directions (with the exceptions of the Dehesa Boyal and the first route to the Laguna San Lázaro) begin from the roundabout to the north of the town.

START

To reach this roundabout from the El Rocío direction you should take the road to Villamanrique, which is on the right, approximately 2kms to the north of El Rocio. Follow this road for 21 kms until you reach a petrol station and a small roundabout. Turn right and after 100 metres there is a second roundabout. Turn left (3rd exit) and continue for 1 km until you reach the roundabout referred to in the main directions.

By going straight ahead at this roundabout, on the road marked "Isla Mayor" you will be able to access all of the sites in the northern marshes area and also reach the ferry that crosses the Río Guadalquivir and leads to the eastern sector.

Villamanrique - Access to northern sites

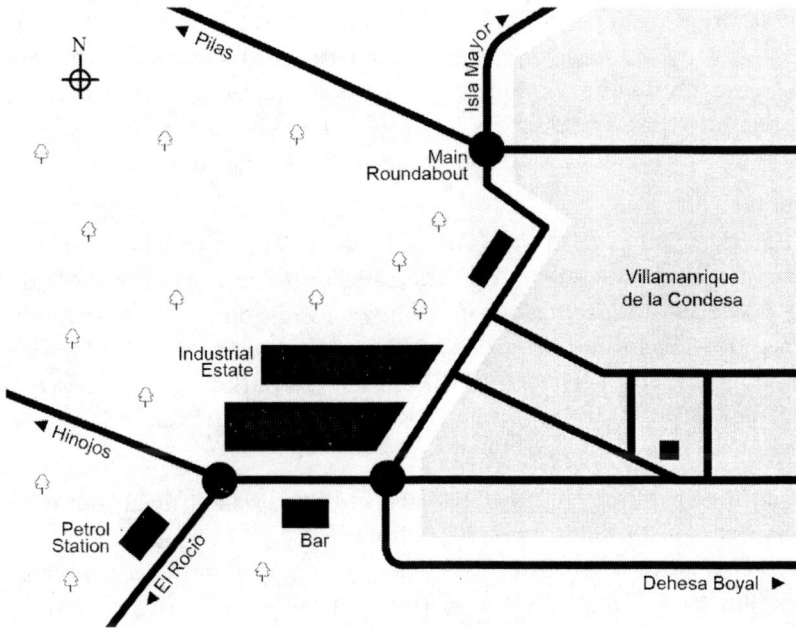

It should be noted that many of the sites in this section involve "off-road" driving on dirt tracks that are perfectly safe to use in normal conditions, but may cause driving problems during certain times and in certain conditions, especially during and just after wet weather. You would be advised to read the notes regarding road/track conditions in the "General Information" section before visiting each site.

Centro De Visitantes Dehesa Boyal.
Villamanrique De La Condesa
North 1.

This a fairly modern visitors centre situated on the eastern outskirts of the village of Villamanrique. It was opened in the spring of 2003 and its facilities include a snack bar, drink vending machines, toilets, information desk and a permanent exhibition hall.

The centre is set in open countryside with scattered holm and cork-oak trees, beside the Villamanrique municipal park. It is the starting point of two interesting nature walks that can produce a wide variety of bird species.

Access

Access is by way of the El Rocío-Villamanrique road. As you approach Villamanrique you reach a small roundabout at a petrol station. Turn right, passing the Mesón de Gato to your right. At the next roundabout you turn right again and follow this road for about one kilometre until you reach a third roundabout. Go directly ahead and the visitors centre is 200 metres further along on the left-hand side of the road.

Walk one.

Behind the visitors centre you will see a long wall, on which a mural has been painted. Here you will find the gates to the municipal park. These may be closed but there is a gap in the hedge, beside a gatepost that allows entry. The birds that are commonly found in the park include Iberian Magpies, Southern Grey Shrikes, Crested Larks, Zitting Cisticolas, Hoopoes, Little Owls, Serins, Black and Common Redstarts, Spotted Flycatchers and Sardinian Warblers.

Continue walking through the park until you reach the far boundary fence. Here you will find an exit point which leads to a sandy track and open scrubland. If you turn right here you will come to a tarmacked road that leads directly back to the visitors centre. Turning left will lead you along the track between forested and agricultural areas. To the right there is the Arroyo de Gato, a seasonal stream, which attracts many species of birds when water is present. Continue along the track for about 700 metres until you reach a tarmacked road. Turn left and after 300 metres there is a dirt track on the left. Follow this track, keeping the fence on your left and you will be led back, across the Dehesa Boyal, to the Centre.

Other birds that are often recorded on this walk are Green and Great Spotted Woodpeckers, Short-toed Treecreepers, Jays, Golden Orioles, Great Spotted and Common Cuckoos, Bee-eaters, Tree Sparrows, larks, finches, tits (including Crested) and warblers. Raptor species are often present and you may find Red and Black Kites, Marsh and Montagu's Harriers, Buzzards, Kestrels, Sparrowhawks and both Booted and Short-toed Eagles.

This walk is 2.3 kilometres long and the time taken depends entirely on how much time you spend watching the birds.

Walk two.

From the front of the Centre, walk to the right, beside the fence, across the Dehesa Boyal, until you reach a tarmacked road. Turn right and continue until you reach a bridge over the Arroyo de Gato. Once across the bridge turn left onto a track that leads into a stone-pine forest. Keeping the stream on your left, continue until you reach another tarmacked road. Turn right here and after a few hundred metres you reach the Laguna San Lázaro. The lagoon is seasonal and will almost certainly be dry from late May onwards. However, when water is present you can find White Storks, Black Storks (winter only), Little Grebes, Kingfishers, Green, Common and Wood Sandpipers, herons and egrets. Otters are sometimes seen in the lagoon and the Arroyo de Gato, but these should not be confused with the more common Egyptian Mongooses that also live in the area.

The pine forest holds the usual array of warblers, finches, tits and larks and many of the previously mentioned species can also be found here. Nest boxes have been fixed to some of the trees and these are most commonly used by Tree Sparrows. Numerous trails lead through the forest which can also be followed.

The area is a popular picnic/barbeque spot with local families at weekends and may be noisy at such times. Inevitably, a certain amount of rubbish is left behind, but anything edible is usually scavenged by the resident population of Iberian Magpies and some of the non-edible waste may be collected by White Storks, to be used as nesting material. Unfortunately, I have yet to find any bird willing to dispose of the empty beer and wine bottles that have been discarded.

To return to the Centre you should re-trace your tracks. This walk is approximately 3 kilometres each way, over fairly flat terrain and you should allow yourself at least four hours to complete it.

I should point out that the two walks can be combined to make one longer walk. When you reach the tarmacked road, as described in walk one, you are very close to the bridge over the Arroyo de Gato, as described in walk two. By following the remaining directions for walk two, you will reach the Laguna San Lázaro.

Centro de Visitantes, Dehesa Boyal (N-1)

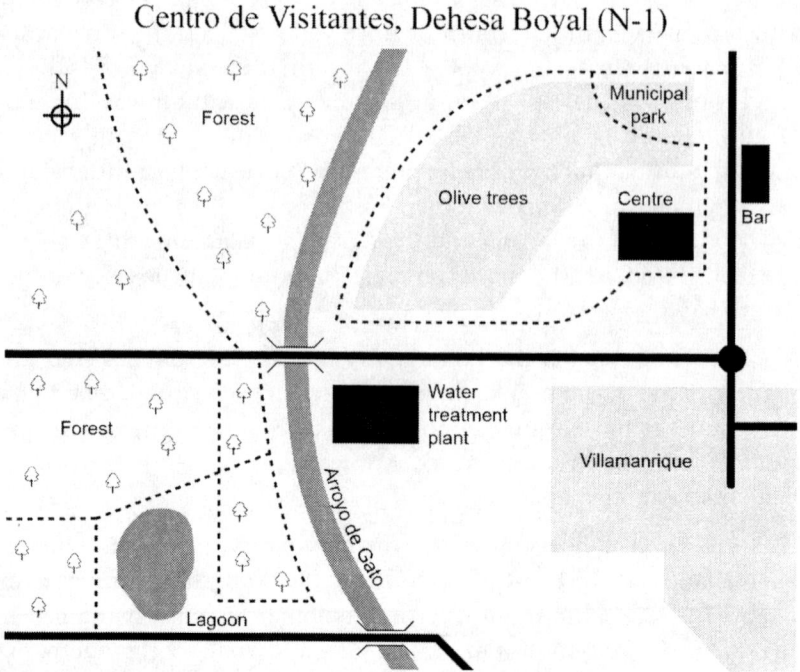

General Information

The visitors centre is usually open from 10.00 to 14.00hrs and the bar is open from 10.00hrs (summer) and 09.00hrs (winter) until late in the evening, but is closed on Mondays. If the centre is closed there is a bar/café just opposite where you can get a cooling drink after your walk.

Although the terrain is fairly flat, the tracks are of soft sand and rutted earth. There could also be a bit of scrambling involved, which would prove to be impossible for wheelchair birders.

When To Visit

The walks are of interest throughout the year but the hot summer months of July, August and September are the least productive. During the warmer months of the year I would recommend visits in the morning or evening.

Laguna San Lázaro
North 2.

The Laguna San Lázaro is a shallow seasonal lagoon situated just a few kilometres to the southeast of Villamanrique. It is seldom more than 50 centimetres deep and is set in a forest of stone pine and mixed oak trees which support a good selection of birds and other wildlife. The lagoon is dependent on rainfall, but even after the wettest winters the area is normally dry from the end of May onwards. To the east of the site there is a small stream, the Arroyo de Gato, which also attracts birds. There are numerous interesting walking trails throughout the forest and around the lagoon itself which invite inspection and there are several picnic tables and a large car park. Although there is a designated parking area, you are able to drive directly into the forest and park.

The resident birds include Iberian Magpies, Hoopoes, Little Owls, Common Buzzards, Tree Sparrows, Green and Great Spotted Woodpeckers, Jays, Short-toed Treecreepers, Zitting Cisticolas, Dartford, Sardinian and Cetti's Warblers, Serins, Crested Tits, Common Buzzards, Ravens and various lark and finch species.

The winter visitors to the lagoon, if water is present, can include Little and Cattle Egrets, Grey Herons, White and Black Storks, Common, Wood and Green Sandpipers, Ringed Plovers, Redshanks, Little Grebes, Kingfishers and other wader and duck species. Amongst the winter visitors to the forest and surrounding scrubland are Black Redstarts, Firecrests, Stonechats, Meadow Pipits, Southern Grey Shrikes, White Wagtails, Woodlarks and Red Kites.

Passing migrants and summer visitors include Golden Orioles, Pied and Spotted Flycatchers, Reed and Willow Warblers, Common Redstarts, Woodchat Shrikes, Iberian Chiffchaffs, Common and Great Spotted Cuckoos, Nightingales, Yellow Wagtails, Black Kites and Booted and Short-toed Eagles.

Other forms of wildlife, such as foxes, lizards, bats, snakes (non-poisonous), turtles, tortoises, hedgehogs and Egyptian Mongooses may also be seen.

Access

The lagoon can be visited as a walk which starts from the Dehesa Boyal Visitors Centre (see description for that site) or by driving directly to it via a different route. There are two driving routes that will lead you to the site. The first is via the El Rocio - Villamanrique road. Travelling from El Rocio, continue along the road for 16 kms towards Villamanrique until you reach the first roundabout, where you should turn right. The *"Bar La Pará"* is your landmark. Follow this road until the next roundabout and go straight across. Continue further and go straight across the next mini-roundabout. The lagoon can be found on the left-hand side about 1 km further on.

The second route is easier. From the main roundabout to the north of Villamanrique take the road to Isla Mayor. After 3.9 kms you reach a large cotton processing factory. Turn right here and proceed for just over a kilometre and you will find the lagoon on the right-hand side. There is ample parking and you can also drive right in to the forest.

Laguna San Lazaro (N-2)

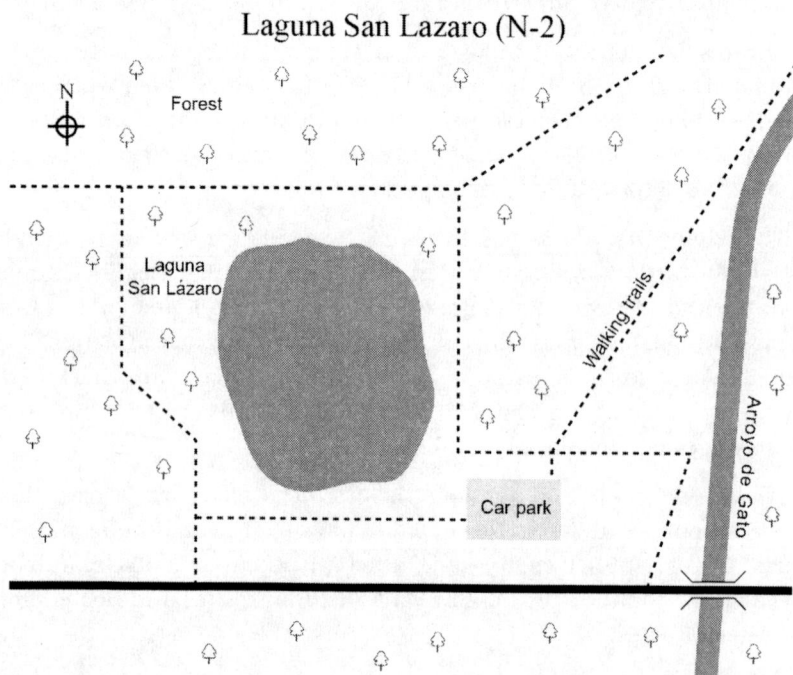

General Information

Although good birding is possible throughout the year, the site is of maximum interest during the winter, when water is present. Generally, this is a very quiet area and you may find yourselves to be the only people present. However, weather permitting, the area is widely used by local families for picnics and barbeques at the weekends and during school holidays. Some camping also takes place in the forest at these times and the noise level may be such that serious birding is not possible.

The terrain is fairly flat and should not prove to be too much of a problem for wheelchair birders to access some parts of the site, although the softer sandy tracks should be avoided.

When To Visit

The site is of greater interest when water is present, usually between October and April, but as the lagoon is totally dependent on rain water it can remain dry if we have insufficient rain in the winter. Morning and evening visits are usually the most productive for birds.

Laguna De Mancho Zurillo, Laguna De Quema And The Corredor Verde De Guadiamar
North 3

These are two man-made lagoons/reservoirs to the east of Villamanrique, where a large range of waterbirds, passerines and raptors can be found.

The lagoons adjoin the Corredor Verde de Guadiamar and are set in a mixture of varying habitats that include open scrubland, meadows, forests and agricultural land. In the first of these lagoons, the Laguna de Mancho Zurillo, there are a number of ancient cork-oak trees that were left in the valley when it was dammed and flooded. Although long dead, the trees are still standing in the water and provide excellent night-time roosts for many birds, the surrounding water protecting them from predators such as foxes, otters and mongooses. Numerous Little and Cattle Egrets roost here each evening in the winter and they are often joined by varying numbers of Grey Herons, Cormorants, Ospreys, Red and Black Kites, Buzzards and Booted Eagles.

Other birds that are regularly found in and around this lagoon are Hoopoes, Iberian Magpies, Sardinian, Dartford, Cetti's and Willow Warblers, Chiffchaffs, Zitting Cisticolas, Woodlarks, Woodchat and Southern Grey Shrikes, Black Redstarts, Coots, wagtails, ducks, grebes, waders, tits and finches. In the spring of 2006, a new breeding colony of White Storks was established here, with seven pairs building nests in the trees at the far end of the lagoon.

Laguna de Mancho Zurillo (N-3)

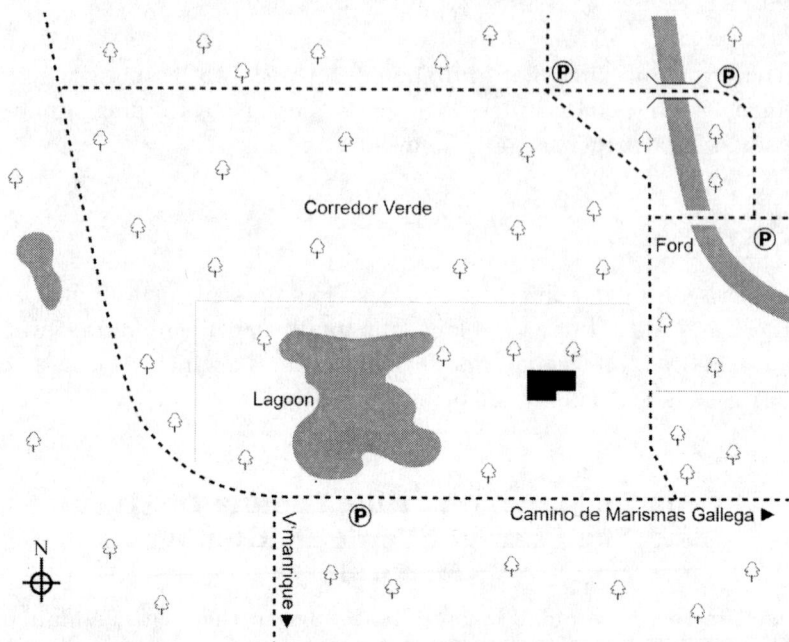

The second lagoon, the Laguna de Quema, is set amidst a very large fruit farm, which is on private land but part of it can be viewed fairly well from a dirt road that passes by the site. The main interest here is the number of duck and grebe species that can be found, mainly between September and April. These have often included Tufted Ducks, Teal, Wigeon, Shovelers, Pintails, Gadwalls, Common and Red-crested Pochards, White-headed and Ferruginous Ducks, Greylag Geese and Great Crested, Little and Black-necked Grebes.

This is a regular hunting ground for the Ospreys that roost at the first lagoon and I have seen up to three hunting simultaneously at this site on numerous occasions. The surrounding fruit trees attract many insect and seed-eating species, the more common ones being Gold and Greenfinches, Hawfinches (winter only), Serins, Tree Sparrows, Blackcaps, Great Tits, Hoopoes and Crested Larks. The giant reeds and tamarisk tees at the edge of the water hold small numbers of resident Cetti's, Spectacled and Dartford Warblers. Nightingales and Subalpine Warblers are usually present in the summer. This area also attracts raptorial species such as Kestrels, Marsh, Hen and Montagu's Harriers, Sparrowhawks, Black Kites and the much scarcer Black-shouldered Kite.

Access

The starting point for the lagoons is at Villamanrique de la Condesa and there are two routes that will lead you to them. The easiest, and probably the best route in wet weather, is by taking the Villamanrique - Pilas road (A-8060) that starts at the roundabout at the northern edge of the village, turning off to the right 1.5 kms along the road. The turning is signed as a crossroads but leads onto a dirt track, the Camino de la Marisma Gallega. Follow this track, which leads alongside vast olive plantations, for 3.5 kms until you reach a turning on the left, signed to the Corredor Verde. At this point I suggest you continue straight ahead and after a further 1.7 kms you will see the first lagoon on the left. Along this route you may see egrets, finches, larks, shrikes, chats, warblers and raptors.

The second access route is more difficult but can be far more interesting for birds. From the same roundabout as described above, take the road that is signed for Isla Mayor. After about one kilometre you will see a White Stork nesting colony in the trees on the right. These trees are in the gardens of the Palacio de Orleans and you can park here, at the entrance to the Cruzcampo beer distribution depot to view the colony and get very good photos.

Continue along the road for about 400 metres until you reach a crossroads where you should turn left, beside a white building. This is a dirt track that leads uphill and then forks. Take the left-hand track, which then leads downhill and then into a forested area known as Los Labrados y Torrejones. Follow the main track, keeping a rather crude fence to your right at all times, for 2.2 kms. At this point you reach a gate. Pass through the gate and continue for another 1.1 km. At the end of the track, turn right. This is the *"Camino de la Marisma Gallega"* and the viewing point for the first lagoon is 150 metres along the road on the left.

You can park anywhere along the route or even walk or drive into the forest, which holds a good selección of birds, ie. Iberian Magpies, Hoopoes, Crested Tits, Short-toed Treecreepers, Tree Sparrows, Green and Great Spotted Woodpeckers, Common Redstarts, Firecrests, Spotted Flycatchers, Buzzards and Ravens, to name just a few.

Please note that this track can be a problem during and just after heavy rain. The wet sand and mud is very soft and unless you have a 4x4 vehicle you may get stuck. If it looks bad it is probably twice as bad as it looks. Don't risk it. Go back to the roundabout and take the safer route.

From the first lagoon, you should continue along the track for about 500 metres and then take the first turning on the left. At the bottom of the hill you pass through a set of gates into an area of the Corredor Verde de Guadiamar (the Green Corridor). This is a fairly new "wildlife reserve" area that was created in 2002, following the contamination spill from the Boliden mine at Las Frailes, Aznalcóllar in April 1998 (see the "Pollution in Doñana" section). Following the disaster, the affected land was bought by the Andalusian Government and the area has been replanted with trees, bushes, shrubs and wildflowers and is maintained by the "*Agencia de Medio Ambiente*". The area has now fully recovered and has become a wildlife haven, with habitats which are now perfect for partridges, quail, shrikes, finches, sparrows, warblers, larks and ovehead raptors. It is also a regular breeding site for several pairs of Black-shouldered Kites.

At the end of this particular part of the Corredor Verde you pass through another gate and after 250 metres you should fork right and then turn right. This leads across a bridge over the Río Guadiamar. The bridge itself offers good birding opportunities for Nightingales, Black-crowned Night Herons, Little Bitterns, Kingfishers, Golden Orioles and Penduline Tits, depending on the season. Continue for 200 metres and you will notice a shrine on the right. This area is called the Vado de Quema, a very important part of the pilgrim route during the religious pilgrimage and festival that is held in El Rocío each year. The travellers stop here and conduct their ceremonies at the shrine, before walking and riding through the river to reach the opposite bank. At quieter times of the year the birding can be very good here, with Zitting Cisticolas, Blackcaps, Nightingales, Cetti's Warblers, Serins and other finches, larks and warblers usually present.

Laguna de Quema (N-3)

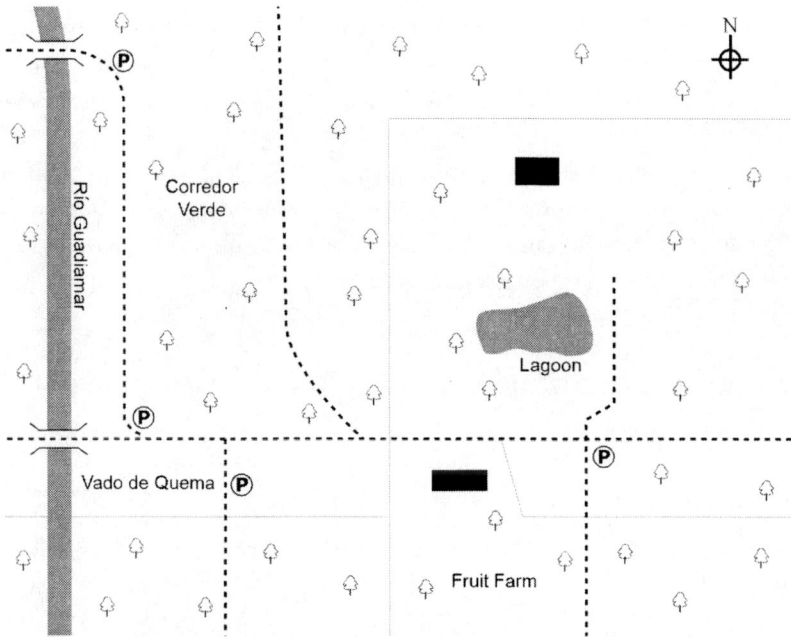

Continue along the track for 1.5 kms, passing the large "Afrexport" farm buildings at the top of the hill. The road now leads downhill and after 500 metres there is a gateway on the right where you can park. The lagoon is on the other side of the road, mostly hidden by fruit trees, but by walking 50 metres or so up the road you can get good views of a large part of the open water.

After you have visited the second lagoon, return the way you came and after crossing the bridge, turn left to re-join the Camino de la Marisma Gallega. Turn left at the top of the hill and continue along the track for 5.8 kms until you reach a main road. This is the road that leads from Villamanrique to the Isla Mayor and to other sites in the northern marshes.

To the left-hand side of the entire length of the track is a continuation of the Corredor Verde, with the Río Guadiamar running parallel with the road. This is one of the favoured breeding areas for Black-shouldered Kites, with at least four nesting pairs being present in 2005 and 2006.

Numerous small bridges cross the river and it is always worth a few minutes to check these for Kingfishers, Red-rumped Swallows, Spoonbills, herons, egrets, waders, grebes and ducks.

Along the last 800 metres of this track, the far bank of the river is covered with tamarisk trees. This is a favourite winter roost for Black-crowned Night Herons, with up to 500 birds being present in favourable years. You can park here and get out of your vehicle without causing too much disturbance to the birds and enjoy the spectacle from less than 50 metres.

The vast expanse of varied agricultural land to the right of the track can be very productive for birds at certain times of the year, especially Red-legged Partridges, Common Quail, larks, wagtails, finches and raptors and should also be checked carefully.

General Information

Both of the lagoons are on private land, surrounded by fences. Please respect the "*Paso prohibido*" signs and confine your viewing from the public areas.

Most of the area is flat and should not present a problem to wheelchair birders.

At weekends you may encounter small groups of pilgrims in this area as they make their way to the shrine at the Vado de Quema. Although they are usually very good natured they do tend to be a bit noisy and can have an effect on the birds.

In the spring of 2003, a pair of Black-shouldered Kites bred in the Corredor Verde, raising three chicks. This was the first successful breeding in the Doñana region by this species for almost twenty years. In 2007, the number had increased to six breeding pairs in this particular part of the Corredor Verde, with at least eight chicks being raised. Previously, the kites were only winter visitors to this region from Extremadura and other areas further north. However, since 2003, the breeding birds have remained in this region and we now have a sizeable resident population in Doñana. The number of wintering visitors has also increased over the last few years and it is possible at that time of year to see twenty or more birds in a single day, making Doñana one of the best places in Spain to see this species.

During the warmer times of the year it is advisable to carry a supply of water or other drinks with you as there are no bars or cafes in this area.

When To Visit

The lagoons and surrounding areas provide good birding throughout the year, although the winter produces more species, especially ducks, grebes and waders.

After a long, hot summer the water levels in the lagoons will be very low and birdlife may be minimal.

The large numbers of raptors do not normally become evident until at least an hour after the sun has risen and the land has warmed up, allowing the thermals to form.

The Dehesa De Pilas And The Dehesa De Banco North 4

This is a vast open cattle and horse grazing area to the south-east of Villamanrique, which although generally referred to as the Dehesa de Pilas, also incorporates the Dehesa de Banco and a part of the Arroyo de las Cigueñas. It is an area where one of Doñana's most sought after birds, the Pin-tailed Sandgrouse, is often found, along with Stone Curlews and occasional Little Bustards. The main Villamanrique - Isla Mayor road passes between the dehesas and the arroyo and a few safe parking areas allow you to view most of the area.

The terrain is generally flat, with low scrub vegetation, creating the perfect habitat for the aforementioned species. An isolated copse of eucalyptus trees holds a breeding colony of perhaps 300 pairs of Spanish Sparrows and several pairs of Black Kites, Booted Eagles and Hoopoes. A few scattered farm buildings nearby are used by a few pairs of nesting Common Kestrels and Little Owls. Several pairs of White Storks nest on the nearby electricity pylons.

Larks are very common in this area, with Crested and Calandra being the most noticeable, but careful scanning of the fields may produce small numbers of Greater Short-toed Larks, along with White Wagtails, Meadow Pipits (winter) and a variety of the Yellow Wagtail species during migration periods and in the summer.

Bee-eaters are particularly numerous here during the breeding season, usually between late March and July and this is one of the best places to guarantee seeing large flocks of them at close quarters. The birds burrow in to the soft sand to make their nesting chambers.

Extensive grazing of horses and cattle takes place here and during the foaling and calving seasons there is always a fairly high mortality rate. The resulting carcasses attract Griffon Vultures, Black and Red Kites, Ravens and, occasionally, Spanish Imperial Eagles. The height of summer also produces high mortality rates, when there is a drastic shortage of water and most of the vegetation has died off and what remains holds little or no nutritional value for the animals.

The nearby Arroyo de las Cigüeñas and a few sparsely vegetated irrigation channels provide suitable habitats for warblers, pipits and waders. Small bridges and water culverts offer nesting sites for both Barn and Red-rumped Swallows.

Access

From the roundabout at Villamanrique, take the road towards Isla Mayor. After 7.8 kms you reach a T-junction where you should turn left. As you drive along the road the Dehesa de Banco is on the right and the Arroyo de las Cigüeñas is to the left. The road has a white line on both sides, which means it is illegal to stop anywhere with your wheels on the road. However, there are a few areas where you can pull off the road safely. The first is after 500 metres, where a gateway with the words "Dehesa de Banco" on the gateposts offers limited safe parking and good views of the surrounding terrain.

Dehesa de Pilas and the Dehesa de Banco (N-4)

The sandgrouse can be hard to see if you don't really know what you are looking for and careful scanning of the area may be required to find them in the low scrub and the slightly undulating land. The birds are constantly flying around the area and by far the easiest way to locate the birds is to listen for their distinctive flight call. The birds are not particularly shy and may land within a reasonable distance. I have had small flocks land within 50 metres of my position on numerous occasions, giving first rate views to myself and clients.

Continue along the road for a further 600 metres and there is another gateway where you can park. This area offers a better chance of finding the sandgrouse as the terrain is flatter, with much less vegetation. Do not discount the other side of the road as the birds can sometimes be found along the banks of the Arroyo de las Cigüeñas

800 metres further along the road you reach a turning to the right which again offers good views of the area. The dirt track is in rather poor condition but leads for over a kilometre to the Dehesa de Pilas and a copse of eucalyptus trees where you can find Spanish Sparrows, Corn Buntings, Bee-eaters, Hoopoes, larks, wagtails, wheatears and pipits. Beside the track there is an irrigation channel which is sparsely vegetated with tamarisk trees. These are always worth checking for warbler species, including Cetti's, Subalpine, Olivaceous, Orphean and Willow Warblers. If you follow the track further it will lead you out through the Hato Raton rice fields and eventually to the José Antonio Valverde visitors centre, although this is not the best route to access that site.

The Dehesa de Pilas site can also be reached directly from the end of the previous site, the Lagunas de Mancho Zurillo. Once you have reached the main road at the end of the Camino de la Marisma Gallega, turn right and the track referred to is 1.8 kms along on the left.

General Information

Sandgrouse and Stone Curlews are generally only seen singularly or in pairs during the breeding season, which is April - June, but small family groups can be found once the chicks have hatched. Between September and March the birds tend to flock in wintering groups and it is not unusual to find up to 150 birds feeding in the same field.

The grassy areas beside the Arroyo de la Cigüeñas can be very good during the winter, if flooded, attracting Black-winged Stilts, Little and Cattle Egrets, Grey Herons, Spoonbills, White Storks, Glossy Ibis and many of the smaller wader species.

On the other side of the arroyo, running parallel with the main road, there is a dirt road that passes a turf producing enterprise and some agricultural land. The turf farm has huge mobile irrigators that are constantly watering the grass and offering feeding opportunities for many different species of birds. During the summer you should expect to see Yellow Wagtails, Hoopoes, Crested Larks, Zitting Cisticolas, Spotless Starlings, Collared Pratincoles, Little-ringed Plovers, White Storks, herons, egrets and other waders, along with swifts, swallows and martins.

During the autumn migration periods I have seen flocks of hundreds of Yellow Wagtails, Northern Wheatears, Whinchats and Meadow Pipits, that gather to feed here, sometimes for several weeks, before continuing their migration to Africa. The track that passes the turf farm is called the *"Camino de las Cigüeñas"* and can be reached from either the Villamanrique road or from the Camino de la Marisma Gallega.

The track leading from the main road to the Dehesa de Pilas is fenced with rather crude posts and are popular places during the spring migration for recently arrived migrants to rest. In the past I have recorded Common and Great Spotted Cuckoos, Turtle Doves, Orphean Warblers, Golden Orioles, Rollers, Common Redstarts, Lesser Kestrels, Black-eared Wheatears and Rufous-tailed Scrub Robins along this part of the site.

The main road here is very straight and traffic sometimes moves along at very high speeds, therefore, the limited space that the roadside parking areas offer may not be suitable for wheelchair birders to get out of their vehicle, but much of the area can be viewed from within the car. Once off-road, there is no problem.

This is a vast area and a telescope is always a great advantage here.

When To Visit

This site is of great interest throughout the year and is well worth visiting at any time. Heat haze can be a problem during the middle of the day in the summer and I would recommend early morning and evening visits at this time. This also coincides with the peak activity times of the sandgrouse, although the other species are normally active throughout the day.

Arroyo De Las Cigüeñas / Los Labrados
North 5

This is a seasonal site and is really only an extension of the previous one, but due to the quality of the birding that can be had here at the right time of the year, I have given it special mention. The area known as Los Labrados is a stretch of pasture land, beside the road between Villamanrique de la Condesa and the Isla Mayor. The Arroyo de las Cigüeñas runs through the area and after heavy rains the stream overflows and the pastures in this area flood, creating extensive shallow waterscapes that attract waders and other waterbirds. In good years the water can remain right through to the end of May and many passing migrants use it as a staging point before continuing their journey north, in some cases remaining for many weeks.

The surrounding area is mainly agricultural fields, with rice, cotton and beans being the most common crops. These also attract birds in good numbers, such as Crested Larks, Northern and Black-eared Wheatears, Whinchats, Yellow Wagtails, Red-rumped Swallows, Spanish Sparrows, Bluethroats, Serins and numerous finch and warblers species. Overhead you can usually see storks and raptors, which include Kestrels, Buzzards, Black and Red Kites, Booted and Short-toed Eagles, Ospreys and Marsh Harriers.

Access

From the turning that leads to the Dehesa de Pilas at the previous site, continue along the main road for 1 kilometre and you will come to a gateway to some agricultural land, on the right-hand side of the road. Beside this spot there is a tall white building which should act as a marker for you. Park here, but ensure that your vehicle is right off the road and that you do not obstruct the gateway. The main area for waders is on the opposite side of the road from here.

General Information

The road that passes the site is 3 metres higher than the seasonally flooded area, thereby offering excellent close-up elevated views of the pastures. However, as parking is very limited I would not recommend that wheelchair birders exit their vehicles here as the road is very straight and motorists regularly drive along here at well over 100 kph. A fair amount of the site and the bird activity can be viewed from the safety of a car.

When To Visit

The site is only of real interest if water is present, usually between October and May. Morning visits are recommended as the afternoon sunlight reflecting off the water can spoil your views.

The Entremuros
North 6

The word Entremuros literally means "between walls", referring to the raised dykes on each side of the site, which is approximately 4 kms in length and 1.2 kms in width. The site is a seasonal flood plain and forms a small part of the Corredor Verde de Guadiamar. It is supplied with water from two rivers, the Río Guadiamar and the Brazo de la Torre. Under normal circumstances there is a gentle flow of water along these two watercourses, but after heavy rains the rivers may flood and the whole of the area can become immersed in up to a metre of water and the whole site can be impassable.

To the west of the site there is the main road that leads towards the northern marshes and the JAV. There are a few parking places where you can stop to look out over the area, but the best views are obtainable from the eastern side where there is a raised track, that although in an appalling state, is driveable with care and offers excellent elevated views of the wetland and also a large part of the Isla Mayor rice fields. Numerous lagoons, streams, pools, marshes and the Brazo de la Torre river are all visible and can hold concentrations of Purple Swamp-hens, White Storks, Spoonbills, Greater Flamingos, Glossy Ibis, herons, egrets ducks and waders. Raptors are usually present and at certain times of the year you can see Marsh, Hen and Montagu's Harriers, Booted Eagles, Ospreys, Red and Black Kites, Common Kestrels, Peregrine Falcons and Hobbys.

Other species that may be regularly found along the length of this site include Collared Pratincoles, Whiskered, Black, Little and Gull-billed Terns, Sand Martins, Goldfinches, Serins, Greenfinches, Bluethroats, Penduline Tits, Dartford, Cetti's and Sardinian Warblers and Zitting Cisticolas. Rare birds are likely to appear at any time and in the past I have recorded Solitary, Pectoral and Marsh Sandpipers, Western Reef Herons, an African Spoonbill, Yellow-billed Storks, White-headed Ducks and Spotted Eagles along the course of this site. Little Bitterns (summer) and Great Bitterns (winter, although a few pairs probably breed) can also be found here.

Access

There are only two crossing points that allow access to the far bank of the Entremuros, the *"Vado de Don Simon"* and the *"Vado de los Vaqueros"*. These are sunken roads (fords) that cross the 1.2 km width of the site and are subject to flooding after heavy rain. As both have interesting habitats and birds I will describe each one separately.

Puente de Don Simon

Make your way to Villamanrique and then take the road to Isla Mayor. After passing the Dehesa de Pilas and the Arroyo de las Cigüeñas, the road turns sharply to the right. Continue along the road for about 3 kms until you reach an unsigned turning on the left. This will lead you across the ford which passes through the centre of the Entremuros. You can also reach this point from the southern end of the Camino de la Marisma Gallega, which joins the main road where it turns sharply to the right, as described above.

One hundred metres from the turning you cross a bridge over the Río Guadiamar and 700 metres further along there is a bridge over the Brazo de la Torre. You can park off-road at both of these sites and check out the rivers and surrounding fields and reedbeds. The Entremuros is a popular feeding area for White Storks, Spoonbills, Avocets, Little and Cattle Egrets, Black-winged Stilts, Purple, Squacco and Grey Herons and a host of other wader species. During the winter these are often joined by good numbers of Black Storks, Great White Egrets and a few Great Bitterns.

Puente de Vaqueros

This is the more southerly crossing that is 3.2 kms further along the main road on the left-hand side. The tarmacked road ends here and the track that leads straight ahead is the main route for reaching the José Antonio Valverde Visitors Centre and a number of other northern marsh sites. The large white building on the right is a pumping station belonging to the Cortijo de los Madrigales (site North 11), which is described later.

The Entremuros (N-6)

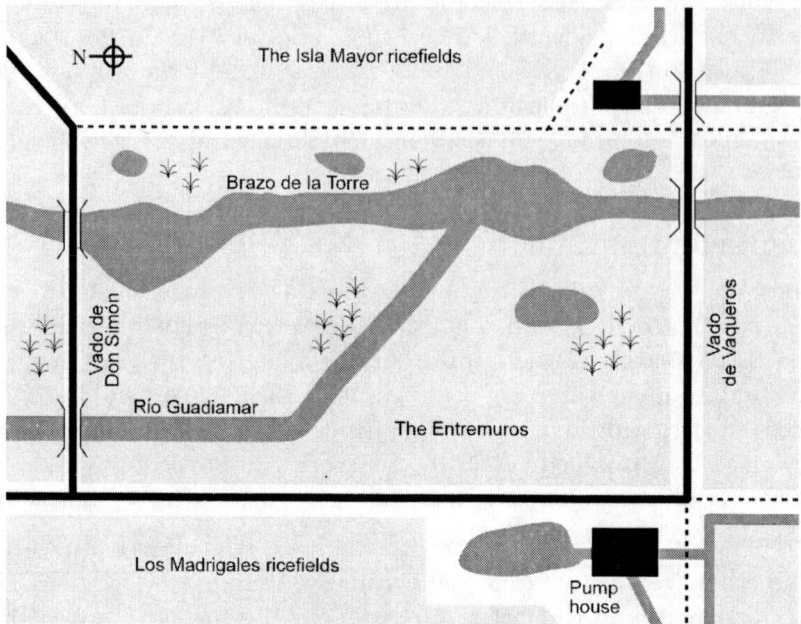

N

The Isla Mayor ricefields

Brazo de la Torre

Vado de Don Simón

Río Guadiamar

The Entremuros

Vado de Vaqueros

Los Madrigales ricefields

Pump house

The two rivers, the Guadiamar and the Brazo de la Torre, merge half way along the Entremuros and you cross the now single river 700 metres along the road. You can park by the bridge and check out the river and surrounding areas. The more interesting area is to the right, where large flocks of White Storks, Spoonbills, herons, egrets and waders often congregate to feed. Raptor activity is normally high and this is a favoured hunting ground for Ospreys and harriers.

Once across the Entremuros, turn right, if you have crossed via Don Simon, or left if you used Vaqueros and drive along the raised dirt track on the far bank. At the southern (Vaqueros) end of the track there is a large pumping station that supplies water to the rice fields of the Isla Mayor. This area can produce good views of Black-crowned Night Herons, Little Egrets and other waders, which gather here when the pump is in action to catch small fish that are forced to the surface by the pressurized water as it passes through the water channel.

General Information

Apart from the obvious attraction of the marshy areas and watercourses of the Entremuros, there are also the rice fields of the Isla Mayor to add to your interest. These fields are flooded and seeded from late April and are kept irrigated until the harvesting season, between late September and the end of November. During the summer, when the Entremuros usually dries out, the rice fields hold large concentrations of birds and are the main feeding grounds for many species.

Obviously, how you view this area is entirely up to you, but my favoured route is to cross the Entremuros by the more southerly crossing (Vaqueros), drive along the east bank and then visit several other sites, such as the Dehesa de Abajo, the "reedbeds" and the "gravel pits", before turning back and re-crossing the Entremuros using the Don Simon road. This enables you to visit the sites in the order in this guide book.

The track that runs alongside the eastern bank of the Entremuros is in very bad condition and care needs to be taken when driving along here. In wet weather the mud/clay surface, especially the middle section, is particularly bad and is often impossible to negotiate. To avoid the risk of getting your car stuck in the deep mud I would recommend that you avoid this road if wet. There is plenty to see elsewhere without taking unnecessary chances.

When To Visit

Due to the combination of the marshes, rivers, ricefields and irrigation channels the site always has something to offer birders as some parts of the area will always hold water. In the winter, the Entremuros is the main attraction, but in the summer, when the marshes dry out, the adjacent irrigated rice fields provide excellent birding.

On sunny days I would recommend that you visit the site during the early part of the day, as after about 14.00 hrs, the sunlight reflecting off the water can spoil your viewing.

The Isla Mayor Rice Fields
North 7

The Isla Mayor (the big island) is the largest of the rice producing areas within the Doñana region and during the growing and harvesting periods can produce some of the most spectacular birding you could wish for.

The rice fields, which extend for over 16 kms in a north/south line and for 10 kms from east to west, are prepared, flooded and seeded from late April onwards, providing essential wetland feeding and breeding areas for thousands of birds of many species. The fields are constantly irrigated and kept under about 3 centimetres of water for the whole of the five month growing process. Many drainage ditches and irrigation canals criss-cross the region, creating other feeding habitats for numerous wader species. As the natural marshes dry out during the heat of the summer the birds move over to the rice fields and great flocks can usually be found with ease.

To the west, the fields are bounded by the Entremuros and the Brazo de la Torre and to the east, the boundary is formed by the Río Guadalquivir. A network of tracks lead through the area and many of these are public, allowing you to get right into the heart of this region where Greater Flamingos, Common Cranes, White and Black Storks, Glossy Ibis, Spoonbills, Black-winged Stilts, Purple Swamp-hens, herons, egrets, waders and ducks can sometimes be found in their thousands.

Raptor activity is usually high throughout the year, especially in the breeding season and during the rice harvesting in autumn. The more common resident species are Marsh Harriers, Booted Eagles, Kestrels, Buzzards and Peregrine Falcons. The winter visitors include Merlins, Hobbys, Red Kites, Black-shouldered Kites, Hen Harriers and Ospreys, whilst in the summer there are Montagu's Harriers, Black Kites, Short-toed Eagles and Lesser Kestrels.

Access

Use either of the two crossings of the Entremuros to enter this area. Access is also possible from Sevilla via Puebla del Río and from the road that is signed for Isla Mayor and Las Minas Golf that leads from the roundabout to the south of the town of Aznalcázar.

General Information.

It would not be helpful or practical to try and highlight any particular location in this area, due to the vast expanse of land involved and constant bird movement. A field that may be holding up to 20,000 feeding birds today could be totally deserted tomorrow. Probably the best course of action is to just drive around the area looking into the fields or watching for flocks of flying birds and noting where they land. The terrain is very flat, but the banks that hold the water in the fields are sometimes a few feet high and there could be thousands of birds within a few hundred metres of your location that are hidden from view by these banks.

One of the methods that I regularly employ to locate the feeding birds is by driving into the Dehesa de Abajo, which is right on the northern edge of the rice fields. The hills here are some 35 metres above sea level and by parking by the, as yet, unopened visitors centre you are able to scan a very large area of the rice fields to see where the flocks are gathered. The elevated position can also help you to establish a way of getting close to the birds, ie. which track to take.

Don't be afraid to get off the main roads. Most of the tracks leading through the rice fields are public and are usually driveable without any problems. Of course, if any track has a sign saying *Privado, Paso Prohibido* or *No pasar*, you should respect these signs.

Many of the farm workers are very tolerant of birders and although they may not understand our pleasure in merely watching birds, instead of shooting and eating them, they will often try to help you. I can recall numerous occasions when I have been way off road and a car has stopped and the driver has informed me that there are many flamingos or storks further along the track, or something similar.

During the autumn and winter (October to March), good numbers of Short-eared Owls are present and one of the best places to see these is from the Isla Mayor end of the Vado de Don Simon. Once across the ford, park off-road by a large Doñana sign and check out the area of La Cangrejera, a vast tract of scrubland to the left. It is best to view this area during the last hour of daylight, when the owls become active. Normally, there will also be other raptors present and in January 2006, 4 clients and I stopped here at 17.00hrs, for an hour and recorded 6 Short-eared Owls, Booted Eagles, Red Kites, Black-shouldered Kites, Marsh Harriers, Hen Harriers, Common Buzzards, Common Kestrels, a Peregrine Falcon and Southern Grey Shrikes, all hunting in the same fields.

When To Visit

The most productive times for the birds is during the sowing and harvesting seasons. The fields are usually flooded and seeded from about the 20th of April. The seeding is carried out by a fleet of aircraft that fly low over the flooded fields scattering the seeds in an aerial bombardment. At first there is very little bird activity in the fields as the water is almost sterile, but after a few days the food chain starts to develop and the birds move in. For the next 6 - 8 weeks, until the plants grow too high, thousands of birds can be found feeding in any field throughout the region. These include herons, egrets, stilts, plovers, wagtails, terns and gulls.

During the summer there is still plenty of activity, as the fields become the sole source of food for some birds and breeding grounds for others. Unfortunately, the height of the rice hides many of the smaller species.

The harvesting season, which can last from late September until early December is by far the optimum time to visit this area and produces one of the greatest birding spectaculars I have witnessed. More information on this can be found in the "Rice production in Doñana" section.

The Reedbeds
North 8

This is a little-known site which is located in the middle of some of the Isla Mayor rice fields. It comprises a 2.5 km stretch of reedbeds that surround a stretch of the Brazo de la Torre river. It has no official name and I refer to it only as the "reedbeds". The site can hold an exceptional number of bird species throughout the year and as human disturbance is minimal, several of the more "secretive" species, such as Little Bitterns, Spotted Crakes, Water Rails and Bluethroats can be found here at the appropriate times of the year.

The resident birds of interest are Purple Swamp-hens, Squacco and Grey Herons, Glossy Ibis, Little and Cattle Egrets, Black-winged Stilts, Little Grebes, White Storks, Greater Flamingos, Marsh Harriers, Booted Eagles, Little-ringed Plovers, Green and Common Sandpipers, Kingfishers, Hoopoes, Sardinian and Cetti's Warblers, Zitting Cisticolas and Common Waxbills.

During the breeding season the resident birds are joined by Little Bitterns, Purple Herons, Marbled Ducks, Little and Spotted Crakes, Montagu's Harriers, Reed, Great Reed, Sedge and Savi's Warblers, Yellow Wagtails, Collared Pratincoles, Whiskered, Black and Gull-billed Terns, Red-rumped Swallows, Sand Martins, Bee-eaters, Woodchat Shrikes and Spotted Flycatchers.

The winter and passage periods are usually very good and produce many of the duck and wader species that can be found almost anywhere in Donana. However, because of the isolated location it is a favourable spot to find wintering Bluethroats, Snipe, Penduline Tits, Reed Buntings, Grey Wagtails and Hen Harriers.

The reedbeds also hold a breeding colony of Golden Bishops, members of the weaver family that are a recent arrival/introduction to Spain. They breed much later than all the other species, usually during September and October. Without doubt, one of the highlights of this site is seeing the males, in full breeding plumage of bright yellow and black, conducting their territorial and courtship displays.

Access

The reedbeds can be reached by following the directions to the Dehesa de Abajo/Cañada Rianzuela. There are two separate entry points to the site. To reach the first you should cross over the Puente de Don Simon and continue along the road until you reach a sharp left-hand bend in the road. 500 metres further on the road turns to the right and just beyond this there is a track that leads down to the right, running between a rice field and some reeds. Take this narrow track and continue for 700 metres until you reach an enclosed water pump on the right. Turn to the right, directly beyond the pump and carry on until the next sharp right-hand turn. 30 metres further on you will find a place to park, at the end of a pasture.

The "Reedbeds" (N-8)

N

Quarry

Cañada
de Rianzuela

Rice

Rice

Rice

Brazo de la Torre (P)

Rice

(P)

To find the second access point, continue along the road until you reach the first pull-off point on the left-hand side of the road. Here you will find the sluice-gate for the Cañada Rianzuela. Opposite this point there is a track that leads into the ricefields. Follow this track to the end and then turn left. After 75 metres you will reach the water pump described above.

From the parking place, walk back 25 metres and explore the reeds and the marshy areas to both sides of the track and also the pasture and rice fields, which can both be very good for birds. The Golden Bishops nest in the reeds close to the track and the Common Waxbills are often found in the reeds or at the very edge of the rice fields. The Bluethroats prefer the muddy irrigation gullies whilst a search of the bullrushes and reeds may produce views of Reed Buntings and Penduline Tits.

As the track you are on is closed by a barrier you should re-trace your route to get back to the water pump. You can now turn right and drive carefully along the track, stopping occasionally to check the reedbeds and rice fields. After about one kilometre the track turns sharply to the left and if you follow this track it will lead you right around the fields and bring you back to the water pump.

General Information

During the rice growing season (April - October) the farmers drain water from the Brazo de la Torre to irrigate their crops. Therefore, the water levels can change from day to day, creating different conditions and attracting different bird species.

You can combine this site with a visit to the Dehesa de Abajo and the "gravel pits", which are only a short distance away.

Most of the tracks through the rice fields are made of sandstone and gravel and are driveable, with care, in wet weather. However, the track from the water pump to the first parking area and the track leading around the fields are composed of a very heavy clay compound which, when wet, will clog the treads of your tyres resulting in your vehicle becoming stuck. If the track is wet then I suggest that you park by the water pump and walk the next 200 metres to view the first site, unless you have a good 4x4 vehicle. Sadly, this warning also applies to wheelchair birders, who will find it very heavy going on this surface.

When To Visit

On bright, sunny days, this site is best visited in the morning as the afternoon sunlight reflecting off the water will have an adverse effect on your viewing. In other conditions you can visit at any time.

During the harvesting season (late September to late November) you may encounter heavy agricultural machinery on the narrow tracks. Always be prepared to reverse a long way to allow them to pass, as due to the size of these vehicles, they would find it hard to do so.

Dehesa De Abajo / Cañada De Rianzuela
North 9

The Dehesa de Abajo (the low meadows) was once a large hunting reserve. It is situated on the northern edge of the vast rice producing area of the Isla Mayor, in the municipality of Puebla del Río, Seville.

In January 2000 the site was bought by the Andalusian Government and the management of the area was taken over by the A.M.A. It has now been turned into a natural reserve, complete with nature trails and bird observation hides. A visitors centre and educational classrooms are being constructed, but there is no indication when these will be opened.

The reserve covers an area of 618 hectares (1,527 acres) and contains varying habitats, all of which are important to birds and other wildlife. Amongst these are large areas of wild olive (acebuches), eucalyptus and oak trees, which play host to one of the largest breeding colonies of White Storks in Europe, with perhaps 500 nests. There is also a stone pine forest where Black Kites, Buzzards, Booted Eagles, Iberian Magpies, Jays, Short-toed Treecreepers, Tree Sparrows, Woodchat and Southern Grey Shrikes, finches, tits, woodpeckers and warblers breed.

Open scrubland and meadows attract Hoopoes, Bee-eaters, Black-eared Wheatears, Yellow Wagtails, larks and scrub warblers, especially in the spring when the meadows are in full flower and insect numbers are at their highest.

Alongside the western edge of the dehesa and within the boundaries of the reserve is a large artificial lagoon and marsh area known as the Cañada de Rianzuela. Two bird hides overlook the lagoon and sandy tracks lead alongside the water's edge and marshy areas. This is an important feeding area for thousands of wintering ducks, waders and other waterbirds and is also a regular breeding ground for Marbled Ducks,

Red-knobbed Coots, Little Bitterns, Squacco Herons, Purple Swamp-hens, Black-winged Stilts, Kentish and Little-ringed Plovers, Whiskered Terns and Great Reed Warblers. Small numbers of White-headed Duck are sometimes to be found at this site and in the spring of 2006, for the first time, at least two pairs successfully bred here.

It is common, when water is present, to find large flocks of Greater Flamingos, Spoonbills, Avocets, Black-tailed Godwits, Glossy Ibis, Little Egrets, Cattle Egrets and Ruff. During the winter and autumn passage period you can also find Green, Wood and Curlew Sandpipers, Dunlins, Little and Temminck's Stints, Lapwings and Ringed Plovers.

In the summer of 2004, nine semi-circular "atolls" were created when the lagoon was dry. These now provide roosting and nesting areas for birds, especially Avocets, Black-winged Stilts, Whiskered Terns and Lit-tle-ringed Plovers. They are strategically placed near to the road and the two bird hides, providing good views for birders.

During the spring passage period this is an important feeding area for migrating birds that are moving further north to their breeding grounds. Garganeys, Rollers, Common Redstarts, Whinchats and Great Spotted Cuckoos are amongst the more interesting birds seen here at this time.

Access

The Dehesa de Abajo and the Cañada de Rianzuela are very close to the "reedbeds" and can be visited directly after that site. Simply return to the tarmacked road and turn right. The road now runs alongside the lagoon for 1 km, offering numerous chances to park off-road. From the end of the lagoon you should continue for 500 metres until you reach an arched gateway. This is the entrance to the Dehesa de Abajo site and at the top of the hill you will find a large car park, beside the (as yet un-opened) visitors centre.

Dehesa de Abajo and the Cañada de Rianzuela (N-9)

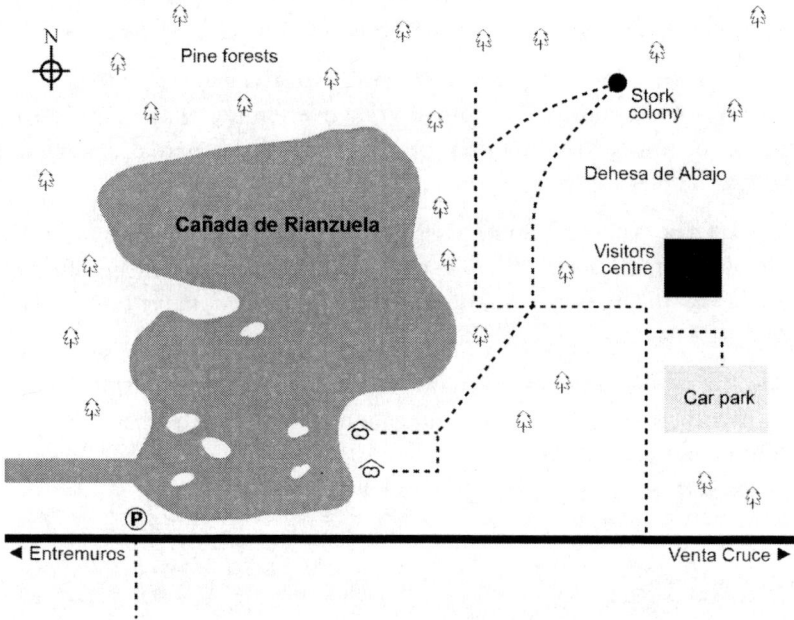

N

Pine forests

Stork colony

Dehesa de Abajo

Cañada de Rianzuela

Visitors centre

Car park

◄ Entremuros

Venta Cruce ►

From the visitors centre car-park, part of the White Stork nesting colony can be seen in the wild olive trees. Walk past the centre and you will find an information board with a map of the area. The two bird hides can be reached by following the left-hand trail. The central track leads directly to the lagoon, but in wet weather this is sometimes flooded. To gain further access you may have to walk along a raised boardwalk which bears off to the right, from the central track. This leads to a *mirador* that looks out over a large part of the stork colony, but you will also find numerous tracks that will lead down to the water.

The main track leads alongside the lagoon, through open scrubland, for about 1 km before reaching the pine forest. Although you will be further away from the lagoon, it is sometimes better to find an elevated position from which to view the marsh and open water.

The distances involved in walking all of the trails is about 4 kms, but the highest point of the site is only 35 metres above sea level so there is no real strenuous effort required.

The area is extensively grazed by horses and cattle from the small farm that is within the reserve's boundary. In spite of my previous warning about cattle, these animals pose no threat to humans and at times can be very helpful when they flush out birds that are hidden from view.

General Information

As this is a fairly flat site, it is suitable for wheelchair birders, although some difficulty may be experienced on the softer sandy tracks.

At the time of writing, the construction of the new visitors centre has been completed but it is not yet known when it will open or whether there will be any food/drink facilities available. It is, therefore, advisable to take a drink supply with you.

During the warmer months of the year, the area is normally very busy with picnicking families, especially at weekends and public holidays. The resulting noise and disturbance is not conducive to good birding and the area is best avoided on days such as these.

The site is also a fairly popular "school day-trip" destination and you may be unfortunate enough to find coachloads of children suddenly descending upon the area. This can result in the same problems as the picnickers.

When To Visit

The site is of great interest throughout the year. In the winter and during passage periods, large flocks of birds are attracted to the site and many birds will spend the whole winter here.

The breeding season can begin as early as late February and can last through until late June/early July. It is during this period that the majority of species can be seen.

During the height of summer, when the water levels are very low, or the lagoon dries out completely, the majority of water birds will move over to the nearby rice-fields, which are constantly irrigated and hold good water levels until the rice is harvested in October and Novemember.

The Gravel Pits
North 10

These are a series of four shallow ponds that begin about 1.5 kilometres north-east of the Dehesa de Abajo entrance and can be viewed from the road. They have no official name and I just refer to them as the "gravel pits". At times, good numbers of herons and egrets feed and roost here and it is also a regular feeding station for smaller waders. The ponds were created by quarrying and the excavation of gravel in the 1970's, and 80's, when large amounts of the soft sandstone that forms the hills in this area were extracted to construct the ricefields and the dirt tracks that give access to them. The gravel pits have since become flooded and well vegetated and some now tend to hold water throughout the year, creating ideal habitats for many bird species. They are regular roosting spots for Black-crowned Night Herons, Squacco and Grey Herons and both Little and Cattle Egrets. During the daytime the birds are often visible in the small tamarisk trees that surround the ponds, usually just above the water-line and especially in sunny weather. Wintering numbers of Night Herons, usually juveniles and a few adults, can be as high as 75 birds.

Other waterbirds/waders that can be found here include Grey Herons, Moorhens, Coots, Great Crested and Little Grebes, Common and Red-crested Pochards, White-headed Ducks, Cormorants, White Storks, Little Bitterns, Black-winged Stilts, Kentish, Ringed and Little-ringed Plovers, Redshanks, Greenshanks, Common, Wood, Green and Curlew Sandpipers, Ruff, Lapwings, Dunlin and Kingfishers.

The surrounding area is of rice fields to the south and low hills and scrubland to the north. Raptors, such as Black and Red Kites, Short-toed and Booted Eagles, Kestrels and Common Buzzards are often seen soaring over the nearby hills. The sandy faces of the quarried areas provide nesting places for Sand Martins and Bee-eaters in the spring, whilst the abandoned buildings are favoured haunts of Little Owls and Black Redstarts. During the winter you may also find Blue Rock Thrushes near the old building close to the road.

Other species to look out for are White and Yellow Wagtails, Meadow Pipits, Sardinian, Willow, Subalpine, Olivaceous, Dartford and Cetti's Warblers, Zitting Cisticolas, Blackcaps, Chiffchaffs, Common Waxbills, Woodchat and Southern Grey Shrikes, Hoopoes, Stonechats, Whinchats, Barn and Red-rumped Swallows, Pallid Swifts, House Martins, Rock Sparrows, finches, tits and larks.

Access

To reach these ponds you should follow the directions to the Dehesa de Abajo (site N-9) and then continue along the road for about 1.3 kms, until you reach the first two ponds on the left-hand side of the road. 400 metres further along the road there is an abandoned quarry building where White Storks nest in spring and Blue Rock Thrushes are sometimes found in the winter. The third pond is 500 metres beyond this building and the last is another kilometre further on. Altogether there are four ponds, spread over a distance of 2 kms.

The "Gravelpits" (N-10)

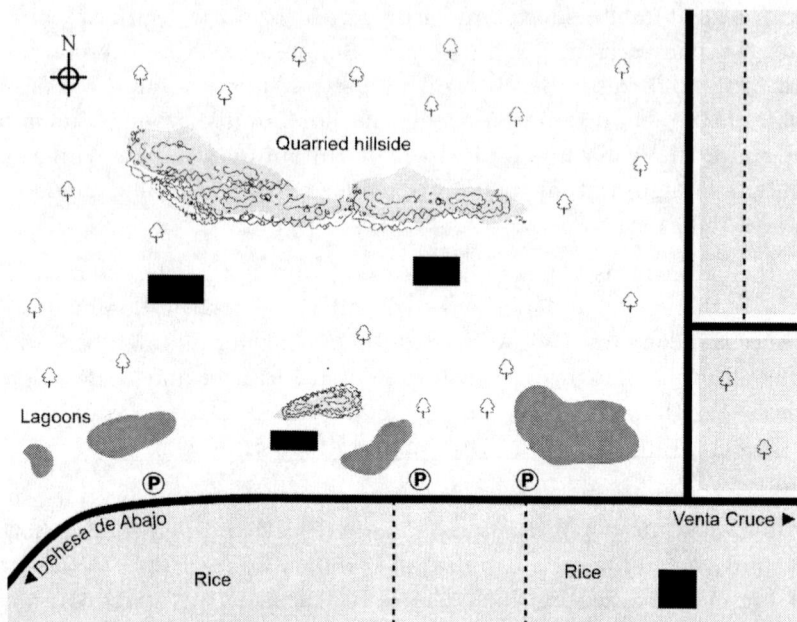

General Information

Even though the road that leads beside the ponds is fairly narrow, the locals tend to drive here at great speeds, so care needs to be taken here. A few parking spaces can be found, but mostly you have to rely on "on-road" parking. The first two ponds are very close to the road and in order not to scare the birds away it is better to pull as far off the road as possible and view from your vehicle. However, if you get out of your vehicle very carefully the birds will often stay.

The last pond is just before a roundabout and is bounded to the east by a number of very tall eucalyptus trees and is protected from the road by a dense hedge of prickly pear cacti. You can park off-road here and approach the pond, using the cacti as a screen. In previous years, two pairs of Red-knobbed Coots have bred here and were highly visible for a number of months. During the same period I also recorded Marbled Ducks, Ruddy Shelducks, Muscovy Ducks, Black Storks and a Marsh

Sandpiper at this site. This pond tends to dry out towards the end of summer and therefore may be of little interest at that time.

One kilometre beyond the last pond there is a bar/restaurant, the "Venta el Cruce," where you can get food and drinks. The outside patio looks out over rice fields, with the possibility to birdwatch and eat at the same time.

Due to the narrow and treacherous road, I would not recommend wheelchair birders to get out of their vehicles at the first two ponds. However, it should be safe to do so at the others.

When To Visit

The ponds are of interest throughout the year provided that water is present, which is usually the case.

The sun is always behind or overhead at these sites, so you will not be affected by reflected sunlight from the water. This makes the area suitable for all-day viewing.

During the hunting season, between October and March, the area is often used for that purpose, especially on Sundays. The disturbance of men, dogs and guns will obviously have an effect on the birds and be disappointing for birders.

Cantarita Ricefields
North 11

The area known as Cantarita is situated in the most southerly part of the Isla Mayor. It is a vast, flat region, where ricefields, vegetated irrigation ditches, canals, reedbeds, scrubland and the Brazo de la Torre offer outstanding birding opportunities throughout the year.

In the spring, the ricefields are flooded and seeded and the area is alive with feeding and breeding birds such as Black-winged Stilts, Avocets, Kentish and Little-ringed Plovers, Squacco and Purple Herons, Little Bitterns and Purple Swamp-hens. The area is also very attractive as a stop-over feeding station for huge numbers of migrating birds that pass through the region at this time, especially many species of waders.

During the autumn (September - November), the ricefields are harvested and, in common with the other rice areas, produce the same spectacle of thousands of birds feeding in the fields on the rich fare that is churned up by the machinery.

From October, we see the arrival of hundreds of thousands of ducks, geese, raptors, waders, storks and cranes, that will spend the winter in this food-rich environment, remaining until March, or even April. This is one of the prime sites for Black Storks and Common Cranes at this time of year.

Access

To access this area, you need to make your way to the town of Villafranco del Guadalquivir (Isla Mayor). This can be reached by the road that crosses the Entremuros (Vado de Vaqueros) or from the road leading from the Venta el Cruce. From the former, turn right onto the main street once you reach the town.

From the latter, continue straight ahead. After 400 metres you will reach a roundabout, where you should take the first exit. Continue for about 400 metres, where you should turn left, at the next roundabout, where signed for "El Matochal". This road passes through an industrial area and then becomes a dirt track, which leads through ricefields and is in fairly good condition.

Cantarita ricefields (N-11)

Continue for about 4 kms until you reach a large single building, just after crossing an irrigation canal. Now follow the main track until you reach an abandoned building. Just after this, turn left, onto the larger of the two tracks. The track now continues for about 3 kms, with electrical pylons on the left, until you reach a sign indicating "Cantarita". Turn right here and continue until you pass through a large area of reedbeds. This is a part of the Brazo de la Torre and should be investigated for warblers and waterbirds.

Once you have passed through the reedbeds, turn right and continue for about 400 metres and then turn left. The track now leads straight ahead for about 4.5 kms, passing through ricefields and beside the Cortijo de Cantarita, with its palm tree lined frontage, until you reach the end of the route, by the Brazo de la Torre. Here there are dense reedbeds and open areas of water and scrubland. Park here and explore the immediate area on foot.

General Information

Depending on the water levels in the ditches and the Brazo de la Torre, you may find ducks, waders, herons, egrets and storks. In the reedbeds, you should look for Purple Swamp-hens, Little Bitterns, Little Crakes, Water Rails, Cetti's, Savi's, Reed and Great Reed Warblers, Bluethroats, Zitting Cisticolas, Penduline Tits, Common Waxbills and Reed Buntings.

Birds of prey are often present and depending on the time of year, you may find Common Buzzards and Kestrels, Marsh, Montagu's or Hen Harriers, Hobbys, Peregrine Falcons, Merlins, Black and Red Kites, Ospreys, Griffon Vultures and Booted and Short-toed Eagles.

Stopping anywhere along the route can be beneficial, especially beside wet ricefields, where waders may be feeding. The distances can sometimes be great, so a telescope would be a great advantage here.

Although the site is easily accessible, there are three main problems that you are likely to encounter. They are: dust in the summer, mud in the winter and the large number of heavy agicultural machines on the tracks during the rice harvesting period.

Due to the very flat nature of this area and the fact that the tracks are usually quiet and are in reasonable condition, it is suitable for wheelchair birders.

This is a very isolated area, without services, so you would be advised to ensure you have enough fuel for your vehicle and an ample supply of drinking liquids.

When To Visit

The area is of great interest for most of the year, as there will always be good numbers of birds present. July and August are the least productive months, due to the excessive heat and the height of the rice, which tends to hide many of the birds that are feeding in the fields. Visits in the morning and evening are preferable, as there will be more bird activity at those times.

Cortijo De Los Madrigales And The Puente De Vaqueros
North 12

This is only a small site consisting of a few rice fields, a pumping station, reedbeds, agricultural land and irrigation channels, but it can produce some tremendous birding at times. It is situated opposite the junction of the Puente de Vaqueros that leads across the Entremuros, just where the dirt road that leads to the JAV Centre begins.

You can park off-road, directly in front of the white building, which is a large pump house, and explore the area from there. To the right of the pump house there are a few large tamarisk trees that regularly hold a few roosting Black-crowned Night Herons and behind these there are reedbeds where Purple and Squacco Herons, Little Bitterns, Reed, Savi's, Cetti's, Sedge and Great Reed Warblers may be found.

To the left and in front of the building, there is a series of irrigation channels and drainage ditches that are favoured by Squacco Herons, Green Sandpipers, Redshanks, Greenshanks and Common Snipe. The large area of rice fields beyond the water courses should be scanned for Purple Herons, Little and Cattle Egrets, Black-winged Stilts, Purple Swamp-hens and Spoonbills. Collared Pratincoles, Sand Martins, Red-rumped Swallows and terns can often be seen feeding over the fields and these can include Whiskered, Black, Little and Gull-billed Terns.

The open agricultural land holds Woodchat and Southern Grey Shrikes, Corn Buntings, Stonechats, Spanish Sparrows, Calandra Larks and Meadow Pipits.

By walking up to the road you can find more muddy ditches, reedbeds and waterscrapes which are regularly frequented by wintering Bluethroats. From this vantage point you also have an elevated view of a large part of the Entremuros.

Access

This site is at the junction of the Puente de Vaqueros and the start of the dirt road that leads to the JAV. It is so easily accessible that you could visit it several times in a day as you visit the Entremuros and on your way to and from the JAV.

You can park beside the road, at the entrance to the site, but you can also drive through the gates and park in a safer place. Just beyond the pump house there is a second set of gates that you can walk through to check the various watercourses.

General Information

Although the pump house is on private land, the owners are tolerant of birders provided that they are on foot and keep to the main tracks, which allow perfectly adequate viewing opportunities of most of the site.

The tamarisk trees where the Night Herons roost during the day also serve as a night time roost for good numbers of both Spanish and House Sparrows. In April and May the trees are often used by migrating Turtle Doves and warblers. During the winter months you should look carefully for Barn Owls, as they, too, prefer tamarisks to roost in.

During the rice-seeding and early growing season (late April to June), the pump-house is usually in operation for most of the day. The water is pumped through large pipes to a main irrigation channel to the left of the building. Night Herons and egrets regularly gather at this point, as small fish and insects, stunned by the water pressure, are forced to the surface and make easy meals for the birds.

When To Visit

There is usually plenty of bird activity at this site and any visit here should produce a good list of birds. As with the main rice fields of the Isla Mayor, the seeding and harvesting periods are exceptionally good, but my favourite time here is a few days after the rice stalks have been ploughed back into the earth, usually in October or November, creating the feeding frenzy spectacular that I have described earlier. After the more aggressive meat and insect eaters have left the fields in search of fresher areas, the more sedate Purple Swamp-hens, which are mainly vegetarian, have their time and are often seen feeding on the remaining stalks and roots in groups of up to 400, usually in the early mornings and evenings.

Casa De Bombas
(The pump house)
North 13

The Casa de Bombas is the main water pumping station in the Doñana region and is situated beside the Brazo de la Torre on an elevated dirt track that leads out towards the JAV and the other northern marshes sites. The building is old, large and imposing and looks to be abandoned, but it is still in working order and is used almost weekly to pump water from a large irrigation canal into the Brazo de la Torre.

Many of the windows have been smashed by stones and gunshot and this has allowed access and created an ideal nesting site for up to 8 pairs of Common Kestrels, which can always be seen in this area.

In front of the pump house there are reedbeds and a few river inlets where Spoonbills, Little and Cattle Egrets, Grey, Purple, Squacco and Black-crowned Night Herons, Purple Swamp-hens, Glossy Ibis and several duck and wader species may be found feeding throughout the day. The area can also be an excellent spot for finding Great Bitterns during the winter period, when as many as six have been present in previous years.

The vast open area beyond the reedbeds is constantly quartered by Marsh Harriers and these are joined by Hen Harriers in the winter and Montagu's Harriers in the summer. Large flocks of Common Cranes and White Storks can sometimes be seen feeding and often include small numbers of Black Storks in the winter.

Casa de Bombas (N-13)

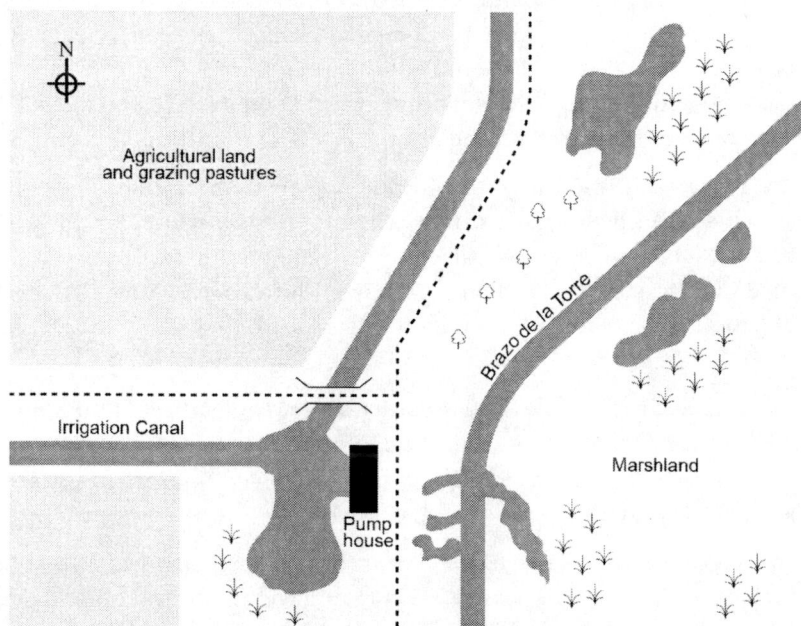

N

Agricultural land
and grazing pastures

Brazo de la Torre

Irrigation Canal

Marshland

Pump
house

Behind the building, the irrigation canal widens out to create a reed-fringed pool that sometimes attracts Little Bitterns and several warbler species. The water level fluctuates from week to week and when the water level is low, muddy margins are exposed where Bluethroats and Yellow Wagtails feed. Great Bitterns also visit this spot and Little Crakes have been recorded here on many occasions.

The dry scrubland is used mainly for cattle grazing and this should be checked for Zitting Cisticolas, Spectacled Warblers, Stone Curlews and both Greater and Lesser Short-toed Larks.

To the sides of the building there are several tall electricity pylons that provide lookout posts/perches for Ospreys, Peregrines, Black and Red Kites and Short-toed Eagles.

Access

The pump house is about 7.5 kms along the track that runs southward from the Cortijo de los Madrigales site. Just follow the directions that are given for the José Antonio Valverde Centre. You can't miss it.

General Information

The track leading to the pump house and the track beyond run alongside the Brazo de la Torre and the Corredor Verde. The elevated track affords good views of the river, canals, irrigation ditches, pools, reedbeds and marshes and I would suggest that several stops should be made on the way to scan the surrounding area, especially if water is present.

The fenceposts, tamarisk trees and the scrub vegetation alongside the track should be checked during the migration periods for passing Common Redstarts, Rufous-tailed Scrub Robins, Turtle Doves, Great Spotted and Common Cuckoos, Spotted Flycatchers, Northern and Black-eared Wheatears, Whinchats and warblers, including Subalpine, Olivaceous, Orphean, Melodious and Icterine.

Numerous rarities have been recorded recently at this site, including 2 Yellow-billed Storks, an African Spoonbill, a Marabou Stork, 3 Western Reef Herons, a Solitary Sandpiper, a Long-legged Buzzard, a Greater Spotted Eagle and a Red-winged Blackbird.

The whole of this area is very flat and the dirt road surface, although pot-holed in places, is in a fairly reasonable condition and should not cause too many problems. There are also numerous parking places along the route which are suitable for wheelchair birders to get out of their vehicles without any danger

When To Visit

Although the largest number of birds (and species) will normally be present during the winter, any time of the year should produce a good list of birds. Sunshine reflecting off the water can be a bit of a problem in the mornings, but after midday there should be no problems.

Huerta Tejada
North 14

This is a vast area of open marsh and scrubland that runs for about 5 kms alongside the northernmost boundary of the national park and usually holds several interesting species. A large Medio Ambiente educational centre, La Casa de Huerta Tejada, and two farms, the Finca de las Caracoles and the Finca de Cochinato, are the only buildings in this area and these, along with several small bridges that cross irrigation channels that lead to the farms, should be checked for the resident Hoopoes, Spotless Starlings, Barn and Little Owls and nesting Red-rumped Swallows.

The two rough fields on the right, between the Huerta Tejada and the farm, are excellent areas for wintering flocks of Stone Curlews, with regular sightings of 300 or more between November and March. In the fields beyond the farm you can often find massive flocks (up to 2,000 of each species) of Calandra Larks and Corn Buntings. Also, careful scanning may produce Pin-tailed Sandgrouse and, if very lucky, Little Bustards.

The land on the other side of the road is known as the Las Caracoles fields, an area of land that has recently been incorporated into the national park. After heavy rains, much of the land will flood to a depth of a 10 - 15 centimetres and attracts many wader and duck species, including Great White Egrets. Greylag Geese are often found here in thousands during the winter and careful scanning of the flocks may reveal one or two Lesser Whitefronts, Barnacle and Brent Geese, or even Ruddy Shelducks.

The dirt road that serves this area and the fences alongside are good places to look for larks, pipits, wagtails, shrikes and wheatears. Crested and Greater Short-toed Larks in particular enjoy using the road surface for dust bathing and White and Yellow Wagtails are regularly seen hunting for insects. Beside the road there is sparse vegetation, mostly salicornia, and this habitat offers the opportunity to look for the various resident scrub warblers that can be found here. The most abundant are Sardinian Warblers and Zitting Cisticolas, but Dartford and Spectacled Warblers are also present.

Huerta Tejada (N-14)

Large numbers of wintering Common Cranes can often be seen feeding in the general area and raptors are always in evidence. The more common species being Red and Black Kites, Marsh, Hen and Montagu's Harriers, Buzzards, Kestrels, Peregrine Falcons and both Booted and Short-toed Eagles. Much scarcer, but also regularly seen are Spanish Imperial Eagles, Hobbys and Merlins.

Much of the area is pastureland, used mainly for the grazing of horses, sheep and cattle. There are also herds of Fallow and Red Deer within the boundaries of the park.

Access

This area is just a few kilometres along the road from the Casa de Bombas and is on the way to the Lucio del Lobo and the JAV centre. From the pumping station, continue for just over 4 kms until you reach a junction where you can only turn right. The track ahead used to give access to the Lucio de Cangrejo, but the surrounding land was acquired by the national park in 2005 and the road has now, unfortunately, been fenced off. However, from the junction you have good views to the left of some wetlands and marshes, which are part of the Corredor Verde/Entremuros/Brazo de la Torre.

The educational centre is approximately 1 km along the road and it is from that point where I suggest you start to look for birds, making frequent stops along the route to the Lucio del Lobo.

General Information

The land to the left of the road has recently been acquired and added to the national park and during 2005 work took place at certain locations along the route, close to the road, to create water scrapes that hopefully, in the wetter times of the year, will attract waders and other birds to these sites.

Mid-way along the route towards the Lucio del Lobo you reach a line of concrete electricity pylons on the right. These offer perching/lookout posts for birds of prey and are regularly used by Common Kestrels, Buzzards, Peregrines, Black Kites and Short-toed Eagles.

This is an extremely flat location, devoid of trees or hills and offers good views across the whole of the area. It is ideal for wheelchair birders, although the road surface is rather bumpy in one or two areas.

When To Visit

The site is productive at any time of the year, even during the hottest months of June, July and August. The spring migration is a particularly good time for finding Subalpine, Olivaceous, Icterine, Orphean and Willow Warblers, Rollers, Turtle Doves, Tawny Pipits, Whinchats, Common and Great Spotted Cuckoos, Black-eared Wheatears and Rufous-tailed Scrub Robins. These birds arrive from Africa after the long sea crossing and tend to use this area as a feeding/resting point before continuing their journey northward.

Autumn migration is also of interest as some species, such as yellow Wagtails, Whinchats, Sand Martins and Northern Wheatears, tend to congregate here in large numbers in September and October, before heading south. This period also sees the passage of Short-eared Owls, which arrive for the winter period and have been seen in the fields in groups of up to 24 birds.

Lucio Del Lobo
(Pool of the wolf)
North 15

The Lucio del Lobo is a vast seasonal wetland situated in the northern marshes area of the Doñana region. It is just within the national park boundary and can produce some spectacular birding when water is present. The water is never more than a metre deep but it attracts thousands of birds during the breeding season and is a regular nesting site for Red-knobbed Coots, Avocets, Black-winged Stilts, Kentish Plovers and Collared Pratincoles.

In the winter, when the water is plentiful, thousands upon thousands of ducks, Greylag Geese, Greater Flamingos, Common Cranes, Spoonbills and other long-legged waders can be found feeding in the central areas, whilst smaller waders, such as Dunlins, Little Stints and Ringed Plovers occupy the shallower parts of the lagoon.

During the spring migration and in the breeding season, as the water slowly evaporates, large numbers of Ruff, Curlew Sandpipers, Black-tailed Godwits, Greenshanks and both Common and Spotted Redshanks congregate to feed and come into breeding plumage prior to continuing their northward migration to their breeding grounds. This can result in over 30,000 birds being present .

Numerous gull species also use the lagoon and it is not unusual to find small numbers of Slender-billed Gulls amongst the more common Lesser Blackbacks, Yellow-legged and Black-headed Gulls. Terns are often present in the spring and I have recorded Whiskered, Black, Little, Gull-billed and even Caspian Terns at this particular site.

Birds of prey and vultures are often present, amongst them are Peregrine Falcons, whose main prey targets appear to be Teal and Black-winged Stilts. Nest thieves, such as Black Kites and Marsh Harriers are present in good numbers, often targeting the nests of the Avocets, Lapwings and Stilts. The Black Kites in particular seem to work in teams and one kite will swoop low over the breeding ground, immediately being attacked by large numbers of the other species. Whilst the breeding birds are distracted by the lone kite, others suddenly appear and attack the unguarded nests.

Other birds that are regularly seen around the lucio include Greater and Lesser Short-toed Larks, Zitting Cisticolas, Yellow Wagtails, Spectacled Warblers, Whinchats, Northern and Black-eared Wheatears and Pin-tailed Sandgrouse.

Access

The lucio is just 0.5kms west of the Doñana Biological Station and just 2.2 kms east of the JAV centre and visits to the lucio are best incorporated with visits to the JAV and various other sites in this area. Therefore, you should consult the access directions for the JAV to reach this site.

General Information

The lucio is just within the park boundaries where there are free-ranging herds of both Red and Fallow Deer and numbers of these are regularly seen feeding in the marshland or drinking at the pool.

The track that leads alongside the site is slightly elevated and offers good views of the whole wetland area, making it very well suited to wheelchair birders. Traffic density is extremely low and you can park anywhere on the side of the road without causing problems to others.

About halfway along the pool there are four or five small scrubby tamarisk trees that should always be checked for warblers. On one of my tours with a group of birders during the spring migration, we discovered Orphean, Olivaceous, Willow and Subalpine Warblers, Blackcaps, Woodchat Shrikes, a Nightingale and 2 Turtle Doves in just one small tree, all viewed from less than 10 metres.

When To Visit

This site is only of any value if water is present. During the summer the pool dries out completely and, apart from a few larks, is usually devoid of birdlife. However, the pool is usually artificially part-filled with water via a pumping system from early September onwards. This then provides a feeding/drinking site for many passage migrants returning to Africa and for the birds that are arriving from the north to spend the winter here.

Morning and evening visits are recommended for the best viewing. During the afternoon the sunlight reflecting off the water can have a detrimental affect. Heat haze may also be a problem from late spring to early autumn.

Centro De Visitantes "José Antonio Valverde" (Cerrado Garrido) North 16

This visitors centre, often referred to as Cerrado Garrido or the JAV, is many kilometres out into the Doñana marshes and is not easy to reach due to the lack of up-to-date maps, insufficient directions and a complex system of tracks that lead to the site.

Many people are under the impression that the site can be accessed directly from El Rocío, via the Raya Real and then by a connecting track through the national park which leads out to the northern marshes. This used to be the case, but the track through the park was closed to the public in 2002 in an effort to preserve the breeding territories of the resident Spanish Imperial Eagles and the Iberian Lynx. More recently, the Raya Real track leading from El Rocío has also been closed to the public. The new route involves a drive of 60 kms from El Rocío and takes about one hour (without stops) to reach the centre. Rough maps and directions to reach the JAV are available from the other visitors centres but I would strongly advise you to disregard these as they guide you along some of the worst tracks in the region where many visitors have suffered damage to their vehicles or have become stuck in deep mud or sand. Also, the directions are not clear and I have, many times in the past whilst on my tours, come across birders who had become completely lost trying to follow the instructions. The route that I will describe later is the one that I use and is the simplest and safest way of getting to the JAV from El Rocío.

The José Antonio Valverde visitors centre was opened in 1994 and has a bar/cafeteria, toilet facilities, an information desk, temporary and permanent exhibitions and audiovisual shows. Inside the building there are large plate glass windows that look out directly onto a large reed-fringed lagoon where many species of herons, egrets, ducks, grebes, terns and waders can be seen at very close range.

Centro de Visitantes "José Antonio Valverde" (N-16)

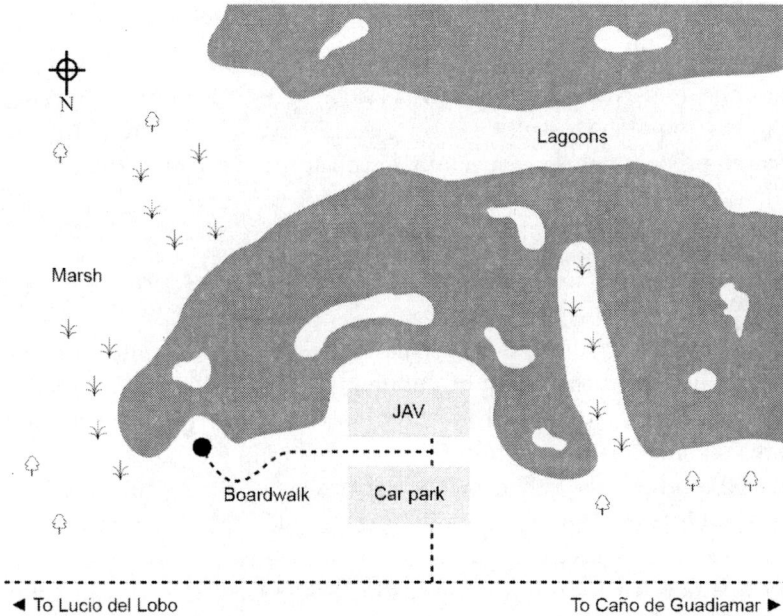

The reedbeds to the right of the centre is a major breeding site for Little and Cattle Egrets, Purple, Squacco and Black-crowned Night Herons, Little Bitterns, Glossy Ibis and Purple Swamp-hens. From mid-March until June, spectacular elevated views can be had of this mixed breeding colony from just 30 metres away, behind the plate glass windows. It is estimated that there may be up to 1,000 nests in total, in an area no bigger that three football fields. In the spring of 2004, over 1,000 Glossy Ibis chicks alone were "ringed" at this site.

To the left of the centre there is a short boardwalk that leads alongside more reedbeds. Here you will find a screen fence with "windows" that allow you to see into the reedbeds without unduly disturbing the birds. This sometimes offers the best chance of getting close to some of the more secretive species, like the Little Bitterns and Cetti's Warblers.

Other breeding species that can be found at this site include Red-knobbed Coots, Garganeys, Marbled Ducks, Red-crested Pochards, Collared Pratincoles and Reed, Great Reed and Savi's Warblers. Throughout the year, water permitting, you may also see Greater flamingos, Spoonbills, White Storks, Avocets, Black-winged Stilts and numerous other wader species and during the winter you should keep an eye out for Great White Egrets, Common Cranes, Black Storks, Black-necked

Grebes, Great Bitterns, Stone Curlews, Bluethroats, Reed Buntings and Penduline Tits.

Birds of prey are always present and, depending on the time of year, you may see Ospreys, Spanish Imperial, Booted and Short-toed Eagles, Black and Red Kites, Common Buzzards, Marsh, Hen and Montagu's Harriers, Common Kestrels, Peregrines, Hobbys and Merlins. Vultures are often present nearby, especially in the spring and summer, with the Griffon being by far the most common.

Access

Easy access to the JAV is via Villamanrique de la Condesa. At the roundabout just to the north of Villamanrique take the road signed for Isla Mayor. Follow this road for 7.8 kms until you reach a T-junction where you should turn left. Continue on this road for 9.5 kms until the surfaced road ends and becomes a dirt track. Take this track and after 7.5 kms you pass a large white building, the "Estación de Bombas", the Casa de Bombas pumping station. A further 4.5 kms along the track you come to a turn-off to the right, which is signed "Centro de Visitantes, José Antonio Valverde - 10 kms." Follow this road to the centre. Please disregard any other roadside sign for the JAV that you may see, except this one. The dirt roads that you will be travelling on can be rather bumpy in places and some care needs to be taken, but they are in far better condition than those described in the hand-outs from the other visitors centres.

As you travel along this road you will be passing several more sites that are described in this book, such as the Dehesa de Pilas, the Arroyo de las Cigüeñas and Los Labrados, the Vados de Don Simon and Vaquero, the Casa de Bombas, the Brazo de la Torre, Huerta Tejada and the Lucio del Lobo. Obviously, time allowing, it makes sense to combine all of these sites into a one-day trip.

General Information

The visitors centre is open from 10.00 - 18.30hrs every day, with the exception of the 25th, 26th and 31st of December, the 1st, 5th and 6th of January and the week of the annual El Rocío festival, which is during whitsun.

There are no nature trails here although the raised road to both sides of the centre offers good views of the surrounding marshes and agricultural land. In the spring and summer you should take note of the birds feeding or dust-bathing on the dirt roads. More often than not, these will be Crested and Greater and Lesser Short-toed Larks. The terrain is very flat with uninterrupted views, which is ideal for wheelchair birders, although the distances can be great and a telescope would be a big advantage at this site.

When To Visit

The site is of major interest throughout the year, with the possible exception of July and August, when parts of the surrounding wetlands usually dry out.

The lagoon in front and to the sides of the Centre usually holds water throughout the summer, courtesy of an irrigation system that pumps water into the lagoon. The most spectacular time for birders is during the breeding season (March to June) but excellent birding is also provided during the winter, when large flocks of Stone Curlews, Corn Buntings, Calandra Larks and Common Cranes can be found.

Between October and March, when the sun is lower in the sky, sunlight reflecting off the lagoon can impair your views during the afternoons. During the summer and on cloudy days, this problem does not occur.

Caño De Rosalimán
(Marismas de Hinojos)
North 17

The Caño de Rosalimán is a seasonal watercourse that extends southeastwards from the Madre de las Marismas at El Rocío. It is surrounded by a vast area of seasonal marshland, the Marismas de Hinojos, which is wet in the winter and spring and dry and dusty during the height of summer. The area is within the protected boundaries of the national park but large areas can be viewed from an elevated track that runs alongside it for over 4 kms.

During the winter this is a prime site for Common Cranes, Pin-tailed Sandgrouse, flamingos, geese, ducks and waders and it is also a favoured hunting ground for Peregrine Falcons, which seem to prefer Teal and Black-winged Stilts as their main prey targets. Marsh Harriers are regular visitors to the area and Spanish Imperial Eagles, from their nesting sites in the stone pine forests to the north, south and west, may also be found, hunting for rabbits.

Up to 60,000 Greylag Geese winter in the Doñana region and it is not unusual to find a quarter of these feeding in this area. These are sometimes joined by very small numbers of Lesser Whitefronts, Bean and Brent Geese and Common and Ruddy Shelducks. If the water conditions are right there may also be up to 30,000 Greater Flamingos here. Wader species and numbers are usually high and I have recorded flocks of thousands of Black-tailed Godwits, Little Stints, Golden Plovers, Ruff, Dunlins, Curlew Sandpipers and smaller numbers of Grey, Ringed, Little-ringed and Kentish Plovers, Turnstones, Temminck's Stints, Wood Sandpipers, Whimbrels, Glossy Ibis, Spoonbills, Avocets, Greenshanks and both Common and Spotted Redshanks.

Caño de Rosalimán and the Caño de Guadiamar (N-17, N-18)

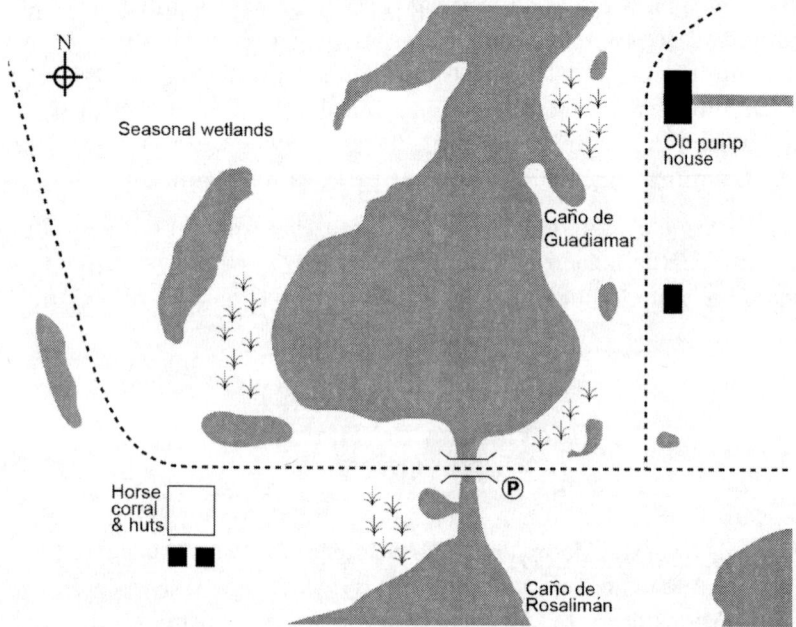

The spring and early summer is a very busy time at this site, with thousands of breeding birds being present. Perhaps the most notable are Marbled Ducks, Red-knobbed Coots, Whiskered, Black and Gull-billed Terns, Collared Pratincoles and Purple Swamp-hens. Raptor activity is usually high, with Marsh Harriers and Black Kites being the most prominent as they raid the other birds' nests for eggs and chicks. Other birds of prey include Common Kestrels, Montagu's Harriers and both Short-toed and Booted Eagles.

Thousands of horses, sheep, cattle and deer roam wild in this area and death is common during the summer, when blazing heat, the shortage of water and the lack of nutritional vegetation takes its inevitable toll. Carcasses do not remain undetected for long and within a day or so there will be large numbers of vultures present. The Griffons are by far the most common, with sometimes up to 100 birds feeding at a carcass, but they are occasionally joined by the larger Cinereous (Black) Vulture and the smaller Egyptian Vulture. Other regular feeders at carcasses are Red and Black Kites, Ravens and Spanish Imperial Eagles.

Access

This area runs westwards from the José Antonio Valverde Centre and should form part of your visit to that site. Approximately 600 metres from the JAV you pass over a bridge that crosses the Caño de Guadiamar. From this point the Marismas de Hinojos run parallel to the left-hand side of the road for some four kilometres. The dirt track is in a fairly bad state and care needs to be taken whilst driving here.

About a kilometre along the track you pass a large enclosure with a few huts (chozas), where horses and cattle are often herded and penned. The many fenceposts surrounding the enclosure are always worth checking for vultures and raptors, which often use the posts as perches. At the end of the track you reach a gate, which is the control point for entry into the national park. The gate is not locked but you may not enter, as only people with the appropriate permits may pass this point. The area here is known as Cancela de Escupidera and is one of the better places to watch for the Spanish Imperial Eagles, which nest in the distant forests to the north and west and can sometimes be seen hunting over this area. The area beyond the gate, within the park boundary, is called Veta Zorrera (the vixen's island) and is always worth checking for waders, raptors and for herds of both Red and Fallow Deer.

The village of El Rocio is less than 5 kms from this point and it is very frustrating for those who wish to return to the village to have to turn round and travel nearly 60 kms to get back to the village, but please respect the "No entry" signs. If caught in this protected area you face a hefty penalty.

General Information

This is a vast, flat area of seasonal marshland, overlooked by an elevated track that borders the national park. The track, although very bumpy in places, should not prove too much of a problem for wheelchair birders and it is wide enough to stop anywhere and get good views from within the comfort of your vehicle whilst still allowing other traffic to pass safely.

Distances are great and a telescope would be a great advantage here, although heat haze is a major problem during much of the year.

When To Visit

This site is of great interest throughout most of the year but the area is more productive during the winter and spring when water is present. Large wintering flocks of ducks, geese, waders and passerines can be seen from late October until late March and breeding birds are present from mid-March to mid-June. However, afternoon visits on sunny days during this time of the year can prove disappointing as the sunlight reflecting off the water will mar your views. In the summer the sun is much higher in the sky and the problem is not so bad until much later in the evening. On cloudy days, good viewing is possible at any time.

July, August and September are the least productive times to visit. Most of the birds have completed their breeding and the marshes will have been baked dry by the intense summer heat. You should also consider the fact that mid-summer temperatures can reach 50° Centigrade (120°F) and that there is no shade to be found in the marsh areas.

Caño De Guadiamar
North 18

This is a vast open area of seasonal marshland that stretches for some 5 kilometres to the north-west of the José Antonio Valverde Visitors Centre (JAV). It is part of the natural park and receives some protection, but the shooting of geese and ducks is allowed during the hunting season. It borders the national park and is adjacent to the Marismas de Hinojos, being divided from that area by a track that runs westward from the JAV. Together they constitute part of what I generally refer to as the northern marshes and form one of the finest overall birding sites in the Doñana region. During the spring this is a major breeding ground for several attractive species, including Marbled Ducks, Red-crested Pochards, Glossy Ibis, Little Bitterns, Avocets, Black-winged Stilts, Pintailed Sandgrouse, Purple Swamp-hens and Red-knobbed Coots.

Numerous rarities have been recorded in this area over the last few years, amongst which were Yellow-billed Storks, Western Reef Herons, a Marabou Stork, a Lesser Yellowlegs, Ruddy Shelducks, a Desert Wheatear, Spotted and Lesser Spotted Eagles, White Pelicans and a Red-necked Stint.

Other birds that are seen quite regularly are Griffon Vultures, Spanish Imperial and Short-toed Eagles, Red Kites, Great White Egrets, Squacco and Black-crowned Night Herons, Spoonbills and Greater Flamingos. The area is also exceptional during the migration periods, especially during the spring passage, as this is the first major feeding/resting site that many birds reach after crossing over from Africa.

Passage migrants regularly include Turtle Doves, Rufous-tailed Scrub Robins, Whinchats, Orphean, Melodious, Willow, Olivaceous, Bonelli's and Subalpine Warblers, Rollers, Tawny Pipits, Northern and Black-eared Wheatears, Curlew Sandpipers, Ruff, Whimbrels, Spotted, Little and Baillon's Crakes and Egyptian and Black Vultures.

Several important reedbeds can be found along the edges of the marshes, which are nesting sites for Cetti's, Reed, Great Reed and Savi's Warblers. In the surrounding shrubs and scrub that border the driveable tracks there are usually Spectacled and Dartford Warblers, which also breed here.

During the winter, hundreds of thousands of ducks and geese can be seen, along with hundreds of Common Cranes, Stone Curlews and large flocks of Corn Buntings, Calandra Larks, Dunlin, Little Stints, Ringed Plovers, Black-tailed Godwits and numerous other wader species. Other wintering birds include small numbers of Short-eared and Barn Owls, Great White Egrets and Great Bitterns.

Access

To reach this site you should follow the directions to the José Antonio Valverde Centre (JAV) and it is best incorporated together with visits to that site and the Marismas de Hinojos. On leaving the JAV, turn left and proceed for 500 metres, until you reach a track on the right. This track leads alongside the Caño de Guadiamar. By continuing straight along the road from the JAV, instead of turning right, you can also look out over the Marismas de Hinojos, which hold many similar species.

General Information

The track that leads north, alongside the Caño de Guadiamar, is in a fairly good condition, but care should still be taken. Along this track there are several areas that are worth mentioning. The first is after 500 metres, where a reed-fringed canal on the left often holds good concentrations of Squacco, Grey and Black-crowned Night Herons, Spoonbills, White Storks, Black Storks (winter) and egrets.

Further along the track, on the right, there is an old, abandoned pump-house. A pair of Little Owls regularly nest underground, beneath the old pump machinery and one or two Barn Owls usually roost in the tallest part of the structure during the winter months.

During the spring and summer, look out for Short-toed Eagles on the tall electricity pylons and also for the Red-rumped Swallows, that nest under the culvert at the pump-house. Peregrine Falcons often use the pylons as look-out posts during the winter.

After a further two kilometres the track turns away from the water and 150 metres to the left you will see a few tamarisk trees. These are favoured roosting places for several egret and heron species.

Please note that this is a very flat area, which makes it easily accessible for wheelchair birders. Most of the area can also be adequately viewed from a car. However, the flatness of the area, without trees or other forms of shade, means that it can get oppressively hot at times. Fortunately, wherever you are, the JAV (where you can get food and cold drinks), is never more than five kilometres away.

When To Visit

The site is of maximum value during the winter and spring, when water is usually present. However, sometimes the winter rains fail and much of the area can be arid and very short of birdlife, except for larks, warblers and raptors. During June, July, August and September, most of the water will have evaporated in the constant heat of the summer.

Good views can be had during most of the day as the sunshine does not affect the site until later in the evening. For more information I refer you to the notes for the previous two sites.

Hato Ratón Rice Fields And Partido De Resina
North 19

These are two reclaimed marshland areas that have been converted into agricultural land. They are situated between the Caño de Guadiamar and the Dehesa de Pilas. The extensive ricefields of Hato Ratón offer the same birding spectaculars as the others in the region, although they tend to be planted, and subsequently harvested, later than the fields of the Isla Mayor. The Partido de Resina covers many hectares of flat, open land which is mainly used for the growing of cereal crops and for the grazing of cattle. This area offers the chance of finding steppe species such as Pin-tailed Sandgrouse, Stone Curlews, Calandra Larks and Little Bustards.

The area is serviced by a large central track and many smaller tracks lead off from this, inviting further investigation. The low scrubby vegetation along the edges of the tracks are ideal habitats for Zitting Cisticolas and Dartford, Sardinian and Spectacled Warblers. Numerous irrigation channels flow around the fields and these often hold Green and Common Sandpipers, Redshanks, Black-winged Stilts, Common Snipe and Kingfishers. The Caño de Guadiamar runs parallel with the main track for about 10 kms and the open water and muddy banks are good places to find Grey and Purple Herons, White Storks, Little and Cattle Egrets and other waders, such as Ringed, Little-ringed and Kentish Plovers, Curlew and Common Sandpipers, Dunlins and Black-tailed Godwits. In some places, the riverbank is heavily vegetated with reeds and harbours Purple Swamp-hens, Little Bitterns and several warbler species. There are several large bridges that cross the river and these provide regular nesting locations for House Martins, Barn Swallows and the much scarcer Red-rumped Swallows.

There is usually significant raptor activity in this area, especially amongst Red and Black Kites, Marsh, Montagu's and Hen Harriers, Buzzards, Kestrels, Peregrines, Merlins and Booted and Short-toed Eagles. The Spanish Imperial Eagles are regularly recorded here as the overall site forms part of their hunting territory. The presence of sheep and cattle, with the inevitably high mortality rate amongst these animals, especially during the lambing/calving season and in the height of summer, attracts scavengers such as Ravens and Griffon Vultures. Both Barn and Little Owls are fairly common and Short-eared Owls are often present during their passage period in October and November.

Passage migrants are usually plentiful during both the spring and autumn periods and, apart from the more common birds, such as Whinchats, Yellow Wagtails, Northern Wheatears, Turtle Doves and Willow Warblers, you may also find Rollers, Great Spotted Cuckoos, Rufous-tailed Scrub Robins, Black-eared Wheatears, Icterine, Subalpine and Orphean Warblers and even Rufous-tailed Rock Thrushes.

Access

There are two main ways to reach this area. The first is by continuing straight on for 1.5 kms from the Dehesa de Pilas (see site North 4) until you reach a small bridge. After crossing the bridge you should turn left and continue for about 500 metres. After crossing a second bridge you should then turn right. This area is part of the Partido de Resina and by following the track for another 6 kms you will reach the Hato Ratón rice fields.

Hato Ratón ricefields (N-19)

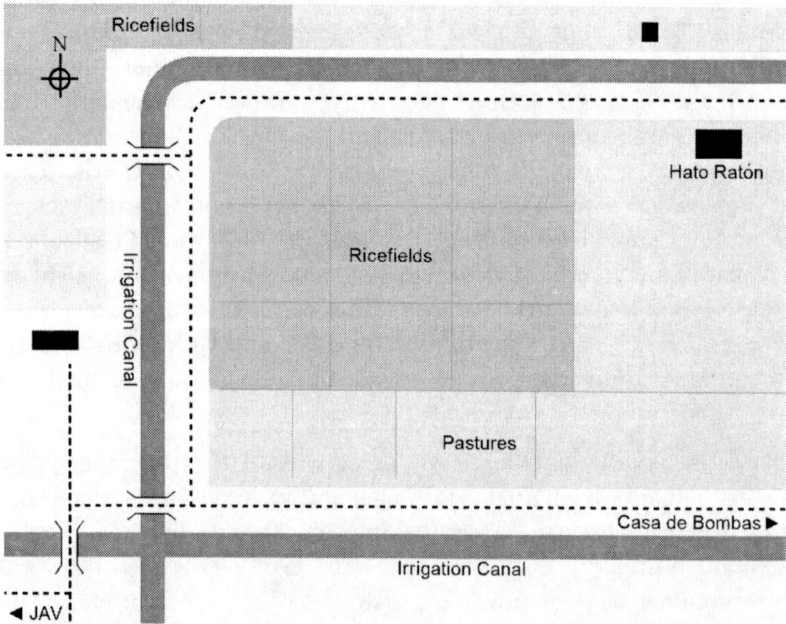

The second way to reach this area is the one that I prefer and can form part of a circular tour of the northern marshes. After visiting the Caño de Guadiamar (North 17), continue along the track for 5 kms until you reach a bridge. Turn left here and then immediately right, across a second bridge. Now turn left, following the sign for Villamanrique and after 2 kms you reach the start of the Hato Ratón rice fields. If you follow this road further you will reach a large orange building that is part of the Hato Ratón farm complex. Once past this point you are entering into the Partido de Resina. At the end of this road there is a T-junction, where you should turn left and after a further 500 metres, turn right. This track will lead you past the Dehesa de Pilas and back to the main Villamanrique/Isla Mayor road.

General Information

The whole of this site/route is on dirt tracks, some of which are in a bad state of repair and extra care needs to be taken whilst driving here. A kilometre beyond the large orange building there is a public "waste plastic" dump, where tractor loads of old plastic sheeting and irrigation piping from the surrounding farms are dumped. Unfortunately, the waste plastic is seldom collected and often the careless dumping results in the road becoming completely covered, creating a major driving hazzard.

The next 2 kms of track, up to the T-junction at Partido de Resina, is in a particularly bad condition, with large, deep potholes. In dry conditions this is not a major problem, as you can at least see the hazzard, but after recent rainfall the potholes may be full of water and mud and you have no idea of how deep the holes are. This could result in your car getting very firmly stuck and I strongly advise you not to take the risk of continuing unless you have a 4x4 vehicle. An alternative and sensible plan would be to turn around and drive 9 kms back to the bridge and then turn left. This will lead you directly back to the Casa de Bombas. From there you should turn left to get back to the main road.

When To Visit

Although the major interest is during the breeding and rice sowing/harvesting seasons, this site will always provide good, all day birding at any time of the year.

The Eastern Sector

The sites that I have included in this section are all situated on the eastern side of the Río Guadalquivir. Sites 1, 2 and 3 are in Sevilla province whilst the others are in the Parque Natural de Doñana region in Cádiz province. Habitats are similar to those in the previous chapter and bird densities can sometimes be as good, depending on the season.

Access from the main Doñana region to the Isla de los Olivillos, Brazo del Este and the El Lago Diego Puerta sites is by way of the municipal ferry that operates from the town of Coria del Río. Other routes, from Sevilla and the main Sevilla-Cádiz road can also be found.

To reach this area from Villamanrique you need to follow the directions to the Dehesa de Abajo. Go past that site and continue along the road until you reach the Venta el Cruce. At the roundabout take the road that is signed for Sevilla and after about 8 kms you reach the town of Puebla del Río. Pass through the town until you reach a roundabout at the top of a hill. Go straight across and after 100 metres you reach a second roundabout with a very large statue of King Alfonso X in the middle. On the roundabout, take the first turning off to the right, which leads downhill into Coria del Río, where you need to catch the ferry across the Río Guadalquivir. The ferry is not advertised but can easily be found by following the instructions below.

Continue towards Coria until you reach the second set of traffic lights, where you should follow the main road to the right. You now pass through the centre of the town and you should continue until you reach the next set of traffic lights. Go straight across and then, after 100 metres, take the first turning on the right. This will lead you directly to the ferry which operates throughout the year from 06.00 to 21.00hrs in the winter and until 23.00hrs in the summer. The crossing takes less than 5 minutes and you should never have to wait more than 10 minutes for the next ferry. The present cost for a car and driver is 2.10 euros with an additional cost of 0.40 cents per passenger. Once across the river, follow the road for 5kms until you reach a bridge over the Río Guadaira. My directions to these sites begin at this point. The road leading directly ahead will take you to the Isla de los Olivillos. You have to cross over the bridge to reach both parts of the Brazo del Este site.

These sites can also be reached from the E5/A4 road from Sevilla to Cádiz by taking the exit at junction 553 and then following signs at the roundabout to Isla Menor. After 1.5 kms there is a T-junction where you should turn left. After 3.5 kms there is a turning to the left, signed for Coria, with a picture of a ferry. By turning right here you will reach the bridge over the Río Guadaira referred to above and the road that leads to the Isla de los Olivillos. By continuing straight ahead you can reach both entry points for the Brazo del Este.

If you are based in Doñana and plan to visit the sites near Sanlúcar de Barrameda, you can use the ferry to cross the Río Guadalquivir, but you may well find it quicker to drive up to Sevilla and then take the E5/A4 toll road to Cádiz, turning off for Jerez de la Frontera at junction Km 84 and then following the signs for Sanlúcar. This would involve a drive of about 2 hours.

9

Isla De Los Olivillos
East 1

The Isla de los Olivillos is situated on the eastern side of the Río Guadalquivir and visits here are best incorporated with visits to the Brazo del Este sites. The site itself includes several interesting habitats and holds a wide variety of resident and migrant bird species throughout the year.

The area is mainly agricultural and boasts a spectacular mixed nesting colony where breeding Squacco and Night Herons, Little and Cattle Egrets and Spoonbills can be viewed from less than 100 metres away. Also breeding in the vicinity are Cetti's, Savi's, Reed and Great Reed Warblers, Zitting Cisticolas, Common Waxbills, Golden Bishops and Marsh Harriers.

Most of the area is bounded to the east by the Río Guadaira and to the west by the Río Guadalquivir. A 4.5 km elevated track runs alongside the Guadaira, offering good views of some of the more sought after waterbirds, ie. Purple Swamp-hens, Squacco and Black-crowned Night Herons and Spoonbills, etc.

A large lagoon offers the chance to see numerous duck species during the winter months, with Common and Red-crested Pochards, Mallards, Pintails, Shovelers and Gadwalls being the most common. The lagoon is also a fairly reliable spot for small numbers of White-headed and Ferruginous ducks in the winter and migrating Garganeys in the spring and autumn. All three of our grebe species, Great Crested, Little and Black-necked can also be found in good numbers in the colder months of the year and small numbers of each species remain to breed in the spring.

Birds of prey are usually evident, with Red and Black Kites, Ospreys, Common Buzzards, Booted and Short-toed Eagles, Peregrine Falcons, Hobbys, Common and Lesser Kestrels and Marsh, Hen and Montagu's Harriers being present at the appropriate times of the year.

The surrounding agricultural land, mainly rice, cotton, sunflowers and sweetcorn, attracts large numbers of larks, finches, waxbills and waders throughout the growing season and Collared Pratincoles breed on rough open land within metres of the main track.

Access

Once you have crossed the Río Guadalquivir by ferry you should drive for 5 kms until you reach a bridge over the Río Guadaira. Do not cross the bridge, but continue straight ahead. Follow this road for 4.2 kms until you reach a number of eucalyptus trees where the road turns sharply right. At this point, take the dirt track to the left, which leads alongside the river and proceed as far as the track will take you.

Isla de los Olivillos (E-1)

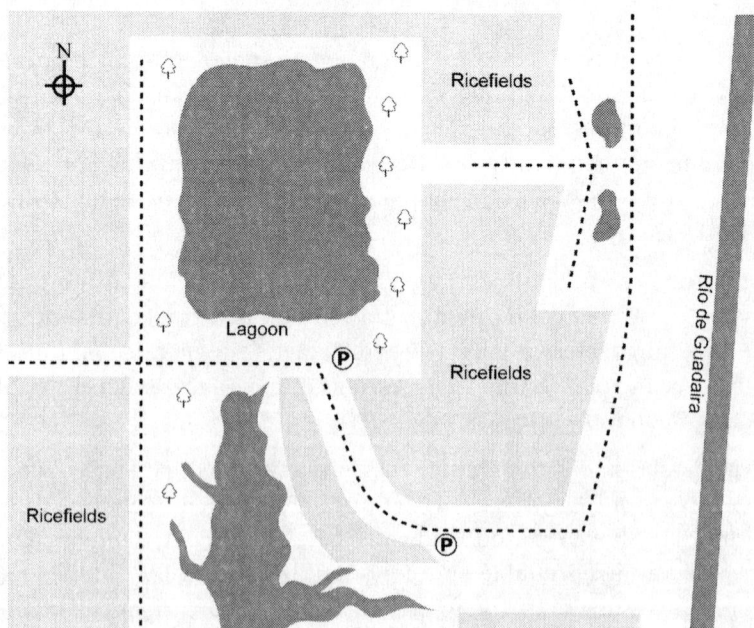

After 4 kms the track swings away from the river and leads uphill. At the top of the hill there is a brick-built construction and a number of large white bollards. Stop here and look directly across the rice field to the trees and reedbeds. This is the mixed nesting colony that I referred to earlier. It is usually in use from March to July and excellent views of the breeding birds can be had at this time.

Continue for another 300 metres and you reach a set of gates which signifies the end of the driving route. Park here and scan the lagoon on the right and the reedbeds to the left. There is a trail that leads into the nearby eucalyptus forest, which will take you closer to the water whilst providing some cover to get nearer to the birds. A bird hide was situated in the forest but it was vandalized a few years ago. Now only the frame and a few floor-boards remain. It may be that at some time in the future this hide will be re-built, but I have had no news on this matter.

If the gate at the end of the route is open, you can walk alongside the end of the lagoon and then explore the western side. The track leads through small ricefields and ends at the northern limit of the lagoon, beside the Río Guadalquivir.

General Information

The site is normally very quiet and at certain times of the year you may be the only person present. However, during the spring and autumn, there is likely to be a lot of activity when the planting and harvesting of the agricultural land occurs.

Ospreys are fairly common here and tend to roost on electricity pylons or on a few dead trees at the far end of the lagoon. Even in the summer you may still find one or two non-breeders that regularly remain in the area rather than migrating north.

This is a fairly reliable site for wintering Black Storks that arrive in October and remain until March and I have personally counted over 50 birds in one day in this area.

Most of the site is flat but the dirt roads can become very muddy after wet weather. Although it is driveable at all times it may cause problems for birders in wheelchairs. However, this should not spoil your viewing of the area, as there is so much that can be seen without leaving the car.

When To Visit

The site is of great interest at most times, except perhaps in July and August, when soaring summer temperatures and the lack of water tend to keep the birds under cover.

The migration and breeding season, March to early July, is an excellent time. As well as the passage and nesting birds there are still late-staying winter visitors to be seen. In April and May there are many thousands of waders in the area, waiting to gain their full summer plumage before moving off to their northern breeding grounds.

From mid-September until the end of November is the rice harvesting season. This attracts huge numbers of birds to the fields and it is not unusual to find mixed flocks of up to 25,000 birds in one field alone. During the winter you can expect to see impressive numbers of ducks, geese and waders that have arrived from the colder northern regions to take advantage of the milder climate and abundant food supply. Large flocks of Greater Flamingos, Spoonbills, Purple Swamp-hens, Glossy Ibis, Spanish Sparrows and Calandra Larks also form at this time.

Brazo Del Este
East 2

The Paraje Natural del Brazo del Este is situated on the eastern side of the Río Guadalquivir in the province of Sevilla. It covers a surface area of 1,336 hectares and is in two distinct parts, the northern and southern sections, with several entry points and a network of tracks leading through it. I shall give directions to each site separately in the access section below.

The northern section comprises a 2 km stretch of water and reed-beds that is walkable or driveable in dry conditions. The southern part comprises over 13 kms of marshes and has to be viewed separately. It includes an area sometimes referred to as the Pinzon marshes, due to its close proximity to the tiny hamlet of Pinzon. This area is on better tracks and is driveable even in wet conditions. Overall, it is one of the best sites within the region for storks, herons, egrets, ducks, waders and other waterbirds. It was declared a Paraje Natural in 1989 and comes under the protective umbrella of the A.M.A.

The water levels change throughout the seasons and are dependent on rainfall and water from the Río Guadaira and the run-off from the nearby rice fields. The habitats consist of canals, lagoons, irrigation ditches, reedbeds, marshes, rice fields, scrubland, scattered eucalyptus and tamarisk trees and the Río Guadaira, a tidal river that flows along the western side of the site.

The overall area is a major breeding ground for Purple Swamp-hens, Black-crowned Night Herons, Little and Cattle Egrets, Squacco and Purple Herons, Little Bitterns and White Storks. Other notable breeding species include Marbled Ducks, Red-knobbed Coots, Collared Pratincoles, Avocets, Black-winged Stilts, Kentish Plovers, Gull-billed and Whiskered Terns, Great Reed Warblers, Penduline Tits, Common Waxbills, Golden Bishops, Marsh Harriers and Glossy Ibis.

Between October and April the area is a very important winter feeding ground for Spoonbills, Black Storks, Common Cranes, Great White Egrets, Ospreys, Hen Harriers, Booted and Short-toed Eagles and thousands of ducks and geese. At this time and during the spring migration, large flocks of waders, such as Little Stints, Ringed, Little-ringed, Kentish and Grey Plovers, Whimbrels, Snipe, etc. congregate in this region. The migrating birds normally arrive here in winter plumage and remain until they are in full breeding plumage before setting off for their breeding grounds in the north. This gives you the opportunity to see Black-tailed Godwits, Ruff, Curlew Sandpipers, Dunlin and Spotted Redshanks in their finest colours.

Recent rarities that have been recorded at this site include an African Spoonbill, a Sacred Ibis, White Pelicans, Yellow-billed Storks, a Marabou Stork, Western Reef Herons, a Saddle-billed Stork, Spotted Eagles, a Blue-winged Teal, Pectoral Sandpipers a Black-headed Bunting, a Dupont's Lark, a White-winged Black Tern and a Rosy Starling.

Temminck's Stints, although rare in many parts of Europe, are common winter visitors and flocks of up to 25 birds are often recorded.

Access

Once you have crossed the Río Guadalquivir by ferry and arrived at the bridge over the Río Guadaira you need to cross the bridge to access both parts of the Brazo del Este.

The northern marshes site

Cross over the bridge and then turn immediately right onto a dirt track that runs alongside the river. Continue for 4 kms until you join a tarmacked road. The start of the Brazo del Este is 500 metres along on the left, signed by a notice board with a map. Just beyond this point there is a small track on the left that leads through this part of the site, with the wetland to the left and rice fields to the right. The habitats of the marsh change as you pass along the track.

The first 500 metres is usually shallow water with exposed muddy banks that attract the smaller waders and dabbling ducks. As you turn a sharp left-hand bend the water becomes deeper and attracts the longer-legged species, such as Greater Flamingos, Spoonbills, herons and also diving ducks. In the middle of the water you will notice a line of wooden posts. These are often used as roosting perches by numerous species and should be checked for Whiskered and Black Terns in the summer and Ospreys and Cormorants during the winter months.

As you pass further along the track the vegetation becomes denser, culminating in extensive reedbeds. This is the favoured spot for Purple Swamp-hens, Little Bitterns, Purple Herons and Water Rails. The reedbeds also hold Cetti's, Savi's, Sedge, Moustached and Reed Warblers, Penduline Tits, Reed Buntings, Common Waxbills and Golden Bishop weaver birds.

The track finishes at the end of the rice fields and it is necessary for you to turn around and re-trace your route back to the road.

Brazo del Este north (E-2)

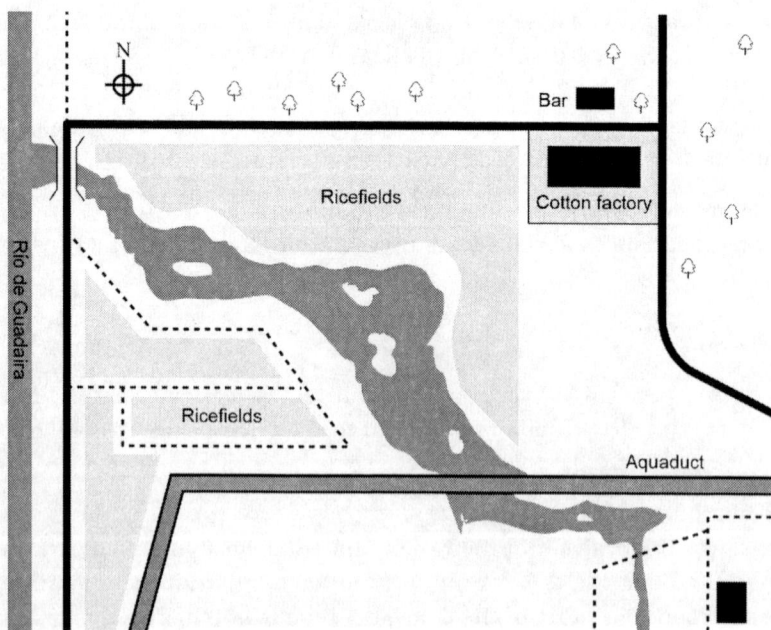

A word of caution. If the track beside the Río Guadaira and the track leading into the Paraje Natural are wet after rain, do not attempt to drive on them unless you have a 4x4 vehicle. You will almost certainly become stuck in thick clay-like mud. The alternative route to reach the site is to continue for 1 km along the road after crossing the bridge, until you reach a T-junction. Turn right at the junction and follow the road for 4 kms until you reach a small built-up area. Keep to the right and continue for about 3 kms until you reach the first part of the site, beside the Río Guadaira. You can then walk along the track to view the site.

This alternative route is also part of the route that will take you to the southern section. If you wish to visit the southern area directly from the northern sector you should return to the built-up area, turn right towards Adriano and then follow the directions below.

The southern marshes site

From the bridge over the Río Guadaira, follow the road for 1 km until you reach the T-junction and then turn right. Continue for 4 kms until you reach a junction which is signed for "Sector B II" and Adriano. Turn left here and after 3 kms, having passed some large silos on the right, you reach a "T" junction onto a raised track. Turn right and continue for about 400 metres until you reach an irrigation channel crossing on the left. After crossing the water channel there is a junction where you should follow the track to the right.

The main track now passes numerous waterscapes and ditches and after 2.5 kms you will reach a large sluice gate. At this point the rice fields begin and just 100 metres beyond the sluice gate there is a long, scrubby lagoon on the right which is a major breeding site for Whiskered Terns, Kentish Plovers and Squacco and Black-crowned Night Herons. Small numbers of Red-knobbed Coots and Marbled Ducks have also bred here in the past.

Continue for another 2 kms and you reach well-vegetated marsh areas on both sides of the track. These areas attract Great Crested, Black-necked and Little Grebes, Gull-billed and Little Terns, Spoonbills, Purple Herons, Glossy Ibis, Purple Swamp-hens and many wader and duck species.

After a further 2 kms there is another large area of marshes, sometimes referred to as the Pinzon marshes, which produces much the same bird species as the previous area. Just beyond the marshes there is a track that cuts back sharply to the left. Follow this track, which has marshland to the left and ricefields and an irrigation channel to the right, for 1.5 kms until you reach an open area of shallow water. This is probably the finest site for close-up views of waders, terns, gulls, egrets and herons, if water is present.

You can follow this track for almost 4 kms and it will bring you back to the large sluice gate referred to earlier. However, I do not recommend the final 2 kms of this track in wet weather as it becomes very muddy and could result in your car getting stuck in the mud. It would be wiser to turn around to rejoin the main track.

Brazo del Este south (E-2)

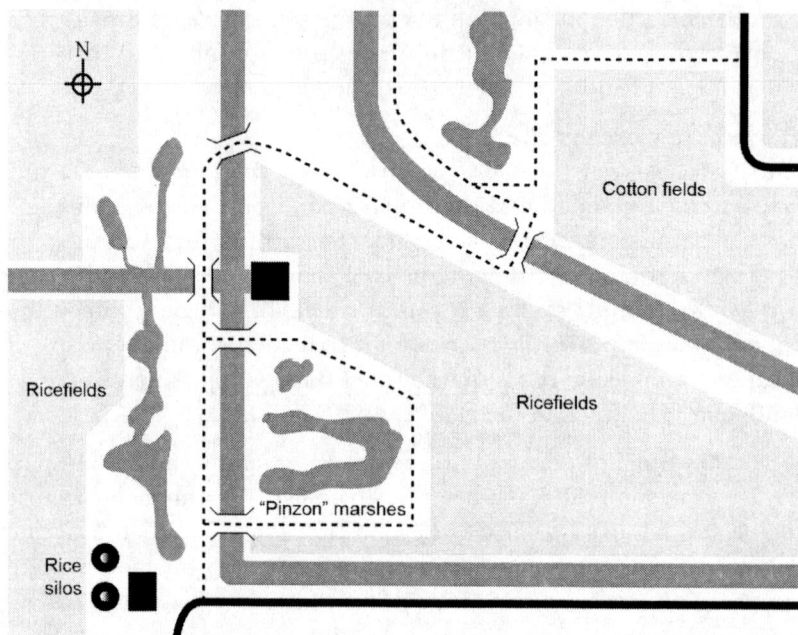

From the turning into the Pinzon marshes, the main track continues for a further 3 kms, passing more marshes, waterscapes and rice fields, until it meets a tarmacked road and a large rice-storage depot. This point signifies the end of the Brazo del Este site.

General Information

This site is of great interest throughout the year and its sheer size means that a whole day could be spent here without seeing everything that it has to offer. For every main track that is described there are smaller ancillary tracks that also cry out to be investigated. Small irrigation gullies contain wintering Bluethroats and Green Sandpipers, with Collared

Pratincoles and Whiskered Terns nesting just metres from the tracks. Glossy Ibis, Purple Swamp-hens, Greater Flamingos and Black-winged Stilts feed in great numbers in the marshes and rice fields.

The reedbeds hold Penduline Tits, Cetti's Warblers, Reed Buntings, Great Bitterns, Common Waxbills and Golden Bishops in the winter and there are Little Bitterns, Purple Herons and Savi's, Moustached and Great Reed Warblers during the breeding season.

Raptor activity is usually very high, with both Lesser and Common Kestrels, Peregrine Falcons, Marsh, Hen and Montagu's Harriers, Red and Black Kites, Booted and Short-toed Eagles, Hobbys, Ospreys and Griffon Vultures being present at the appropriate times of the year.

The area is very isolated, being mainly farm land, and it would be advisable to ensure you have adequate liquid refreshment with you. There is a small bar at the junction that leads to Adriano and there are a few bars/cafes within a 10 km radius, but this means leaving the sites to find them.

The main planting of the rice and other agricultural crops takes place during April and May and the main harvesting season is between September and November. At these times you are almost certain to encounter heavy farm machinery, so please ensure that you park sensibly to allow wide vehicles to pass.

The area is completely flat and apart from muddy track surfaces after rain there should be no problems for wheelchair birders.

The ferry at Coria del Río operates from 06.00hrs until 21.00hrs in the winter and until 23.00hrs during the summer.

When To Visit

This site is of great interest as the water courses and rice fields usually contain varying levels of water throughout the year, even during the long, hot summer.

The winter period is usually the most productive for ducks and waders, when thousands of birds can be present. The spring is usually the most interesting as, although there may be fewer birds, there is a greater diversity of species and many birds are conducting their mating rituals.

7

El Lago De Diego Puerta
East 3

This is a medium-sized lake with a surface area of about 2 hectares, that is situated just to the north of the town of Los Palacios y Villafranca in the province of Sevilla. The lake usually holds water throughout the year but the level may become very low during the summer. It is surrounded by tamarisk trees, a few of which stand in the middle of the lake, creating roosting sites for several heron and egret species. Small areas of the water's edge are vegetated with reeds, sheltering resident Purple Swamp-hens, Little Grebes and Cetti's Warblers and summer visitors such as Little Bitterns, Purple Herons and Reed, Great Reed and Savi's Warblers. Waterfowl are very common at this site and have included Marbled, Ferruginous and White-headed Ducks, along with the more numerous Shovelers, Gadwalls, Teal, Pintails and Mallards.

El Lago Diego Puerta (E-3)

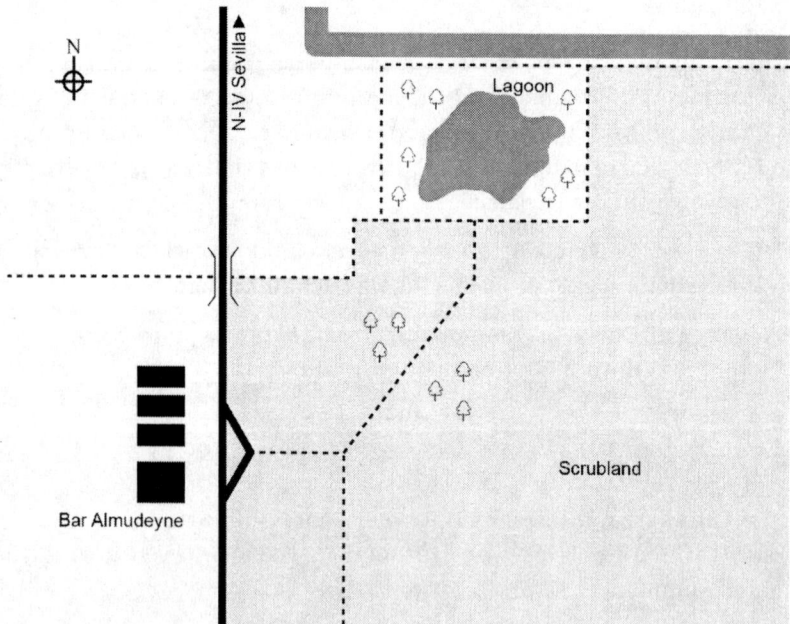

Part of the surrounding area is open scrubland, where larks, wagtails, warblers, chats, redstarts, shrikes and finches can usually be found. To the east of the lake there is an irrigation canal that often attracts storks, egrets and several species of smaller waders. Beyond the canal there are cotton fields, that also attract many bird species.

In the summer, the sky above the lake is usually very busy with feeding Barn and Red-rumped Swallows, House and Sand Martins, Pallid Swifts, Bee-eaters and Whiskered Terns. Raptor activity is usually very good, with Kestrels, Buzzards and Marsh Harriers being the most common birds seen, but Montagu's Harriers, Booted and Short-toed Eagles, Black Kites and Peregrines are also sometimes present.

Access

The lake is less than 2 kms to the north of the town of Los Palacios and can be reached by taking the road from the centre of the town that leads north towards Sevilla and joins the N-IV road. However, I usually visit the lake after visiting the Brazo del Este, as it is only 16 kms away from the end of that site. At the southernmost end of the Brazo del Este there is a T-junction. Turn left and continue for 14 kms, passing the small hamlet of Pinzon and town of Chapatales until you reach Los Palacios. On the right is the local football stadium and just beyond this there is a roundabout. Turn left here (3rd exit) and after 200 metres turn right (1st exit) at the next roundabout. From here, continue for 1.1 km until you reach a large roundabout with a white walled fountain in the middle. Turn left (3rd exit) and continue until you reach the edge of the town.

Proceed for another 200 metres and you will see the Bar/Restaurant "Almudeyne" on the left. Just beyond this there is a filter-lane to the right. Take this lane and after 50 metres turn sharp right onto a dirt track and then turn immediately left. Now follow the track for 1.1 kms until you reach the lagoon.

You can also reach this site by taking the N-IV Seville - Cádiz road and turning off to Los Palacios at km 566. The Bar/Restaurant "Almudeyne" will now be on your right and you will need to turn around at this point to reach the entry track on the opposite side of the road.

General Information

Although this is only a small site, it should produce an hour or so of interesting birding. A large part of the lake can be viewed from the southern end, but by walking or driving right from the main parking area you can get views from the eastern edge. It is also possible, if the water level is not too high, to walk in amongst the tamarisk trees and by using them as cover, get much closer to the birds.

Although the entry to this site is along a dirt track, it is usually driveable at all times. However, soft mud may present some problems for wheelchair birders around the edges of the lake.

When To Visit

The site is usually of some interest throughout the year, provided, of course, that there is water present in the lake. As the main viewing areas are from the south and east of the lake you are not affected by adverse sunlight conditions, except in the late afternoons or evenings.

Salinas De Bonanza
East 4

This area is a large expanse of active commercial salt-pans situated beside the east bank of the Río Guadalquivir, just a few kilometres north of Sanlúcar de Barrameda in the province of Cádiz. Entry into the salinas is not allowed without a permit, but many of the saltpans are right beside the road and the area is so rich in birds that you can often see many of the species without even entering the area. The area is renowned for the vast concentrations of waterbirds that can be found here in the winter and spring, such as Greater Flamingos, Spoonbills, Black-winged Stilts, Avocets, Little and Cattle Egrets, Slender-billed and Audouin's Gulls, Caspian and Whiskered Terns, Marbled Ducks, Red-crested Pochards, and Red-knobbed Coots, along with good numbers of many of the more common European waders.

Summer visitors include Little, Black and Gull-billed Terns, Purple and Squacco Herons and Collared Pratincoles.

Non-water birds, such as Bee-eaters, Tawny Pipits, Crested Larks, Dartford and Sardinian Warblers, Meadow and Water Pipits, Zitting Cisticolas, Woodchat and Southern Grey Shrikes, Pallid Swifts and Red-rumped Swallows are also normally present at the appropriate times of the year.

Raptor activity is generally evident, with Marsh Harriers, Common Kestrels, Red and Black Kites and Ospreys being the most common species, although Peregrine Falcons and Lesser Kestrels are also often recorded here.

Access

Sanlúcar de Barrameda (from now on only referred to as Sanlúcar) can be reached either from the C-441 Lebrija/Sanlúcar or the A-480 Jerez de la Frontera/Sanlúcar roads. As you reach the town you should look out for and follow directions to Bonanza and Algaida. Once through Sanlúcar you reach the small town of Bonanza and at a T-junction you should turn left and then almost immediately right. This road will lead you directly to the salinas, which are easily seen on the left-hand side of the road, the entrance to which is well signed.

Salinas de Bonanza - El Puntal (E-4, 5, 6, 7 & 8)

General Information

If you wish to gain entry to the area you will require a day permit issued by the company that operates the salinas. There is an office in a white build-ing on the right, 50 metres before the entry point, where you can apply. You will need to give your name, address, passport number and vehicle registration. The whole process can be completed in under 10 minutes, but this, of course, depends on (a) the office being open and (b) a person being available who is authorized to issue the permit. It may, therefore, be prudent to write and ask for a permit well in advance of your visit.

The postal address is:- Aprovechamientos Marinos S.A. Apartado 111, 11540 Sanlúcar de Barrameda, Cádiz.

Due to the increased work activity in the salinas during the summer and the threat of interference to breeding birds in the spring, the company sensibly restricts visits into the salinas to the winter months only, ie. from November to March.

Wheelchair birders should have no problems if you can access the site by car, as you can reach most of the areas, but the vastness of the site, the uneven surface of many of the tracks and the constant activity of large trucks and other heavy plant machinery may prove dangerous if trying to negotiate the area in your wheelchair.

When To Visit

Winter and spring visits are the most rewarding due to the very large number of birds that overwinter and breed here. At this time of the year the day-time temperatures are not so high and viewing is generally very good. During the hotter times of the year your views can be badly affected by heat haze and I would suggest that morning visits should be considered. Afternoon and evening viewing from the road in the summer will also prove frustrating due to the sun reflecting off the water.

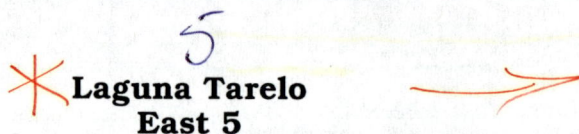

Laguna Tarelo
East 5

This is a medium sized lagoon, covering about 5 hectares, situated near the eastern bank of the Río Guadalquivir at the entrance to the Pinar de la Algaida forest. It was created in the 1980's when thousands of tonnes of earth and gravel were excavated from the site for use in the various forms of agriculture that exists nearby. After digging down more than 3 metres, the excavators reached the water table and work ceased. Over the years, the remaining crater filled with water and is now a well vegetated permanent lagoon that attracts large numbers of waterbirds throughout the year.

A comfortable observation hide has been erected on the eastern side of the lagoon which gives good views of most of the open water. Directly in front of the hide, about 50 metres away, there is a small island where many egrets, herons and ducks come out of the water to rest. This is also the best spot for feeding waders such as Common and Green Sandpipers, Ringed Plovers, Dunlins and Redshanks,

It is one of the most reliable spots in the Doñana region in which to find both Marbled and White-headed Ducks in reasonable numbers. In the case of the latter, there have been sightings of more that 200 birds on many occasions. Other resident species you may expect to find include Great Crested and Little Grebes, Grey, Squacco and Black-crowned Night Herons, Little and Cattle Egrets, Purple Swamp-hens, Red-knobbed Coots, Red-crested Pochards and Spoonbills.

Seasonal visitors include wintering Great White Egrets, Wigeon, Pintails, Tufted Ducks, Teal, Shelducks, Snipe and Cormorants. Amongst the summer visitors and passage migrants you may find Purple Herons, Little Bitterns, Whiskered, Black and Gull-billed Terns, Collared Pratincoles, Pallid Swifts and Red-rumped Swallows.

The surrounding reedbeds and other vegetation hold resident Hoopoes, Cetti's and Sardinian Warblers, Crested Larks, Tree Sparrows and Corn Buntings. These are joined by Willow, Savi's, Reed and Great Reed Warblers, Woodchat Shrikes and Red-necked Nightjars in the summer and Reed Buntings, Penduline Tits, Bluethroats and Blackcaps in the winter.

Access

From the previous site at Bonanza, continue along the road, passing through the town of La Algaida. The main road is very straight and all the streets in the town run directly at 90° angles to the main road. Strangely, the streets do not have names and are marked merely as Calle A, Calle B (street A, street B) etc. After 4.5 kms you come to the end of the town and reach the entrance to the Pinar de la Algaida, a large stone pine forest. A gateway and a large "Parque Natural de Doñana" sign mark the entrance. Twenty metres after you pass through the gates, turn to the left and park beside some low wooden barriers. Here you will find the path to the lagoon leading to the left.

General Information

This is an excellent all-year site that should keep any birder happy for an hour or two and produce a good bird list. The surrounding stone pines and scrub should not be ignored, as they also hold several interesting species.

The observation hide is not fully enclosed. Although it does have a roof and sides, it is open at the back and only offers limited protection against rain. However, it does have bench seating and the windows are at a good height for most people, including wheelchair birders, who can also get between the seats to reach the windows.

Morning visits may prove uncomfortable on hot, sunny days as the hide offers very little shade and the sun is directly on your back. In the late afternoon and evening your views may be impaired by sunlight reflecting off the water. Therefore, I would recommend, both for comfort and viewing, that you visit between midday and 4pm during the summer.

If you leave the forest and head back towards Bonanza, you can take the first turning on the right and follow the track for about 300 metres. This will give you views from the eastern side of the lagoon and also views of other wetlands.

When To Visit

As stated previously, the site is of great interest throughout the year, with only the weather protection factors to be taken into consideration.

In the evening, hundreds of Little and Cattle Egrets, with lesser numbers of Grey and Squacco Herons arrive to roost in the trees and reedbeds, creating quite a spectacular sight. At the same time there is increased activity amongst the Black-crowned Night Herons, which also roost in the trees during the daytime. If you wish to view this activity you should plan to arrive about 45 minutes before dusk.

4

✱ Pinar De La Algaida
East 6

This is a large forested area, predominantly of stone pine and oaks, but with some eucalyptus and other broadleaved tree species. The ground surface is almost exclusively of sand and there is a great diversity of groundcover vegetation that harbours scrub warblers.

The forest extends for about 4 kms and there are no restrictions with regards to walking. Numerous trails lead through the trees, which invite further investigation and exploration. A large information board at the entrance to the forest highlights a pre-planned walk of some 5 kms.

In the past there have been problems with the main track, with some vehicles becoming stuck in loose sand. This problem has now been overcome with the re-surfacing of the track in August 2005.

At the far end of the main forest track there is a rather attractive picnic area and a small chapel. It is laid out with stone tables and bench seating and is a good place to sit quietly and let the birds come to you.

The resident birds of the forest include Iberian Magpies, Black-billed Magpies, Green and Great Spotted Woodpeckers, Short-toed Treecreepers, Crested Tits, Hoopoes Tawny Owls, Serins, Chaffinches, Greenfinches, Southern Grey Shrikes, Tree Sparrows, Sardinian Warblers and Crested Larks.

The summer visitors and passage migrants include Common Redstarts, Spotted and Pied Flycatchers, Golden Orioles, Bee-eaters, Rollers, Scops Owls, Common and Great Spotted Cuckoos, Olivaceous, Orphean, Melodious and Subalpine Warblers, Northern and Black-eared Wheatears, Whinchats, Nightingales, Turtle Doves and Red-necked Nightjars.

In the winter months you may find Black Redstarts, Spanish Sparrows, Siskins, Hawfinches and Chiffchaffs.

Birds of prey are usually present throughout the year. In the summer, the most common are Buzzards, Kestrels, Sparrowhawks, Black Kites and Booted Eagles, whilst small numbers of Red Kites and Black-shouldered Kites are regularly seen in the winter.

Access

From the Laguna Tarelo, drive directly ahead into the forest. The road is wide enough to stop anywhere and explore, without causing disruption to other road users.

General Information

As with all forest areas, there is always the risk of fire, especially during the summer months. If you are a smoker, please be sure that any discarded cigarettes are completely extinguished. If you decide to have a barbecue you should also ensure that it is not left burning when you leave.

Although the main track is now firm and in good condition, all of the surrounding area is of loose sand and would prove to be very difficult to negotiate in a wheelchair.

When To Visit

This is an interesting site throughout most of the year, although in the middle of summer, July and August, it is usually quiet during the day as most of the bird activity takes place in the early mornings and evenings. For the remainder of the time the birds are often well under cover, sheltering from the blazing sun.

Walking or driving through the site just before dusk and after dark can produce good views of Red-necked nightjars and increases your chances of finding owls.

The forest is a popular place with families at weekends and on national/local holidays and you may find hundreds of people enjoying picnics and barbecues at such times, especially at the designated picnic area at the far end of the forest.

3

Salinas De Monte Algaida
East 7

The Salinas de Monte Algaida are situated beside the east bank of the Río Guadalquivir. The area boasts several distinct habitats and therefore attracts a wide range of bird species throughout the year, including all those that can be seen at the larger Bonanza site and often at a closer range and in a more relaxed atmosphere. Many of the salt-pans are no longer in use and have become deeper and more richly vegetated than the working ones. Human activity in the area is much less and has resulted in many birds using the salinas as nesting sites. Regular breeders include Avocets, Black-winged Stilts, Little Grebes, Little-ringed Plovers, Collared Pratincoles, Redshanks, Whiskered and Little Terns and both Audouin's and Slender-billed Gulls.

Beside the salinas there are large areas of saltmarsh, with scattered lagoons and waterscrapes that attract many of the wader species. The vegetation on the saltmarsh is mainly salicornia, which attracts scrub species such as Spectacled, Dartford and Sardinian Warblers and Zitting Cisticolas. Several dead trees stand out in this area and are ideal perching/feeding stations for Ospreys and other birds of prey.

Open scrubland, which is also mainly of salicornia, attracts warblers but can also produce good views of Stone Curlews, Greater and Lesser Short-toed Larks, Tawny Pipits, White and Yellow Wagtails, Stonechats and Northern and Black-eared Wheatears.

The river, which is never more than 100 metres away, offers good opportunities to watch waders such as Kentish Plovers, Sanderlings, Curlew Sandpipers, Ruddy Turnstones and Dunlins. During the winter there are usually Black-necked Grebes, Razorbills and Red-breasted Mergansers to be seen on the river and, occasionally, you may find Common Scoters.

The Doñana National Park is on the opposite side of the river, just over a kilometre away, and the Spanish Imperial Eagles that live in the park are often seen flying over the treetops and even venturing to this side of the river in search of prey.

At the far end of the salinas there is a bird observatory that looks out over an area that is particularly favoured by many bird species and it is not uncommon to find large concentrations of Spoonbills, White Storks, Greater Flamingos, egrets, herons, terns, gulls and waders roosting here.

Access

Following on from the last site, once you have passed through the Pinar de la Algaida you come to a tarmacked road. Turn left here and proceed for 2.2 kms until the road turns sharply to the right. As you travel along this road there is a watercourse on your right that is fairly well vegetated with reeds. It is always worth making a couple of stops to look for Squacco and Black-crowned Night Herons, Green Sandpipers and Reed and Sedge Warblers.

The open areas to both sides of the road are part of the Marisma de Adventus, which stretches for about 6 kms. During the winter this is usually wet, but in the summer it is normally dry.

At the point where the road turns sharply right, you will see a dirt track leading straight ahead. There is a sign advertising the "Observatorio Salinas de Bonanza. 6.1 kms". Take this track and after about 70 metres you reach a small observation hide that looks out over wetlands and dense salicornia.

Continue along the track for 2.5 kms until you reach the first large saltpan. On the way you should make several stops to check the surrounding terrain, not forgetting the few dead trees, where the Ospreys can often be found.

Once you have reached the first saltpan you have a choice of options. You can park here and explore the area on foot, or you can continue by car. The main observation hide is still 3.5 kms away and my preferred option is to drive off the main track (to the right) and follow a well-worn path through the sparse scrubland, but only if the surface is dry. I would not recommend driving along the slightly elevated track that goes straight ahead as it is very narrow and bumpy and the banks are crumbling in some places. Also, the sight of your vehicle is likely to put any feeding or roosting birds to flight.

There is one obvious disadvantage in taking the route that I suggest and that is that the saltpans are mainly hidden from view, behind the raised bank, but frequent stops will allow you to climb the bank to check the activity beyond. As you approach the bird observatory, the track surface changes from baked mud to loose sand. I would strongly urge you to park here and walk the remaining 400 metres to the hide as by continuing by car, unless you have a 4x4, will almost certainly result in you becoming stuck in soft sand. And as you are many kilometres away from the nearest road and very few people visit this area, you are unlikely to get any help recovering your vehicle.

General Information

In wet weather, the 2.5 km track leading to the first saltpan is perfectly driveable. However, the track through the open scrubland should be avoided, even if it only looks wet, as the soft mud will quickly pack the treads of your tyres and you will become stuck.

Once at this site you are far away from any inhabited areas, so I would suggest that you carry a supply of drinks with you.

Apart from the first 2.5 kms, this site cannot be viewed satisfactorily by wheelchair birders, due to the raised bank obscuring your views and the soft sand leading to the observation hide.

When To Visit

The site is of great interest throughout the year and will always produce a good bird list. The winter is renowned for the very large concentrations of birds, but even in the height of summer there will be enough birds present to keep most birders entertained.

Early morning sunlight reflecting off the water of the saltpans can cause major problems on sunny days and heat haze can also impair your views, as can evening sunshine reflecting off of the river. I always try to time my visits to this site for the afternoon, when the sun is directly overhead. Of course, on cloudy days, the sunshine will not be a factor.

El Puntal, The East Bank Of The Río Guadalquivir East 8

El Puntal is an area of almost permanent lagoons, water channels and scrapes that covers a 2 km stretch of the east bank of the Río Guadalquivir, between the river and the road. The varying depths of the water regularly attract large numbers of many different bird species, especially waders, throughout the year and can easily be viewed at close quarters from an elevated road that runs alongside the site.

It is a regular breeding site for Black-winged Stilts, Whiskered Terns, Collared Pratincoles, Avocets and Kentish Plovers, along with Coots, Moorhens, Great Crested and Little Grebes and several duck species, including Red-crested Pochards and Marbled Ducks. Garganeys are often recorded here during the spring migration, but as yet I have not heard of any remaining in the area to breed.

Inland from the site there is the vast area known as Marismas de Adventus, a seasonal wetland that supports wildfowl and waders in the winter when wet and Stone Curlews and Pin-tailed Sandgrouse in the summer, when dry. Little Bustards have also been recorded in this area. The marshes are often overflown by hunting raptors, which include Spanish Imperial, Short-toed and Booted Eagles, Marsh, Hen and Montagu's Harriers, Peregrine Falcons, Hobbys, Common and Lesser Kestrels and Buzzards. Griffon Vultures from the nearby hills are often seen soaring overhead or feeding on carrion in the open marshes.

Also in the marshes and alongside the road you can find Crested, Calandra and both Greater and Lesser Short-toed Larks, Spectacled and Sardinian Warblers, Hoopoes, Woodchat and Southern Grey Shrikes, Meadow, Water and Tawny Pipits, Spanish Sparrows, Bee-eaters, Sand Martins, Barn and Red-rumped Swallows, Common and Pallid Swifts, Rufous-tailed Scrub Robins, Zitting Cisticolas and Barn, Little and Short-eared Owls.

There is always bird movement along the river and you should look out for Yellow-legged, Audouin's and Slender-billed Gulls, and both Caspian and Sandwich Terns.

Access

This site can be looked upon as an extension of the previous site and can be found by returning to the tarmacked road and turning left over a small bridge, or, if coming directly from the Pinar de la Algaida, by turning sharp right at the end of the road leading toward the river.

The bridge is always worth investigating and a few minutes spent here could be very worthwhile. To the right of the bridge there are dense reedbeds where Cetti's and Willow Warblers, Chiffchaffs and Squacco Herons are often seen. To the left the area is muddy and attracts such waders as Green and Common Sandpipers, Redshanks, Greenshanks and Dunlins.

The wetlands start just beyond the large Co-operativa buildings, after you have crossed the bridge. They are in an inter-tidal area between the river and the road, where disused saltpans and gravel excavation sites have created an ideal environment for birds. On one particular visit here in August 2005 there were hundreds of coots present, including two Red-knobbed Coots, along with good numbers of Glossy Ibis, Greater Flamingos, Black-tailed Godwits, Little-ringed and Kentish Plovers, Purple, Grey and Black-crowned Night Herons, Curlew Sandpipers and an unprecedented 37 Marbled Ducks, feeding no more than 50 metres from the road.

After 2 kms the wetlands end as the river sweeps round to run alongside the road. You can continue further along the road, finding tracks that will take you to Trebujena or Lubrija, but the road is in an appalling state and I would not recommend it.

General Information

To avoid any confusion, the area described as Marismas de Adventus has often been referred to as the Marismas de Trebujena in some other publications. Much of this area has now been transformed into agricultural land and although great swathes of marshland still remain, the future for these cannot be guaranteed.

Various tracks lead inland from the road which give you the opportunity to explore these areas more closely, in search of Little Bustards, Pin-tailed Sandgrouse, Calandra Larks and Spanish Sparrows.

This is a very flat area and overall the views here are very good. Most of the area can be adequately covered without having to get out of your vehicle, which makes this an exceptionally good site for wheelchair birders.

When To Visit

Due to the large number of bird species that can be found in this area, it is worth visiting at any time of the year. Obviously the winter will produce the greatest numbers of birds, due to the very large concentrations of wintering geese, ducks and waders. Stone Curlews, Pin-tailed Sandgrouse and Little Bustards also gather in flocks in the winter, which makes them easier to find.

The spring migration period and breeding season will normally produce the greatest number of species, but the birds become harder to find as they are usually only seen singularly or in pairs at this time.

Sunlight reflecting off the water in the late afternoon/evening may have an adverse effect on your views at the wetlands and heat haze can also be a problem when viewing over the marismas/agricultural land.

← 1ST   SANLUCAR

The Southern Sector

The southern part of the region is perhaps the area most visited by birders and contains some excellent birding sites in and around the town of El Rocío. Here there is easy access to the El Rocío marshes and the main visitors centres at El Acebuche, La Rocina and the Palacio de Acebrón. However, a fair number of lesser-known sites exist within the area and these can also provide equally good birding opportunities. The habitats include rivers, beaches, sand dunes, streams, marshland, woods, forests, dehesas, golf courses, agricultural land, grazing pastures and open scrubland.

El Rocío

The village of El Rocío is situated in the province of Huelva, on the very edge of the national park and has a history going back over a thousand years. It is world famous for the religious pilgrimage and festival that takes place there every year at Pentecost, when over a million people from all over Spain converge on the village to give thanks and offer prayers to the Virgin of the Dew (Virgen del Rocío). Amongst birders it is equally famous as the epitome of Doñana and the birds that are found in this region.

The village itself is reminiscent of an American wild west frontier town from the mid 1800's, with a large prominent church, numerous bars, wide sandy streets, low white buildings and hitching rails outside many of the houses. Horses are still an important means of transport here, although the modern "*cowboys*" now prefer their 4x4 vehicles.

Much of the time the village is quiet, with perhaps only a few hundred residents being present, but at weekends, public holidays and during the months of July and August, the village can be very busy with holiday-makers and day-trippers. Spanish coach tour companies have added El Rocío to their itineraries and you may find numerous groups swarming all over the village, especially by the church and the promenade. Mini pilgrimages by the religious brotherhoods (hermandades) occur on most weekends and the pilgrims' arrival is usually heralded by the ringing of the church bells and loud gunshot-like rockets being set off.

On Sunday, it is traditional for the Spanish to go out to eat, either at restaurants, bars, ventas, or by having barbeques and picnics. Don't be surprised, when driving in the village, if the car in front suddenly stops in the middle of the street and the occupants get out and start setting up their picnic tables and chairs. This is normal behaviour and is part of the charm of the village. Another tradition is spending the weekend riding around on horses or in horse drawn carriages. Often, you may see a couple of horsemen arrive at a bar and be served their beer or sherry whilst still on horseback.

El Rocío is central to several excellent birding sites and is a popular place for birders to spend a night or two whilst visiting Doñana. The most prominent and easily accessible of these sites is the large seasonal lagoon and marsh that borders the southern edge of the village, La Madre de las Marismas del Rocío. Other interesting sites nearby include the road bridge (Puente de la Canaliega), an area of open grazing land (Boca del Lobo) and the national park visitors centres at La Rocina, Palacio de Acebrón and El Acebuche. Other little-known sites also exist nearby and these will be described within this section.

La Madre De Las Marismas Del Rocío (The Mother of The Marshes) South 1

This is the vast shallow lagoon and marsh area right beside the village of El Rocío, known as the Mother of the Marshes. The lagoon is seasonal and is filled by water from the Arroyo de la Rocina, which flows under the road bridge and from the Arroyo de las Cañadas, which enters the lagoon to the east of the village. A very attractive promenade, complete with bench seating and pay-to-view telescopes, runs alongside most of the length of the lagoon, offering excellent viewing possibilities.

The water-level fluctuates with the seasons and can be completely dry at times, especially at the end of a long, hot, rainless summer. During the winter and spring, water is almost guaranteed (although the water is never more than a metre deep) and is an exceptional site for all manner of waterbirds, including Greater Flamingos, White Storks, Spoonbills, Common Cranes, herons, egrets, grebes, coots, gulls, terns, ducks, geese and waders. During the breeding season, the drier areas of the marsh are used by Whiskered Terns, Collared Pratincoles and both Kentish and Little-ringed Plovers as nesting areas.

El Rocío marshes (S-1, 2, 3)

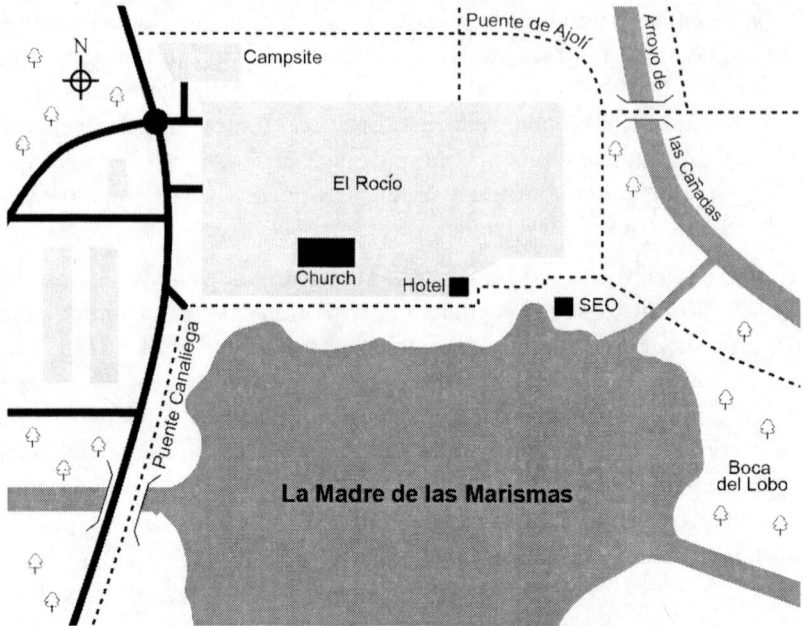

At the western end of the lagoon there are small reedbeds that hold resident Cetti's and Sardinian Warblers, Zitting Cisticolas and Blackcaps. These are often joined in the breeding season by Reed, Great Reed, Sedge and Savi's Warblers. The fenceposts that mark the national park boundary are often used as lookout points by hunting Kingfishers and as roosting sites by both Little and Cattle Egrets. Wintering Bluethroats are often to be found here.

At the eastern end of the lagoon you will find the ruined remains of the SEO bird observatory, which was burnt down (arson) in September 2002 and there has still been no move, as yet, to re-construct the observatory. However, I have recently been informed by a reliable source from the SEO that building plans are now being made. Although the major part of the observatory, which was constructed of large wooden beams, a thatched roof and was fitted with large plastic windows, was completely destroyed, an upstairs brick-built viewing terrace survived and still offers good views of most of the area. The muddy margins here attract good numbers of waders and dabbling ducks and it is not unusual to find large flocks of Avocets, Black-winged Stilts, Dunlins, Redshanks, Greenshanks, Curlew Sandpipers, Snipe, Glossy Ibis, Black-tailed Godwits and Ruff in this area.

This viewing terrace offers the chance of watching passing terns in the spring and summer, as they often cruise by at eye-level, sometimes within a few metres. The terns that are commonly seen are of the Whiskered, Black and Gull-billed varieties. Raptors are constantly in evidence as they hunt and overfly the marshes. During the winter the most common are Red Kites, Common Buzzards, Marsh Harriers, Griffon Vultures, Common Kestrels and Peregrine Falcons. The summer visitors include Black Kites, Montagu's Harriers, Booted and Short-toed Eagles and, occasionally, Egyptian Vultures and Lesser Kestrels. The Spanish Imperial Eagles (7 pairs) live and breed in the stone pine forests at the far side of the marsh and these are sometimes seen soaring over the treetops.

The birding here doesn't have to stop when the sun goes down. The lights along the promenade and the floodlights from the church illuminate the area so well that many of the birds are still feeding late into the night, often very close to the edge of the marsh.

Access

The wetlands are at the very edge of the village of El Rocío and there is ample free parking everywhere. However, at times, you may be asked to pay a small parking fee at the large parking area in front of the church and directly beside the marsh.

When To Visit

The marsh is only of real interest when water is present, usually between October and June, although insufficient, or no rain, can result in the marsh and lagoon being empty, even during these times.

On sunny days, sunshine reflecting off the water can have an adverse effect on your views of the lagoon. I therefore recommend that you visit the old SEO bird hide and the promenade in the mornings and view the lagoon from the Puente de Canaliega in the evenings.

El Rocío has now become a very popular location for tourists at weekends and on public holidays and the resulting noise levels may have an effect on the bird population, driving them further into the middle of the marsh.

Boca Del Lobo
South 2

This area, known as "The Wolf's Mouth", is to the east of the old SEO bird observatory and can be easily reached by following the track from that point. At the very edge of the village you will see a track that runs parallel with the marsh for about 500 metres. The terrain here is flat open scrubland with several small seasonal ponds and waterscrapes that attract gulls, terns, waders, larks, finches, wagtails, pipits and warblers. Cattle, sheep and horses are grazed on this land and these attract good numbers of Cattle Egrets and Spotless Starlings. In the summer you will often find Hoopoes, Bee-eaters, Tawny Pipits, Whinchats and Black-eared Wheatears in this area, especially near the farm buildings on the right of the track. Also to the right there is a small sewage outfall/treatment plant that also attracts birds.

The numerous fenceposts that border the marsh are used as perches/plucking posts by raptors and both Southern Grey and Woodchat Shrikes and should be scanned regularly. Ahead and to the left you will see part of the Coto del Rey forest, where raptors and vultures are normally visible. This offers another chance of seeing the Spanish Imperial Eagle.

Puente De Canaliega
South 3

This is the road bridge just to the south of the village that carries the main A-483 El Rocío - Matalascañas road over the Arroyo de la Rocina, the stream that supplies much of the water to the marsh. The bridge offers excellent elevated views of the whole length of the lagoon, marshes and the flooded pastures, where many species of waterbirds gather to feed. The most prominent are obviously the larger birds, spoonbills, flamingos, ibis, storks, herons, egrets and geese, etc. but careful scanning will usually produce smaller species, such as waders, wagtails and larks. Large concentrations of ducks are usually present in the winter months and these regularly include Pintails, Wigeon, Shovelers, Common and Red-crested Pochards and Teal.

It is a very popular spot for birdwatching, but I should point out that by being on the bridge you are very close to fast-moving traffic and caution needs to be exercised here. To maximize safety, I recommend that you choose an alternative spot to view from. Just before the start of the bridge there is a bar/restaurant on the left-hand side of the road, the "Aires de Doñana". Just beyond this there is a sandy track that leads parallel with the road and will take you to the underside of the bridge and the stream where views, although not so elevated, are still very good.

A word of caution. The sand on this track can be very deep in places and unless you have a 4x4 vehicle I suggest you do not attempt to drive along it. You will almost certainly get stuck in the sand.

Kingfishers and marsh terns are often found here and a few pairs of Red-rumped Swallows nest under the bridge in the breeding season. Looking under the bridge may also produce Purple Swamp-hens in the reeds on the other side.

This site is best viewed in the evenings, especially on sunny days when morning and afternoon sunlight reflecting off the water can impair your views. A great way to finish off a day's birding is to sit on the outside terrace of the "Aires de Doñana" as the sun is going down and enjoy the sight of the birds coming in to roost for the night, or to have their last feed of the day. Take your binoculars and telescopes with you. The staff are quite used to us birders using the terrace as a birding spot whilst enjoying a refreshing glass of beer from the bar.

Puente De Ajolí / Arroyo De Las Cañadas
South 4

The Puente de Ajolí, the bridge that crosses the Arroyo de la Cañada, is situated at the north-eastern corner of the village of El Rocío. To reach it, simply take any of the roads that lead northwards from the marsh and drive as far through the village as you can, until you reach a fenced track. Turn right and the track will automatically lead you to the bridge and the stream.

The stream flows in a north to south line and empties into the El Rocío marsh, just to the east of the old S.E.O. bird observatory. By crossing over the bridge you have access to a sandy track (the Raya Real) that leads directly ahead, toward the Palacio del Rey, passing through the Coto del Rey pine forest.

Another track runs to the left, parallel with the stream, for just over one kilometre. Water is usually present throughout the year and attracts a wide variety of bird species. The land on the eastern side of the stream is mainly open scrubland used for cattle grazing. To the western side it is firstly open land and then there are the fenced boundaries of a small livestock farm.

The main species that are commonly seen here include Little Grebes, Little and Cattle Egrets, Purple, Grey and Squacco Herons, Spoonbills, White Storks, Black-winged Stilts, Common, Green and Wood Sandpipers, Snipe, Kingfishers, Hoopoes, Southern Grey Shrikes, Crested Larks, Zitting Cisticolas and other warblers and finches. Overhead there are usually Red and Black Kites, Common Buzzards, Kestrels and occasional eagles.

The bridge area is fairly well vegetated and is usually a reliable spot for Cetti's and Sardinian Warblers, tits and finches. Kingfishers regularly perch nearby and both Barn and Red-rumped Swallows are often present from March to October.

The track leading toward the Coto del Rey, the Raya Real, is always worth investigating, at least in part, for Iberian Magpies, Red-necked Nightjars, finches, larks, warblers and raptors. You may even catch a glimpse of the elusive Iberian Lynx, but these are now extremely scarce. If the dirt track conditions allow, drive 400 metres to the new bridge that crosses the Arroyo de Partido and check the riverbanks and vegetation for waders and warblers. Looking south from this bridge, you have views of La Dehesilla, which is within the boundaries of the National Park. This is a fairly good spot to find Great Spotted Cuckoos in the spring and Red and Black-shouldered Kites in the winter. Following recent decisions made by the A.M.A., driving beyond this point is no longer permitted, although you are allowed to continue on foot, passing an area known as Matagordas on the right and stone pine forests on the left, where you stand a reasonable chance of spotting a Spanish Imperial Eagle. After visiting this area, you should retrace your route back to the first bridge and continue to investigate the other parts of this site.

The elevated track beside the eastern side of the Arroyo de las Cañadas (across the bridge) can be followed right to the end. The reedbeds and small tamarisk trees, although sparse, are favoured by resident Cetti's Warblers and wintering Black-crowned Night Herons.

Migrating warblers, such as Willow, Sedge, Savi's, Reed and Great Reed may also be found during the passage periods and breeding season.

Arroyo de las Cañadas (S-4)

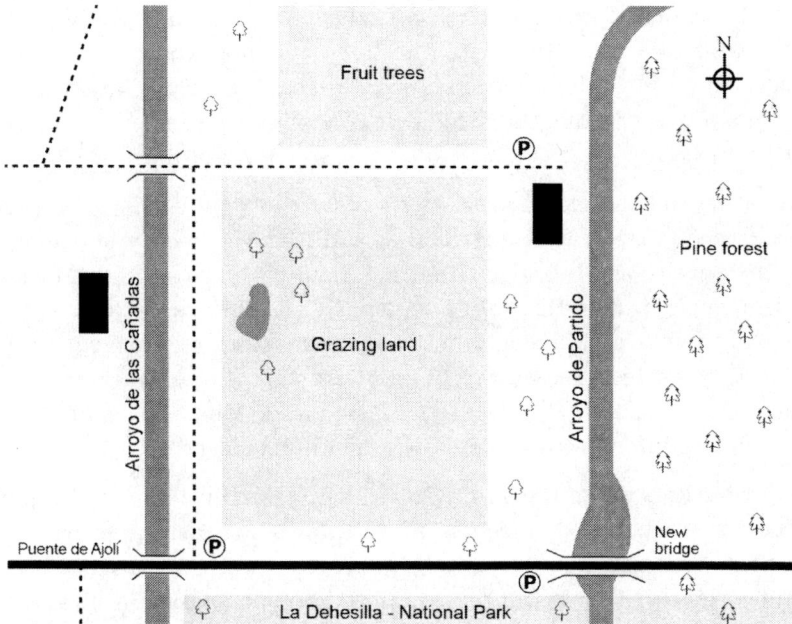

The open scrubland to either side of the stream attracts both Sardinian and Dartford Warblers, Zitting Cisticolas and Chiffchaffs. Southern Grey Shrikes (winter) and Woodchat Shrikes in the spring/summer, can often be found on the fence-posts and mixed flocks of finches are normally present.

The ramshackle animals' buildings and the food barns at the small farm attract insects in great numbers, which in turn attract many insectivorous bird species. Hoopoes are fairly common throughout the year, as are Black-billed Magpies, Jackdaws, shrikes, wagtails and larks.

At the end of the track there is another bridge. If you turn left here and then left at the next turning, the track will lead you through a stabling yard and back to the village. Although somewhat sandy and bumpy in places, this site should not cause too many problems for wheelchair birders and can be driven, with care.

Camino De Moguer
South 5

This is a road/track that leads behind the petrol station from the main roundabout just to the north of the village. For the first few hundred metres it passes an area of stone pine, oak and eucalyptus trees, where Iberian Magpies, Hoopoes and Golden Orioles (summer) are regularly seen. This wooded area can be accessed from a dirt track on the right, just 100 metres along the road. The trees also hold the usual passerines, such as Short-toed Treecreepers, Crested Tits, larks, finches and warblers. Further along the road there is a picnic/barbeque area on the right, which is also a good area to sit and watch for birds.

Just beyond the picnic area, as the surfaced road bends to the left, there is a dirt track to the right that will lead you past a few houses and then over a small bridge. The track then becomes sandy and leads out into open land on the right and densely vegetated areas on the left. You can find paths that lead into the open areas, which are favoured by Cattle Egrets, Black Redstarts, Crested Larks, Sardinian Warblers, Lapwings and Golden Plovers, but the forested area, which normally holds the usual woodland birds, is private land and is fenced off.

About 2 kms along the sandy track there is an entrance into a part of the forest where it is possible to walk for short distances in either direction. This dense area is a reasonable site for Golden Orioles in the summer. During the spring you can find many passage migrants, such as Pied Flycatchers, Common Redstarts, Subalpine Warblers and Rollers. Numerous pairs of Nightingales breed here during the spring and summer and are very obvious in April and May, when they perch openly and sing constantly to proclaim their territories and to try to attract a mate.

Much of this area, including the tarmacked road, is usually productive for Red-necked Nightjars from April to September. These are best seen at dusk, when the birds become active and will often land on the road, taking advantage of the heat from the surface and are sometimes approachable by car to within a few metres.

Centro De Visitantes La Rocina
South 6

The La Rocina visitors centre (pronounced ro-theena) and nature reserve is situated just over a kilometre from El Rocio and is one of three centres within the national park boundaries that are open to the public. The building has toilet facilities, an information desk and an audiovisual display. A soft drinks vending machine is available outside the building.

Within the reserve there is a 3.5 kms boardwalked nature trail, known as the Sendero Charco de Boca, that starts from in front of the office. The route passes through numerous interesting habitats where a wide variety of bird species are to be found. These include algaidas (vegetated streams), pine forests, reedbeds, marshes, lagoons and heathland. There are also four bird hides that look out over the Arroyo de la Rocina, the principal supply of water for the Madre de las Marismas.

The stone pine forest between the office and the first bird hide holds a sizeable population of Eurasian Tree Sparrows and nesting boxes have been supplied to encourage these birds to breed here. The forest is also home to Short-toed Treecreepers, Great Spotted and Green Woodpeckers, Chaffinches, Crested Tits, Sardinian Warblers and Iberian Magpies. The seasonal visitors include Pied and Spotted Flycatchers, Iberian Chiffchaffs, Golden Orioles, Common Redstarts, Hawfinches, Woodchat Shrikes and Olivaceous Warblers.

The first bird hide looks out over fairly open water with a few reedbeds and small islands. Here you may see Purple Swamp-hens, Spoonbills, Glossy Ibis, Little and Cattle Egrets, Whiskered and Black Terns and numerous duck and grebe species. Nearby there is a screen with windows that allows you to look out over more wetland.

To reach the second bird hide you need to cross over the Charco de la Boca, which is a marsh area that is a favoured feeding and roosting site for Squacco, Purple and Black-crowned Night Herons. The vegetation and overhanging trees here also hold Reed, Great Reed, Cetti's and Savi's Warblers, Blackcaps, Winter Wrens and Nightingales.

Once across the causeway you come to another pine forest and the entrance to the second hide. This part of the forest is a nesting area for both Iberian and Black-billed Magpies and as such, is visited by Great Spotted Cuckoos in the spring, as they use both of the magpie species nests to lay their eggs in. The second hide gives a more overall view of the stream and is probably better for viewing the various duck species. Most of the common ducks can be seen here and you may also find numbers of migrating Garganeys in the spring.

La Rocina Visitors Centre (S-6)

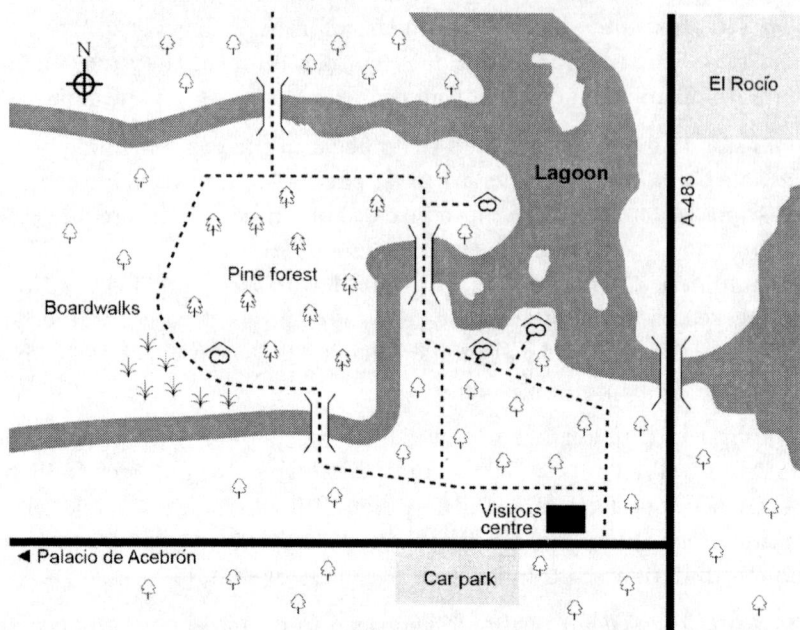

Continuing along the boardwalk you reach a junction. The right-hand route takes you across an *algaida* and then leads you through a vast heathland of scrub and scattered stone pines towards the other two bird hides. The low scrub plants in this area hold Melodious, Spectacled, Sardinian and Dartford Warblers, Red-legged Partridges, Woodchat and Southern Grey Shrikes and Hoopoes. This part of the site is regularly overflown by hunting raptors, of which, Buzzards, Booted and Short-toed Eagles, Red and Black Kites and Kestrels are the most common.

The third and fourth hides look out over the top end of the stream, which tends to hold less water and has more muddier margins. This makes it a more suitable environment for waders and you should look out for Little-ringed Plovers and Green Sandpipers in particular. White Storks nest in the trees surrounding the stream and Kingfishers are often seen on top of the fenceposts on the opposite bank.

Returning along the same track through the heathland, you arrive back at the junction. From here you should go straight ahead. This will lead you through more pine forests and reedbeds before returning you to the visitors centre. En route there is a thatched shelter where you can sit and look out over a dense reedbed and a few scattered cork oak trees.

Access

Access is very simple as the site is only one kilometre from El Rocio. From the village, turn left towards Matalascañas and as soon as you have passed over the bridge (Puente de Canaliega) the entrance gates to the centre are on the right. There is a large parking area 70 metres beyond the buildings.

General Information

The park and office is open everyday, usually from 09.00hrs until dusk, with the exception of December the 25th, 26th and 31st and January the 1st, 5th and 6th and during the El Rocío pilgrimage week. The office closes for an hour (15.00 - 16.00hrs) each afternoon but the park itself remains open.

During the spring and summer this is one of the easiest places to see the Red-necked Nightjars. If these are on your target list then I suggest you drive along the road from La Rocina to the Palacio del Acebrón between dusk and 45 minutes after darkness. At this time, the birds are beginning to become active and they will sometimes land on the road to gain heat from the warm surface of the tarmac. The birds are often loathe to fly and you can sometimes drive your car to within just a few metres of them before they grudgingly take to the air.

Most of the reserve area is fairly flat and all of the trails are board-walked. However, there are three or four short but steep inclines that may cause problems for wheelchair birders, especially if the boards are wet. The bird hides all have a step up or down to get in and out, but the second hide presents other problems as it has a soft sandy floor and there is insufficient room to get a wheelchair between the "fixed" seats. This means that you would have to sit well back from the windows, thereby reducing your field of vision.

The reserve is a very popular attraction for Spanish touring coach holiday companies and you may find you are suddenly surrounded by a group of people who have no interest in birds or nature, but are there solely because it is on the coach company's itinerary. Similarly, coach-loads of schoolchildren are also likely to appear on (dis-) organized outings. My experience is that the teacher in charge is usually interested in nature and becomes so involved in his or her own pursuits that the children are left completely unsupervised. This can result in spontaneous singing, shouting, clapping and dancing amongst the girls and football matches (someone always produces a ball) amongst the boys.

The resulting noise is not conducive to good birding and you may have to abandon the area until the offending groups have left.

When To Visit

The site is of interest throughout the year, especially if water is present. The winter period usually produces the best birding, followed by the spring/breeding season. July and August is the quietest time as the stream will almost certainly be dry at this time.

I personally prefer to visit the site in the early mornings and in the evenings as the area is generally much quieter then and the site is unaffected by sunlight reflecting off the water.

Palacio Del Acebrón
South 7

This rather imposing mansion was built in 1961 as a hunting lodge by a wealthy local merchant from the nearby town of La Palma del Condado. In the following years the estate changed hands several times, until it became a part of the national park in 1978. It has now been restored and turned into an exhibition centre depicting the history of rural life in the Doñana area. There is also an information desk, toilet facilities and a soft-drinks machine. It is set in a mixed forest and has extensive grounds and gardens which are open to the public. There is a nature trail of some two kilometres which passes through the forest and circles the lake of Acebrón (pronounced athey-bron). Bench seats are to be found along the route where you can sit and observe the wide range of forest and woodland birds that can be found here.

Access

Access is from the car park of the La Rocina Visitors Centre. Simply follow the road for 5.2 kms until you reach a large parking area just before the Palacio gates. The road from La Rocina passes through extensive areas of low scrub and gorse with scattered trees and is an excellent area for Hoopoes, Bee-eaters, Great Spotted Cuckoos, Southern Grey and Woodchat Shrikes, Black-eared Wheatears, Zitting Cisticolas and both Sardinian and Dartford Warblers. Also along this road you pass through several *algaidas*, which are the courses of well-vegetated seasonal streams that are always worth checking for warblers, flycatchers, tits and finches. In the summer, Golden Orioles, Nightingales and Red-necked Nightjars are abundant. Raptors are fairly common and can include Booted and Short-toed Eagles, Buzzards, Kestrels, Marsh and Montagu's Harriers and Black and Red Kites.

Palacio del Acebrón (S-7)

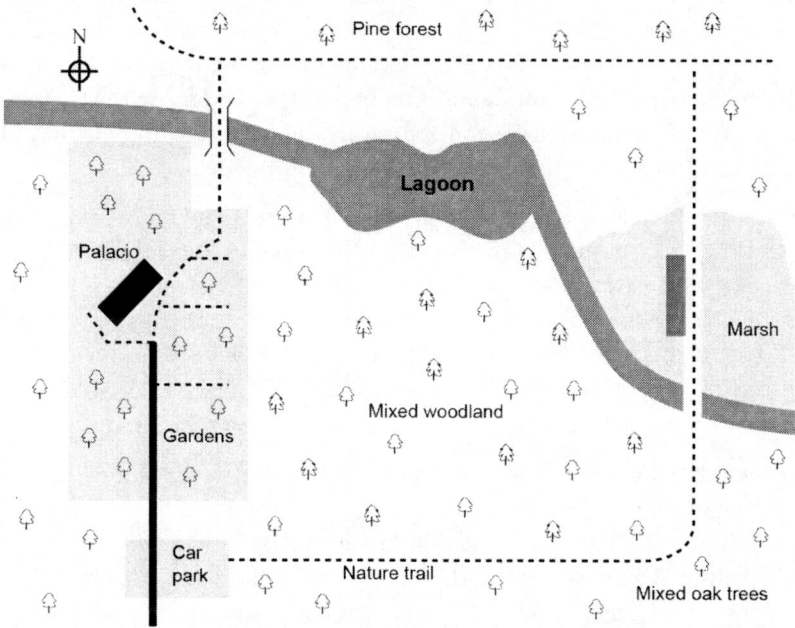

From the car-park of the Palacio, you can choose to either enter the gates and follow the trail around, finishing back at the car-park, or you can take the reverse route, which is my particular preference. At the bottom right-hand corner of the parking area, a track, marked by a sign, leads into the forest. The trees here are mainly cork-oak, some ancient and decaying, but there are several other broadleaved varieties, including poplars, eucalypts and strawberry trees, along with a few stone pines. There is a dense floor covering of several fern species and other undergrowth.

As you pass along the trail you will see several noticeboards giving more information on the vegetation in that particular area. The common birds to be found here, depending on the season, include Robins, Wrens, Spotted and Pied Flycatchers, Short-toed Treecreepers, Firecrests, Common Redstarts, Golden Orioles, Jays, woodpeckers, finches, tits and warblers. In the spring, the forest is alive with the sound of Nightingales calling to proclaim their territories and to attract a mate.

Tree Sparrows are common and use nest boxes or holes in the decaying cork-oaks to build their nests.

After a few hundred metres, the trail turns left onto a wooden causeway that crosses the La Rocina stream and a wide marshy area that is vegetated with willow and alder. This is perfect habitat for Cetti's Warblers, Long-tailed Tits and Blackcaps, which are usually present throughout the year. Once across the causeway you come to a totally different habitat. The surface here is mainly sandy, with pine and eucalyptus species being the dominant trees. The undergrowth includes cistus, broom, halimium, lavender, thyme and other scrub plants. This is the most likely area to find Crested Tits and Serins.

Follow the track to the left which leads downhill and back toward the Palacio. The tree canopy is more open here and gives you a much better chance of seeing overhead raptors. After about 500 metres, turn left and cross back over the La Rocina stream by way of another causeway. There is access to the lake half-way along, but I have always found this to be very unproductive for birdlife, except for a few Mallards, Little Grebes, Bee-eaters and small numbers of swifts, swallows and martins.

After crossing the causeway you arrive at the Palacio and the gardens. The main central track leads for 400 metres back to the car-park, but there are other smaller paths into the gardens that you can follow. At the Palacio end of the track there is a large silky bark oak tree which is covered in orange flowers in the spring and attracts many birds, especially warblers and flycatchers.

The exhibition in the Palacio may or may not be of interest to you, but I would recommend that you go up to the roof where there is an observation platform. This is ideal for watching passing/soaring birds of prey and offers the chance of spotting the Spanish Imperial Eagle.

General Information

The opening times for the Palacio are similar to those of the previous site and the office also closes for an hour between 15.00 and 16.00hrs, although the grounds remain open. There is an information desk and toilet facilities are available, but, at the time of writing, no refreshments are sold here, although there is a soft drinks vending machine at one side of the building.

The central track to the Palacio and some of the small garden paths are perfectly accessible to wheelchair birders, but the forest walk and causeways present many problems and safety risks. At the rear right corner of the building there is a special elevator which is for the use of wheelchair users, enabling you to visit all parts of the Palacio, including the open-air roof terrace.

My preference to take the forest walk in the reverse direction is based on my wide experience of birding at this site. The vast majority of people, birders and non-birders alike, tend to take the orthodox route of visiting the Palacio first and ending up back at the car-park. If you are travelling "with the flow" you can have the (unwanted) company of non-interested noisy tourists with you for the whole route. By taking the opposite direction, you pass these people and then they are gone, leaving you to birdwatch in some modicum of peace. Of course, if enough people buy this book and follow my instructions, you may find yourself walking in the same direction as the majority.

When To Visit

The passage periods and the breeding season are by far the best times to visit this site as these produce the maximum number of bird species, which are often more visible then. If it is pouring with rain and you are stuck for something to do, it may be worthwhile spending an hour or so looking at the interesting exhibition contained within the building.

Centro De Visitantes "El Acebuche"
South 8

The visitors centre and nature park at El Acebuche (pronounced athey-boo-chay) is the largest of the Doñana visitors centres that are open to the public and is an important site to visit, both for the birding and for the information that can be gained here. The new, recently opened complex holds a gift shop, bar/restaurant, information desk, permanent exhibitions, audio-visual displays, park-tour booking office, toilets and an upstairs observation gallery that looks out over the surrounding forest and scrubland.

At the entrance to the visitors centre there is a large car park and picnic area with tables and bench seating. The resident Iberian (Azure-winged) Magpies have become very tame over the years and have learned how to exploit the picnic area, scavenging food from the tables of the picnickers and offering excellent photo opportunities. They are often joined by the Black-billed Magpies that are common elsewhere in Europe. A pair of White Storks regularly breed on the roof of the main building and between May and July the chicks are usually visible in the nest.

Inside the nature park there are about 3 kms of boardwalked trails that can be followed, leading to eleven different bird hides. Seven of these hides look out over the *Laguna de Acebuche*, which is a large expanse of reed-fringed fresh water. There are numerous islands in the lagoon where many bird species breed, including Purple Swamp-hens, Purple Herons, Savi's, Cetti's and Great Reed Warblers, Great Crested and Little Grebes and Little-ringed Plovers.

Raptor species are usually in evidence, especially Marsh Harriers, Kestrels and Buzzards, but the whole of the area is regularly overflown at the appropriate times of the year by both Booted and Short-toed Eagles, Black and Red Kites, Sparrowhawks and even the Spanish Imperial Eagle.

The last two of these hides, to the right (east) of the centre look out over a particularly reedy area. It is here that you have the best chance of finding three of the more elusive breeding birds, ie. Moustached Warblers, Water Rails and Little Bitterns. However, as usual, some degree of patience may be required to see these species.

El Acebuche Visitors Centre (S-8)

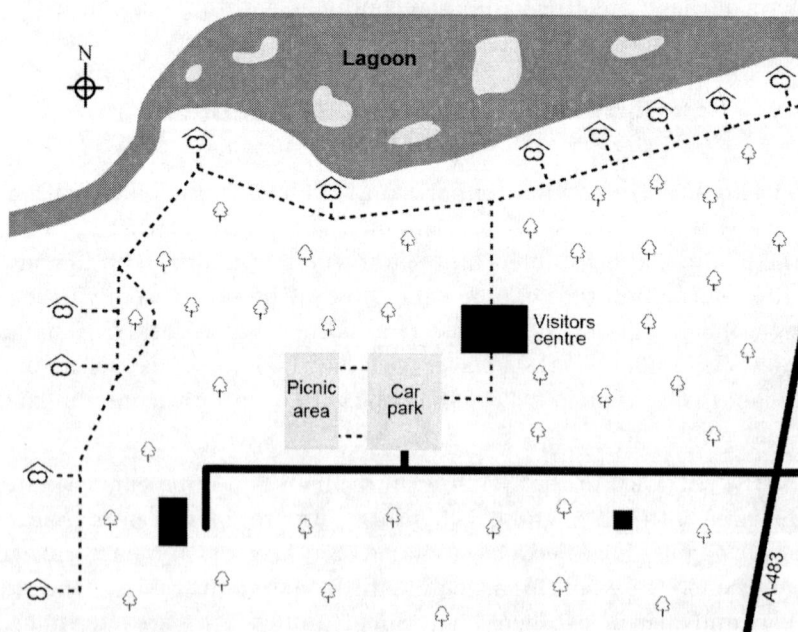

Away from the lagoon there is a further trail *(Sendero peatonal La-gunas del Huerto y las Pajas)* that leads first through a forested area and then into open scrubland. Four more hides can be found along this route that look out over the scrub and also some seasonal marshy areas where other forms of wildlife, ie, foxes, badgers, wild boar, red and fallow deer, lizards, mongooses, etc. can be found alongside the birdlife, which can include Golden Orioles, Common and Great Spotted Cuckoos, Ring Ouzels, Dartford and Spectacled Warblers, Southern Grey and Woodchat Shrikes, Short-toed Treecreepers, Green and Great Spotted Woodpeckers, Wrynecks, Crested Tits, Pied and Spotted Flycatchers, Nightingales, Common and Black Redstarts, Serins, Red-legged Partridges and Turtle Doves.

Throughout the park there are noticeboards that give information on the types of trees, shrubs, herbs, grasses, animals and birds that can be seen at particular locations.

Access

The centre can be reached from the main El Rocío - Matalascañas road (A-483) by turning off, where signed, at km 37.8.

General Information

The centre is open throughout the year, except for December the 30th and 31st, January the 5th and 6th and the week of the religious pilgrimage and festival in El Rocío. Entry is free and all of the facilities are available throughout the day. Opening times vary according to the season, ranging from 07.00hrs in the summer to 09.00hrs in the winter. The park closes at dusk.

The whole of the park is on flat terrain and all of the trails and entrances to the bird hides are boardwalked, making the area suitable for wheelchair birders.

If you have made a reservation to take one of the 4-hour safari trips into the national park, which are operated by the "Cooperativa Marismas del Rocío", then you will start your trip from the main car park here.

Some of the Iberian Magpies that are resident at the visitors centre are so bold that they will come down to the tables whilst you are sitting at them. If you want close-up photos of these birds, sit down quietly, spread a little food on the table and wait.

When To Visit

The park is of great interest throughout the year, but obviously the spring/breeding season will produce the most species. July and August are the two most unproductive months as the very high temperatures, which often exceed 45°C (115°F), tend to keep most of the birds under cover, seeking the shade. Also, you may find the lagoon completely dry at this time.

During the winter, the resident passerines and raptors, together with the winter-visiting ducks and waders will keep you occupied for hours.

Early morning sunlight reflecting off the lagoon can have an adverse effect on your views from some of the bird hides, but this generally only lasts until about 11.00hrs. After that the views can generally be relied upon to be good. Should you be unlucky enough to encounter a rainy day, then the hides offer good protection against the rain and enable you to continue birding.

Matalascañas
South 9

The modern seaside resort town of Matalascañas is situated on the Atlantic coast in the province of Huelva, some 15 kms south of El Rocío. Although collectively known as Matalascañas, it is, in fact, two separate towns, the other being the old town of Torre de la Higuera. For most of the year the resort is quiet, with perhaps only 2 - 3,000 inhabitants, but during Easter and the main summer holiday months of July and August the population can swell to 150,000.

There are several good birding spots in this area, including the extensive stretch of beach, the local golf course, a boardwalked dune walk and the Parque Dunar.

The Parque Dunar contains several walking trails that lead through open land, forested areas and sand dunes and offers the chance of finding Iberian Magpies, Crested Larks, Black Redstarts, Sardinian and Dartford Warblers, Chiffchaffs, Spotted Flycatchers, Serins and other finches. Just inside the entrance of the park there is a raised boardwalk that leads up over the dunes and ends just above the beach. Here you will find a lighthouse which offers a good lookout point for passing seabirds. Just offshore and sticking out from the sea is the collapsed *"Torre de Higueras"*, from which the old town took its name. This ancient man-made structure now serves as a roosting site for gulls and waders.

The golf course can be overlooked from an attractive pedestrian promenade that leads alongside the northern part of the course. Hoopoes, Bee-eaters, larks, finches, wagtails and hirundines are the species that are commonly found here.

The beach and a 1km boardwalked trail through the moving sand dune system of the national park offers the chance to find more passerines and also to observe waders and seabirds. Large gull flocks often gather on the beach and these can include Lesser Blackbacks, Yellow-legged, Black-headed, Audouin's, Mediterranean and, occasionally, Slender-billed Gulls. Various terns are also to be found and although the most noticeable is the Sandwich Tern, there is also the chance of finding Common, Little, Gull-billed, Lesser-crested and Caspian Terns.

Waders are also to be found on the beach, with Oystercatchers, Sanderlings, Turnstones, Ringed, Grey and Kentish Plovers and Dunlins being the most prominent.

Matalascañas (S-9)

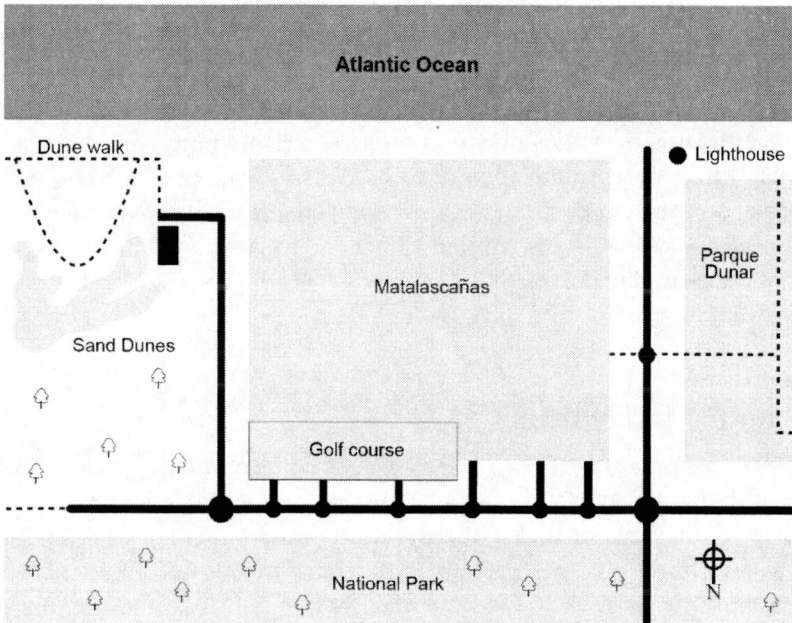

Offshore, especially during the winter, there may be feeding Razorbills, Gannets, Red-breasted Mergansers, Black-necked Grebes and Common Scoters. There is constant seabird movement along the coast as birds head for and return from the Mediterranean Sea. Amongst these there could be Great Skuas and Cory's, Sooty and Mediterranean Shearwaters.

Access

From El Rocio follow the A-483 road to Matalascañas. As you approach the town there is a large roundabout. To visit the Parque Dunar go straight across the roundabout and continue to the next roundabout, where you will find the entry point on the right.

To reach the golf course and beach you should turn left at the first roundabout and follow the road through a series of roundabouts. Just after the fourth one you will see the *Casa de Cultura* building on the right. You can park your car here and walk along the pedestrianized promenade, which passes alongside the golf course, for over a kilometre.

Continue by car until you reach the seventh roundabout, which has a wall with windows and sherry barrels as a feature in the centre of it. Turn right here and follow the road for 600 metres until you come to a T-junction where you should turn left. After 300 metres you should turn right, down a one-way street and at the bottom of the road, turn left. Continue on this road, passing beside the large "Gran Hotel de Coto" until you reach a sandy parking area. Turn right and drive down closer to the beach. In the summer you may be asked for a parking fee.

At this point you will notice a boardwalk. By following this to the left and continuing past the entry point to the national park, you will come to the 1km walk through the dunes and also to the beach. The dunes give a good elevated position for watching passing seabirds and offshore Razorbills, scoters, grebes and mergansers, etc. At this point, the beach forms the boundary of the park and is one of the few areas of the park where one is permitted to walk freely.

General Information

The Parque Dunar offers both a variety of habitats and bird species. However, although a few of the walks in the park are suitable for wheelchair birders, both the boardwalked path and the main circular trail *(La Vial del Dunar)* have quite steep inclines that may prove problematical. The dune walks are over very soft sand and are very hilly. I would not, therefore, recommend this park as being suitable for people in wheelchairs.

The boardwalked sand dune trail at the beach site often gets covered by wind-blown sand, sometimes to a depth of 15cms and becomes totally lost from view for many metres. This makes wheelchair access almost impossible.

At weekends and public holidays during the warmer months of the year the beach is very popular with Spanish families and is best avoided at such times. On Sundays, throughout the year, Matalascañas becomes very busy with people who go there for their Sunday lunches. Normally, at about 18.00hrs, there is a mass exodus from the town which often results in very long traffic queues on the road back to El Rocío, which could see you stuck for an hour or more. I would advise you to depart long before that happens.

When To Visit

All of the sites are of interest throughout the year but visits during the spring migration periods are exceptionally good. For many passerines, crossing over from Africa, this is the first landfall and is used as a resting/feeding point by many birds before continuing their northward journeys. It is not unusual to find Olivaceous, Orphean and Subalpine Warblers, Whinchats, Northern and Black-eared Wheatears, Golden Orioles, Rollers, Nightingales, Woodchat Shrikes, Turtle Doves and Rufous-tailed Scrub Robins all concentrated into these sites during the migration period.

Sunlight reflecting off the sea will obviously have an adverse effect on your views so it would be better to visit the beach and the lighthouse sites during the middle of the day in summer, when the sun is at its highest and reflection is at its least.

Los Guayules
South 10

This is a vast area of pastures, scrubland, forests and small lagoons that, in its entirety, extends from the main El Rocío - Matalascañas road to the Parador near Mazagón. The route follows dirt roads, farm tracks and tarmacked roads and is about 40 kms from start to finish. Due to the varied habitats along the route, this should produce a very good cross-section of bird species, including storks, herons, egrets, ducks, waders, raptors, warblers, wagtails, finches and wheatears. Being aware that not everyone will want to follow such a long route, this site description also offers a much shorter circular tour of about 13 kms that takes in some very good birding areas in the early part of the route.

Access

From El Rocío, take the main A-483 road towards Matalascañas and turn right at km 31.9 and follow this narrow road for 2.5 kms, passing through strawberry fields, orchards and other agricultural land. To the left of the road there is an irrigation ditch which sometimes holds Little-ringed Plovers and both Green and Common Sandpipers. The sparse trees and hedgerows should be checked for Serins, Sardinian and Dartford Warblers, Iberian Magpies, Nightingales, Hoopoes and Bee-eaters. After 2.5 kms you reach a cattle grid and a set of gates which leads into Los Guayules, an area set aside for the grazing of sheep, horses and cattle.

Go over the cattle grid and proceed along the road, which has White Stork nests on nearly every electricity pylon to the right. The low scrub to the left of the road should be checked for resident Dartford, Spectacled and Sardinian Warblers, Crested Larks, Zitting Cisticolas and Southern Grey Shrikes. These are often joined by Subalpine and Melodious Warblers and Woodchat Shrikes in the spring and summer.

Los Guayules (S-10)

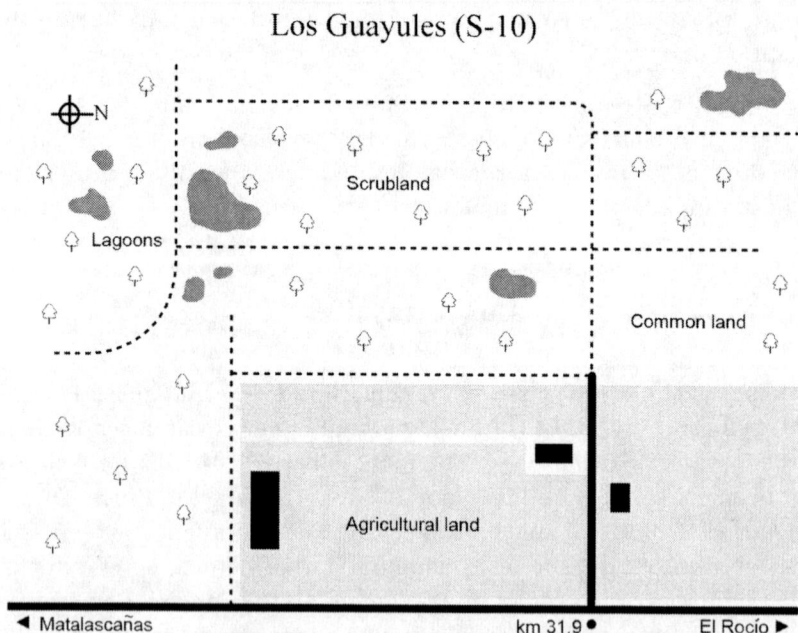

This is one of the few places in the Doñana region where Little Bustards can be found and careful scanning of the scrubland may produce results.

Birds of prey are often present and these can include Black-shouldered, Black and Red Kites, Booted and Short-toed Eagles, Marsh and Montagu's Harriers and Common Kestrels and Buzzards.

The open land to the right often becomes flooded after rain and attracts waders such as Redshanks, Greenshanks, Ringed Plovers and Black-tailed Godwits. In the winter this is a fairly reliable spot for large numbers of Lapwings, Golden Plovers, White Wagtails, Meadow Pipits and flocks of Calandra Larks. Migrating birds, such as Whinchats, Northern Wheatears, Olivaceous Warblers, Rufous-tailed Scrub Robins and Turtle Doves, may be found during the passage periods and Golden Orioles are frequently found in this area during the spring.

After a further 2 kms you reach another cattle grid. Continue along the road, which now becomes a dirt track with open scrubland on the right and a plantation of young stone pines on the left. Once again, this area should be scanned for warblers, chats, larks, shrikes, pipits and Red-legged Partridges.

After another 2 kms there is a T-junction where you should turn left, but before doing so, park and walk 80 metres down the track to the right, where there is a seasonal pool on the left, about 35 metres in from the track. In the past I have seen White Storks, Spoonbills, Little and Cattle Egrets, Grey, Purple and Black-crowned Night Herons and even a pair of Purple Swamp-hens here.

Continue by car for 400 metres until you reach another T-junction. To complete the whole route you need to follow the track to the right, but again you can visit another pool by turning left and following the road for 2.1 kms. The pool (Laguna del Alamillo) is about 50 metres to the left of the track and is partly hidden by trees, but you should be able to see the small reedbed that surrounds it. This pool and several other smaller ones nearby, is largely used as a watering hole by cattle but some interesting birds can be found here, including Reed and Great Reed Warblers, Cetti's Warblers, Chiffchaffs, Stonechats, Hoopoes, Golden Orioles, Little Crakes, Purple Herons and Little Bitterns. I have heard Water Rails calling on several occasions, but as yet I have not actually seen one at this site. The surrounding scrubland holds Southern Grey and Woodchat Shrikes, Black-eared Wheatears, Corn Buntings and Serins.

At this point, you can chose to complete the rest of this site description, or you can drive along a small track beside the pool (see map) that will take you back to the second cattle grid at Los Guayules, where you can then turn left back toward the main road.

If you decide to follow the full site description, you should return back along the road and after passing the junction you will reach an area of eucalyptus and pine forests. It would be worth stopping anywhere amongst the pines to search for Crested Tits, Iberian Chiffchaffs, Firecrests, Short-toed Treecreepers, Spotted Flycatchers, Tree Sparrows, Golden Orioles, Hoopoes and both Great Spotted and Green Woodpeckers.

I have not produced a map of this area, due to its size, but the directions given will easily guide you to all of the important sites along the route.

After 5 kms you reach an area where there are about 12 small foresters' houses. These are mostly abandoned as homes now, but are still used at times by the foresters and the charcoal burners who work here. The road to the right will lead for 1.5 kms to more forests which you can investigate, but you are unlikely to find anything there that you haven't already discovered. Instead, continue along the road and after 3.5 kms you come to another junction. Ignore the road to Ribatehilos on the right and proceed straight ahead. 150 metres after the junction there is a small seasonal wetland on the left, which has often produced good numbers of waders in the past.

Continue for another kilometre and you reach a tarmacked road that leads to Almonte and Mazagón. Turn left and after 250 metres there is a turning to the right that leads into another abandoned forestry settlement called Cabezudos.

This site can be excellent in winter for Black Redstarts, Meadow Pipits, White Wagtails, Robins, Booted Eagles and Red Kites. In the summer it is a major breeding area for Barn and Red-rumped Swallows, House Martins, Common Swifts and Golden Orioles. A large abandoned church stands nearby and usually has a pair of White Storks nesting on the upper tower. Spotless Starlings nest in the adjacent palm trees.

Returning to the main road, you should now head in the direction of Mazagón. Most of the countryside along this road is scrubland with scattered forests and is an excellent place to see Red-necked Nightjars in the summer evenings/nights, as they often rest on the tarmacked road. There are one or two small rivers that flow under the road, but generally they are of little interest, although they may produce a few Blackcaps, Long-tailed Tits, finches, larks and other warblers in the dense vegetation.

The next important stop is 13.5 kms from Cabezudos, where there is a large "Doñana" sign. At this point, a walking route called the "*Via Pecuaria Vereda del Camino del Loro*" crosses the road. Notice boards give information and a map of the area, showing where many small seasonal lagoons can be found. In the winter it is worth seeking out a few of these, but they are usually dry by late April/early May. One of the deepest lagoons, the Laguna de Moguer, can be found beside the road just over a kilometre from the Camino by following the main road. It is never very much more than one metre deep, but in the winter and spring, provided that we have had sufficient rain to fill it, you can find a good selection of ducks, herons, egrets, waterfowl and waders.

The road now continues for almost 5 kms until it reaches the main A-494 Matalascañas to Mazagón road just opposite the Parador. You can either return to the El Rocío area via Matalascañas, or you can turn around and trace your route back.

General Information

The middle section of this route, about 12 kms, is on dirt roads and tracks, which, at the time of writing, are in fairly good condition. However, during the winter the tracks may degrade and care may need to be taken when driving here.

There are no inhabited areas between the El Rocío road and the Parador at Mazagón, ie. no bars, cafes or petrol stations, and I would suggest that you ensure you have enough fuel and take an adequate supply of drinks and food with you.

As most of the area is relatively flat, with reasonable views across the open scrubland, I feel that wheelchair birders will have no problems following this route.

When To Visit

Due to the wide diversity of habitats that occur along this route the site is of year-round interest and should always produce a good and varied bird list, although you are likely to see more birds in the cooler months of the year, ie. October to June.

Arroyo De Santa Maria
South 11

The Arroyo de Santa Maria is a seasonal stream with extensive reed-beds and both sandy and rocky banks and riverbed. The stream, which is bounded by agricultural land and open scrubland, runs in a north to south line and eventually flows through the Coto del Rey forest, where the name changes to the Arroyo del Partido, before reaching the marshes to the east of El Rocío.

The site is easily viewed from a road bridge or from elevated farm tracks that lead both up and downstream. Waders are usually present when the water is in flow and these regularly include Ringed, Little-ringed and Kentish Plovers, Little and Temminck's Stints, Common, Green and Wood Sandpipers, Black-tailed Godwits, Redshanks, Greenshanks, Avocets, Black-winged Stilts, Lapwings and Dunlin.

The surrounding open land supports Hoopoes, Bee-eaters, Tree Sparrows, buntings, wheatears, finches, tits, warblers and larks. Red-legged Partridges and Common Quail are also often present, but the latter is more usually heard rather than seen. During the spring and summer you may find House and Sand Martins and Barn and Red-rumped Swallows, both of which nest beneath the bridge.

Raptor numbers are usually high, with Black and Red Kites, Buzzards, Marsh and Montagu's Harriers, Kestrels and Booted Eagles being the most common.

Access

From El Rocío, take the road toward Almonte and after two kilometres turn right onto the road which is signed for Villamanrique. Continue along this road for just over five kilometres and you reach the bridge over the stream. Parking is easy as there are pull-off areas at both sides of the bridge.

Arroyo de Santa Maria (S-11)

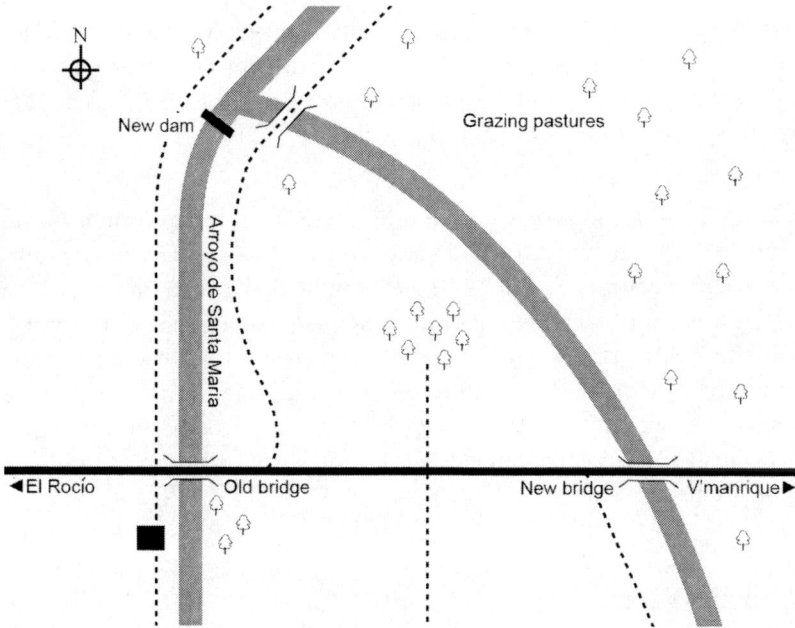

N

New dam

Grazing pastures

Arroyo de Santa Maria

◄ El Rocío   Old bridge   New bridge   V'manrique ►

General Information

The bridge is a good point to start viewing the site, but please be careful. This is a particularly fast stretch of road and the footpath across the bridge is fairly narrow. Other more suitable spots can be found close by to set up your telescope in safety.

The sandy margins and a few small islands in the middle of the water-course are the best places to search for wader species, whilst the reedbeds and other vegetation usually hold resident Cetti's Warblers and seasonal visitors or passage migrants such as Reed, Great Reed, Sedge, Savi's, Willow and Aquatic Warblers. Chiffchaffs are very common in the winter and a small number of Bluethroats may also be present at this time.

The agricultural land and scrubland hold both Woodchat and Southern Grey Shrikes, Hoopoes, Zitting Cisticolas, Crested Larks, White Wagtails, Common Quail and Corn Buntings. Tree Sparrows are often present in good numbers and a few pairs regularly nest in the holes in the nearby electricity pylons.

Elevated farm tracks give easy access to both the up and downstream areas. As you look around the site you will notice many electrical pylons. These should be checked carefully as they are the favoured perching sites of Ravens and raptors.

Although the farm tracks may be a little bumpy in places, they can be negotiated, with care, by disabled/wheelchair birders. The upstream track beside the stream is driveable so bird watching can also be done from the comfort of your car.

In the autumn of 2006, work was completed on a scheme to improve the water management of the area and a new road bridge was built one kilometre along the road to the east of the old bridge. Partial damming of the arroyo occurred about 400 metres upstream and a new canal was excavated, so that in times of heavy rainfall, the excess water will be channelled along the new watercourse and pass under the new bridge, joining the Arroyo de la Partido before finally emptying out into the marshes, rather than just flooding the fields as it does now. It is possible, that if this scheme is successful, a new area of interest to birders will be created at this site.

When To Visit

The site is of most interest when there is steady or slow water flow, which is usually between October and June. After heavy rains, the stream is often a raging torrent and much of its worth as a birding site is diminished until the water returns to a reasonable level, but maybe the water management scheme described above may improve things once the work has been completed.

During the height of summer the stream is usually dry and of very little interest, although the surrounding countryside is still worth investigating. The site is of interest at any time of day, more so in the mornings and evenings, although morning sunlight reflecting off the water can affect downstream viewing from the bridge. The upstream areas do not suffer this problem.

The Villamanrique De La Condesa Road South 12

This is the main connecting road between El Rocío and Villamanrique de la Condesa, which leads on from the previous site. The road is exceptionally straight and in the past was subjected to high-speed driving which resulted in at least five Iberian Lynx becoming road-kill victims in the last five years.

Recent traffic calming schemes, such as speed-bumps and rumble-strips have helped to reduce the speed and other measures have been taken in an attempt to preserve the lynx, which is one of the most endangered wild cats in the world. These include over 35 kms of roadside fencing and underpasses that offer the cats safe routes to get from one side of the road to the other.

Along a large section of the road there are tall electricity pylons that are popular perching/roosting spots for raptors, such as Black Kites, Booted Eagles, Common Buzzards, Ospreys and Common Kestrels. As the road is perfectly straight, you are able to spot these birds well in advance and can usually get quite close to them in your car.

The new fences alongside the road provide feeding and look-out posts for Southern Grey and Woodchat Shrikes, Corn Buntings, Stonechats, Common and Black Redstarts, Bee-eaters, Robins and Spotted Flycatchers.

To both sides of the road there are stone pine forests but access into these is not allowed as they are private hunting grounds. However, by stopping at any convenient parking area along the road you may see Iberian Magpies and other forest birds.

At one point the road is crossed by the Raya Real, which is part of the ancient pilgrim route between Villamanrique and El Rocío, which is often in use by groups of travellers at weekends throughout the year. This tree-lined sandy route is always worth visiting to look for such birds as Crested Tits, Short-toed Treecreepers, Tree Sparrows, Golden Orioles and Firecrests, which are often found in the pines and eucalyptus trees.

A few kilometres further along the road you reach a roundabout near to the Bar La Pará. It is here, at the roundabout, that the sandy track of the Raya Real begins and this is another area that you may wish to stop at to look for the aforementioned species and Black-shouldered Kites, which are reasonably common in the general area between October and March.

Continue straight ahead for another 2.5 kms and you cross over the Arroyo de Gato. This is a seasonal stream that runs to the south west of the town of Villamanrique de la Condesa. It may prove beneficial to stop nearby and check the stream for herons, egrets and waders. The area to the left of the road, with cork and holm oak trees, is the Dehesa de Villamanrique, an area where Hoopoes, Little Owls, Iberian Magpies, Woodchat Shrikes and numerous other woodland species can be found. Villamanrique, which is a kilometre further on, is referred to as the "Gateway to Doñana" by the local people.

General Information

Almost the entire length of the road has white lines painted along the sides, which means "no stopping" with any of your wheels on any part of the road. As frustrating as this may be to birders I strongly urge you to find somewhere to pull off the road completely if you want to stop.

Although the traffic calming systems have had a genuine effect on some drivers, there are still those that drive along at speeds of up to 150 kms per hour. Because of this the road is regularly patrolled by the Guardia Civil police. If they catch you parked on the road you are likely to receive a very hefty on-the-spot fine.

When To Visit

Regardless of when you pass along this road there will always be something of interest present, either perched on electricity pylons and fence posts, feeding on the verges or flying across the road.

The Western Sector

This area covers several sites just outside the recognized boundaries of Doñana, but includes some excellent birding areas that should form part of your visit to this region. The major sites are the Marismas del Odiel, a vast, tidal salt marsh area to the south of the city of Huelva, which is considered to be the second most important area for birds in this region and the Laguna El Portil, a site of major importance during the winter months for Ferruginous and White-headed Ducks. Also included are the Marismas del Río de Piedras, La Rábida, Lagunas de Palos, Estero de Domingo Rubio, El Rompido, La Ribera and the town of Niebla, where a large colony of Lesser Kestrels are the main attraction.

All of the sites are within 100 kms of the main Doñana region and can be reached within one hour. Due to the diversity of the areas, I will give directions to each site individually in the site descriptions.

Niebla Castle
West 1

The town of Niebla is situated just a couple of kilometres from the main A-49 Sevilla - Huelva road and as well as being of great interest to birders it also has great historical interest. Within the town there is an ancient castle with a surface area of over 16 hectares. The town dates from before the time of the Roman occupation and much of the current town, including the castle, now stands on historical Roman sites. The most obvious of these sites is the bridge that leads over the Río Tinto (the red river) to the east of the town. It was built sometime in the 2nd century AD, and it still stands as the main entrance into the town.

The town became a Moorish stronghold during their occupation of Andalucía between the early 8th century and 1262 and much of the castle still shows distinct signs of Moorish architecture. After the Spanish finally defeated the Moors and ousted them from the country, the castle remained intact until 1563, when parts of it were re-developed in a more Spanish style. The castle walls and much of the internal buildings still remain in good condition, but nowadays a complete village exists within the walls.

To birders, the main attraction of the castle is the colony of Lesser Kestrels that breed there. Over 50 birds are regularly seen in the spring and summer, nesting in holes in the castle walls and numerous towers. The kestrels, however, are not the only attraction. There are also breeding colonies of Common and Pallid Swifts, Jackdaws, Spotless Starlings, House Sparrows, Feral Pigeons and a few pairs of White Storks.

Access

From all parts of the Doñana region you should head for the main A-49 road and turn towards Huelva. If you are travelling from Portugal or from the Ayamonte area you should take the A-49 towards Sevilla. The motorway exit to Niebla is at junction Km 60. Follow the road into Niebla, which passes over the Río Tinto and the Roman bridge. Once over the bridge there is a set of traffic lights. Go straight ahead and the castle walls are directly in front of you.

You can park right in front of the castle, where Lesser Kestrels can usually be seen flying around the high defensive walls. One of the best places to watch these birds at close quarters is inside the castle itself. Walk down the road until you reach the main gate and enter through the archway. Within 10 metres you should turn left and walk for 25 metres. On the left there is an open area used as a car park. This gives you excellent views of an ancient bell-tower, where at least 6 pairs of kestrels, Spotless Starlings, Jackdaws and both Common and Pallid Swifts nest in holes in the walls of the tower. A pair of White Storks also nest here, on the highest part of the tower.

If you continue further up the road and take the first turning left and then the first right, you will come to another area where the kestrels also nest and display. Here, you will also find the tourist information office and the ticket office/entrance to visit an interior part of the castle, worthwhile, if just for a closer view of the kestrels.

General Information

Being within the town of Niebla, you are close to all services and amenities and it is sometimes a pleasure to sit at one of the bars in front of the castle walls and enjoy a coffee or beer, whilst watching the impressive flying displays of the Jackdaws, swifts and kestrels in comfort.

When To Visit

The best time to visit this site is between March and July, when the maximum number of birds are present and the breeding season is in full swing. I have always found that morning visits (before midday) and evening visits (after 18.00 hrs) produce the best views of the birds. During the afternoons the birds spend much of the time resting and activity is at its lowest.

During the spring and autumn migration periods (March/April and September/October) you may find a few Alpine Swifts flying and feeding with the other swifts, before moving further north to their breeding grounds. The kestrels are classed as migratory and many do return to Africa between November and February. However, a few do remain throughout the winter, although at this time the interest of this site is somewhat diminished as there are no swifts to be seen.

Laguna Balestrera
West 2

The small nature reserve of Laguna Balestrera is situated just a few kms west of the town of Niebla. It is not a lagoon in the true sense of the word, but a series of small seasonal pools and waterscrapes created by the commercial extraction of gravel many years ago. It covers a surface area of about 3 hectares and the area is now well vegetated with mature reedbeds, grasses and tamarisk trees. The main part of the reserve is fenced off from the general public but there is a bird observation point that offers reasonable views of much of the site.

Waterbirds that are commonly recorded include Purple Swamp-hens, Moorhens, Black-winged Stilts, Green Sandpipers, Redshanks and Little-ringed Plovers, all of which breed here. The reedbeds and tamarisk trees hold resident Cetti's Warblers and Zitting Cisticolas, which are often joined in the migration and breeding periods by Sedge, Reed, Melodious and Savi's Warblers, Common Redstarts, Purple Herons and Little Bitterns.

The surrounding areas are either agricultural or open scrubland and these can produce Northern and Black-eared Wheatears, Crested Larks, Corn Buntings, Black Redstarts, Southern and Woodchat Shrikes, Stonechats, Red-legged Partridges, Bee-eaters, Hoopoes, Meadow Pipits, Serins, Blackcaps and both White and Yellow Wagtails.

To the east of the site there is the Río Tinto (the red river), where several wader species, including storks, herons and egrets, are often found feeding. A visit to the river area can easily be incorporated into your visit to the main site.

Hirundine activity is high in the summer, with House and Sand Martins, Common and Pallid Swifts and Barn and Red-rumped Swallows usually present and many of these nest underneath the nearby motorway bridge.

White Storks build their nests on large electricity pylons close by and the stork nests are shared by House Sparrows and Spotless Starlings.

Lesser Kestrels, from the nearby breeding colony at Niebla, are often seen hunting in this area and Marsh and Montagu's Harriers are also fairly common. Other raptor species include Booted and Short-toed Eagles, Common Buzzards and Black Kites.

Access

This site is just a few kilometres west of the town of Niebla and is best visited directly after visiting that particular site.

From the castle at Niebla, pass through the town and continue along the road (the A-472) towards Huelva until you pass 2 large buildings on the left at about Km 49.6. A few hundred metres further on you should turn left, onto a dirt track at km 49.9. Continue on this track for about 500 metres until you reach a railway crossing. Once you have crossed the railway lines, follow the track to the right until you pass through a tunnel under the main motorway. After passing through the tunnel you are at the site, but you should drive straight ahead for 250 metres until you reach the bird observatory at the bottom end of the reserve.

From the observatory you have views of part of the area, but other aspects of the site can be seen from the top end of the reserve. This can be reached by walking up-hill from the entrance to the tunnel for about 125 metres.

Laguna Balestrera (W-2)

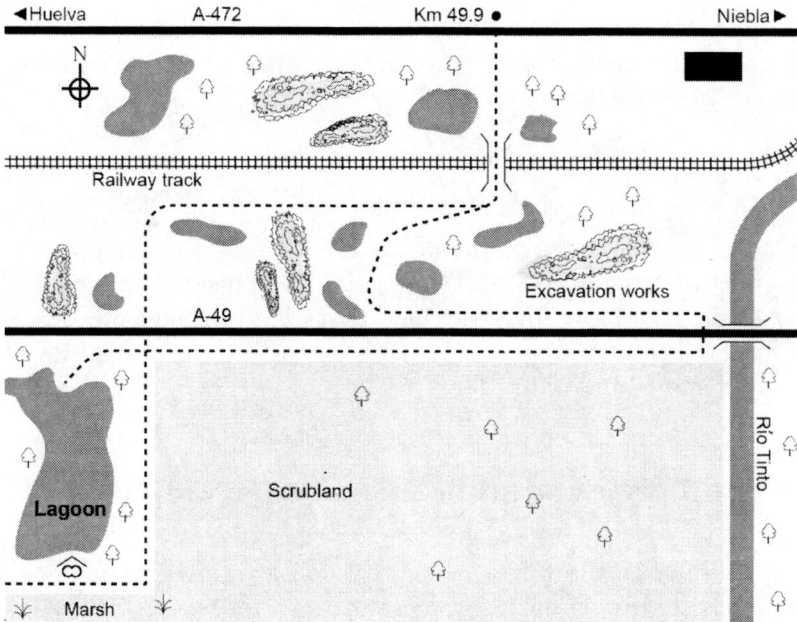

On leaving the site, drive back to the tunnel, but instead of passing through it, turn right and follow the track until you come to the bank of the Río Tinto. Pass under the motorway bridge and then turn immediately left and follow the track back to the railway crossing.

Gravel excavation is still taking place here and you will find many small pools and waterscapes, some new and barren and some older ones with mature vegetation, that should be investigated.

Once back at the road, you can turn right to go back to Niebla, or left, if you wish to go on towards Huelva and the sites in that area. To reach the other sites you should continue for about 8 kms and then follow the Huelva signs until you return to the main A-49 road. Shortly after re-joining the A-49 you should take the H-31 to Huelva at km 77 as described in the Access section for that site and then follow the rest of the directions that are given.

General Information

This is a seasonal wetland site that is entirely dependent on rainfall and most of the pools and gravel pits normally dry out from mid-June onwards. You may find that the river also becomes dry in the hottest months of the year. At this time, the whole of the site is of little interest except for a few passerines and hirundines.

Due to the height of the windows in the observatory and also much of the surrounding vegetation, this site is not really suitable for birders who rely on wheelchairs.

When To Visit

The main site and the surrounding areas are only of real interest if water is present, usually between October and the end of May. As the site is quite small, heat haze is not a problem here. The sun is usually directly overhead or behind you so you are not affected by sunlight reflecting off the water at any time of the day.

Paraje Natural Marismas Del Odiel
West 3

The Marismas del Odiel is a vast area of tidal marshland, situated between the estuaries of the Ríos Odiel and Tinto and the Atlantic Ocean, to the south of the city of Huelva. It covers an area of 7,185 hectares and is partly natural reserve and partly a UNESCO Man and Biosphere Reserve. It is also a RAMSAR site and an EU site of special protection for wild birds.

Various ecosystems exist within the site, ranging from commercial salinas (saltpans), sand dunes, the ocean and rivers, forests, beaches, tidal inlets and the marshes themselves. The accessible parts of the area are located mainly on three islands, the Isla Calatilla, the Isla Bacuta and the Isla de Saltés, covering over 1,000 hectares. Being a saltmarsh, influenced by the daily tides, the flora here is what you would expect to find in saline habitats. The main marsh vegetation consists of cord grasses, glassworts, bullrushes, reeds, cat mint, rosemary and cistus species. In the drier areas there are small forests of stone pine, juniper, tamarisk, oak, broom and mastic trees.

The area has a recorded bird list of over 200 species and the inaccessible area of the Isla de Enmedio holds up to 400 pairs of breeding Eurasian Spoonbills, about 30% of the European breeding population. The site is an important wintering ground for many species and is also a staging post for migrating birds in the spring and autumn. Two of Spain's scarcest gulls, Audouin's and Slender-billed are to be found here, the former with up to 500 birds and the latter in very much smaller numbers.

Access

There are two routes to take to the Marismas del Odiel from the Doñana area. The first is via the main A-49 road towards Huelva and the second is along the coast road from Matalascañas. The former offers the chance to stop off at Niebla, to see the Lesser Kestrels that live in the ancient castle there. The latter allows you to visit the Lagunas de Palos on the way.

The A-49 route.

Follow the A-49 towards Huelva, which passes the turn-off to Niebla at junction km 60. Further along the road, at km 77, the road to Huelva becomes the H-31, which you should follow until you reach junction 84A, signed for Punta Umbria and Ayamonte. Turn off here onto the H-30 and follow for 2 kms until you reach a roundabout, where you should turn left. Continue for 500 metres and at the traffic lights, turn right where signed for "Playas" (beaches) and "Paraje Natural Marismas del Odiel". After 2 kms you reach a large roundabout where you should take the first exit, which is again signed for Punta Umbria and Ayamonte. This is the A-497 which takes you to the bridge over the Río Odiel. Once over the bridge you should take the first turn-off, which is signed "P.N. Marismas del Odiel". This leads to a roundabout where you should take the second exit. This will lead you to another roundabout where you should take the first exit. You are now at the entry point to the marshes.

The Matalascañas route.

From Matalascañas take the A-494 towards Mazagón and Huelva. Once past Mazagón the road becomes the N-442 and leads past the Laguna de Palos sites at km 13, 12 and 11. It also passes the entry point to La Rábida at the roundabout at km 7. Beyond the roundabout the road number changes again, this time to the H-30, the same road referred to in the other route directions above. Continue until you reach the roundabout referred to there and then follow the remaining directions to reach the marshes.

The road that leads along the entire length of the site is called the *"Dique Juan Carlos 1"* and is 25 kilometres long. After leaving the roundabout you pass over a bridge onto the Isla Calatilla and the first point of interest is within 300 metres, with commercial salt-pans *(Salinas Aragonesas)* on the right and scrubby open land on the left. The salinas often hold good numbers of gulls and waders and it is here that you are most likely to spot the Slender-billed Gull. The scrub area should be checked for Southern Grey Shrikes, Sardinian Warblers, Zitting Cisticolas and both Marsh and Montagu's Harriers.

After 2 kms you reach two ponds on the left that can sometimes offer tremendous birding. You can park here, near the entrance to the "Bar/Restaurant La Calatilla", which offers the chance of food, drink and toilet facilities.

La Calatilla Visitors Centre (W-3)

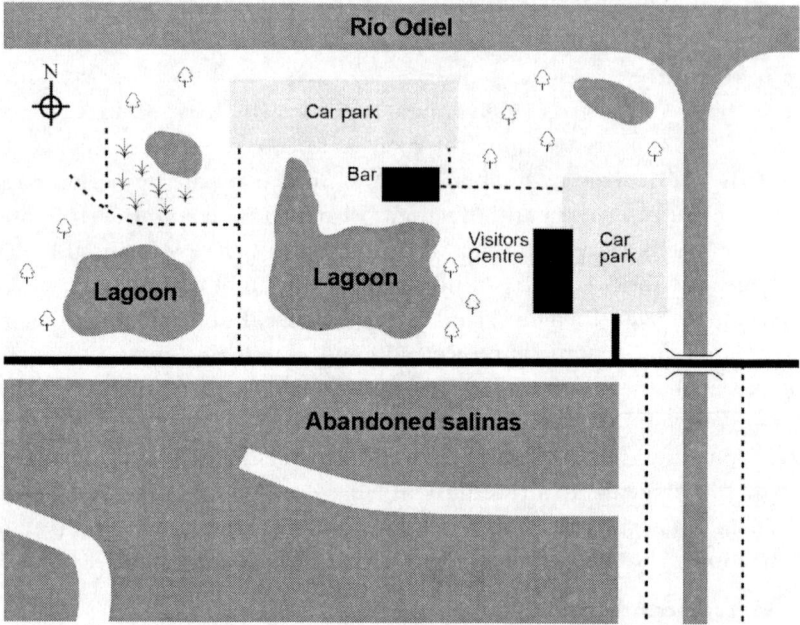

The first pond is rather scruffy looking but is a regular breeding site for Red-knobbed Coots and Red-crested Pochards. The second pond is surrounded by dense reeds and rushes which usually hold one or two pairs of Purple Swamp-hens, which breed here. The reedbeds can hold wintering Penduline Tits and Reed Buntings, as well as resident Cetti's Warblers. In the spring and summer, there is usually at least one pair of Little Bitterns present. The usually wet salinas on the right are regular feeding spots for Greater Flamingos, Black-winged Stilts and numerous other wader species.

150 metres further along the road you will find the La Calatilla Visitors Centre, which, if it is open, is a useful source of handouts and information. The car park in front of the Centre offers views of a tidal river where many waders may be found at low tide. A short walk leads from the Centre to the bar/restaurant and views of the bank of the Río Odiel.

Continuing along the road you pass over a bridge and onto the Isla

Bacuta, where there are many old abandoned salinas which are excellent locations for feeding waders and gulls. You can park anywhere along the road to stop and look at the birds and views are generally very good.

Driving further, you reach a large bridge *(Puente de Burros)* that leads onto the Isla de Saltés, perhaps the better of the three islands for birding.

Six kilometres from the bridge there is an obvious parking area on the right in an area known as *"Cabeza Alta"*, where there is a large tidal inlet to the left of the car park and a boardwalk to the right that leads to another tidal area nearby. These are two of the best places to see large numbers of waders, especially at low tide. At high tide the birds will leave these areas and move to their high-water roosts.

From this point on, the road becomes a causeway, offering elevated views of the Río Odiel and some of the marsh areas. After 3.5 kms you reach another parking area and three distinctly different habitats. To the left are large open sandy fields that have been created to provide nesting sites for various bird species, the most noticeable of which are Kentish Plovers and Little Terns. In recent years there has also been a pair of breeding Stone Curlews here. The low sandy dunes to the right are favoured by Crested Larks, Meadow Pipits, Stonechats and Woodchat Shrikes and the numerous broom trees, beyond a disused building are favoured by warblers.

Marismas del Odiel (W-3)

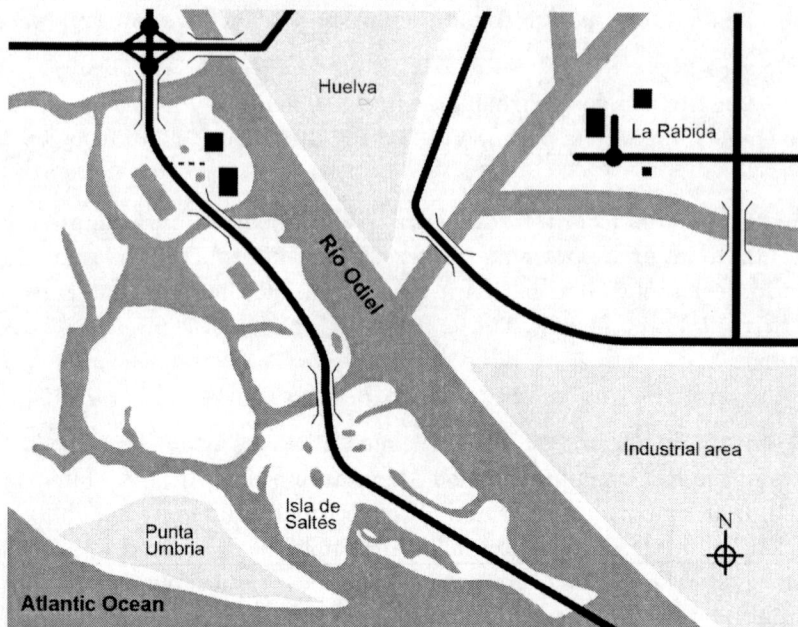

During the spring passage migration this is an outstanding spot for migrating passerines, which can sometimes be found in their hundreds, as they spend time here recovering from the long flight from Africa. Amongst these there may be Northern and Black-eared Wheatears, Woodchat Shrikes, Subalpine, Savi's, Olivaceous, Orphean, Willow and Melodious Warblers, Whinchats, Hoopoes and Rufous-tailed Scrub Robins. The resident passerines include Sardinian, Dartford, Cetti's and Spectacled Warblers, Zitting Cisticolas and Stonechats.

To the left of the causeway there are several sand-bars, which, at low-tide, attract large numbers of gulls, terns and waders. These are good places to look for Audouin´s Gulls, an intermediate sized gull, between Black-headed and Yellow-legged size. The most numerous waders appear to be Sanderlings, but Black and Bar-tailed Godwits, Ringed, Little-ringed, Kentish and Grey Plovers, Oystercatchers, Turnstones, Dunlin, Curlew Sandpipers and numerous other species can regularly be found here.

The road continues for another 3 kms before reaching two large water-scrapes in a fenced-off area on the left. These are also excellent for gulls, terns and waders and are the main nesting sites for Little Terns, with over 200 pairs regularly breeding here each year, along with reasonable numbers of Collared Pratincoles and Kentish Plovers. Seawatching opportunities exist here, although you may have to climb onto the large concrete blocks at the side of the road to get good views. Gannets are usually seen throughout the year and passing shearwaters are also often visible. During the winter there may be Common Scoters, Red-breasted Mergansers and Razorbills on the water and occasional passing Great and Arctic Skuas.

Unless you are particularly interested in passing seabirds, I would suggest you do not go any further along the road. The causeway (Espigón) now continues for another 4 kms until ending at a lighthouse, where you have to turn around and come back the way you came.

General Information

Many people believe that waders are only present in this region in the winter and during passage periods. This is not the case and large numbers of waders can be seen here throughout the year, with many species breeding. However, the winter does produce both the largest number of species and the greater concentration of birds.

The area is very flat and with the exception of the Cabeza Alta site, where there are 50 metres of shale to cross before reaching the boardwalk, it is easily accessible to wheelchair birders.

As this is a coastal site, the wind tends to be stronger and the temperatures a few degrees lower than at many other sites and I would suggest that you take some protective clothing with you as a precaution.

As with all tidal areas, the best birding is to be achieved at low tide, when the muddy tidal inlets and sand-bars are exposed and the birds are feeding.

Sunlight reflecting off the water may be a problem, but this can generally be overcome by moving your position by a 100 metres or so.

Surprisingly, this is not a great site for birds of prey, but Black Kites, Booted Eagles, Common Kestrels, Peregrine Falcons, Common Buzzards, Montagu´s, Marsh and Hen Harriers and Ospreys can all be found here.

John Butler

When To Visit

The site is of great interest throughout the year and a good bird list is guaranteed whenever you visit. The winter and passage periods produce the highest numbers and the most species, especially amongst the waders and seabirds, with over 25 species regularly seen.

The breeding season is notable for the large number of Little and Whiskered Terns, Black-winged Stilts, Avocets, Spoonbills, Little-ringed and Kentish Plovers and Collared Pratincoles that nest here.

July and August are the least productive months in birding terms and is the busiest for tourists, who use the beaches and any available spots for barbecues, picnics and fishing. The sheer weight of numbers makes serious birding almost an impossibility.

Lagunas De Palos Y Las Madres
West 4

These are a series of inland lagoons that run parallel with the Atlantic coast, just to the east of the city of Huelva. They form part of a 693 hectare Paraje Natural that was created in 1989 and are managed by the Agencia de Medio Ambiente of the Andalsian Government. The surrounding vegetation consists of stone pines, junipers, eucalyptus, tamarisk, rosemary, cistus, palms, thyme, broom and phragmites. The area is also extensively used for agriculture and vast areas are utilised for the growing of strawberries.

Other forms of wildlife are to be found in the area, with Otters, Mongooses, Oceolated Lizards, Chameleons, Hedgehogs, Foxes, Spur-thighed Tortoises and snakes being present, but normally secretive.

The most accessible of these lagoons are the Laguna de la Mujer, the Laguna de la Jara and the Laguna de Primera de Palos. The first of these lagoons holds Purple Swamp-hens, Little Bitterns, herons, egrets, ducks, grebes and waders. Apart from the lagoon there are strawberry fields, orchards, forests and areas of open scrubland which can also provide good birding.

The second lagoon is located next to the main Matalascañas to Huelva road and has a bird hide and farm tracks that are walkable and lead to other wet areas and also through a small pine forest. The lagoon offers the chance of Purple Swamp-hens, Little and Great Crested Grebes, Purple and Black-crowned Night Herons, Little Bitterns, egrets, ducks and terns, whilst the surrounding area can produce Iberian Magpies, Hoopoes, Bee-eaters, warblers, tits, finches and larks.

The third and largest lagoon is on private land owned by the Cepsa petroleum company and the refinery borders the western edge of the lagoon. The area is fenced off from the general public but good close-up views can be had of large areas of the lagoon from the southern end and eastern side.

This is by far the most interesting of the three lagoons and usually holds far greater numbers of the previously mentioned birds plus Shovelers, Gadwalls, Common and Red-crested Pochards, Teal, Wigeon, Tufted and White-headed Ducks, Red-knobbed Coots, Water Rails, Glossy Ibis, Squacco Herons and numerous wader species.

Lagunas de Palos y Las Madres (W-4)

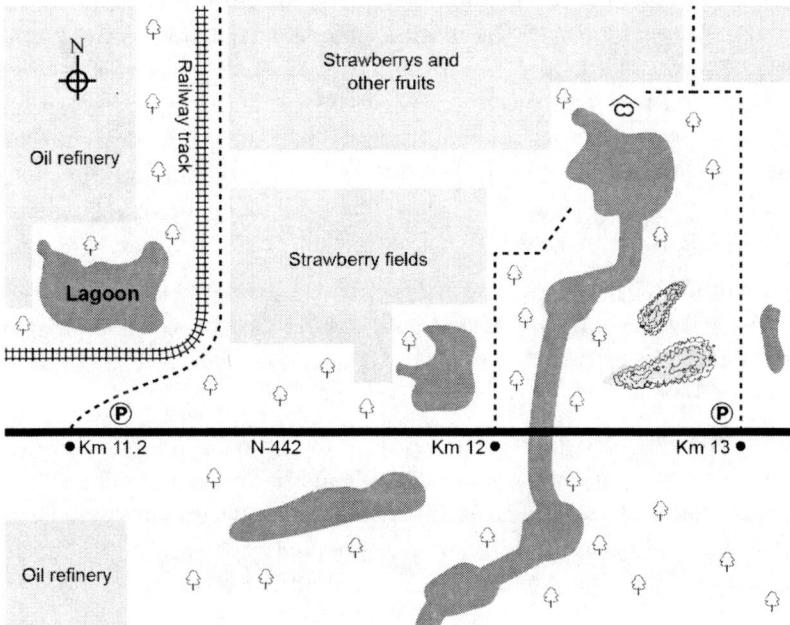

Access

All three sites can be easily accessed from the main Matalascañas - Huelva road and you may wish to visit these sites first if you are travelling to the Marismas del Odiel on the coast road from Matalascañas. However, between Matalascañas and Mazagón the road is the A-494 and from Mazagón to Huelva it becomes the N-442.

Laguna de la Mujer

To reach the first site you should turn right onto a dirt track, exactly at the km 13 marker and park. Walk up the track for about 200 metres, viewing the seasonally wet areas beyond the fence to the right and the rough scrubland to the left, until you reach the start of the agricultural land (orchards and strawberry fields). To the left you will see a small path with a fence beside it that separates the path from the strawberry fields. Follow the path for about 350 metres and you will arrive at a bird-hide that overlooks the reed-fringed Laguna de la Mujer. Beside the hide there is a sandy knoll with a few stone pines. By climbing up here you get a different aspect of part of the lagoon and some seasonally wet areas. You can walk across the open scrubland, passing a small reedy pond, to return to the entrance track.

Laguna de la Jara

To reach this site, continue along the main road until you reach the km 12 marker. Directly beside the marker there is a track to the right. Turn here and park. The lagoon is on the left and there is a series of small well-vegetated pools on the right. By walking along the track you will get good views of most of the site. If you follow the track for about 300 metres, passing strawberry fields, you will come to a white building with a large circular water well. Turn right here and follow the track towards the reedbeds that surround the previous site, the Laguna de la Mujer.

The stone pine forest and the agricultural land should also be checked for birdlife, but be careful. At one point in the forest there is a clearing with about 20 bee-hives. Although the bees are not normally aggressive, you would be advised to avoid this particular area.

From the entrance point, you can cross over the main road where you will find a small gap in the fence. This leads to an area of densely vegetated marshland and irrigation ditches that is always worth exploring for summer visiting Little Bitterns and Purple Herons and Little Crakes and also for Kingfishers and warblers, including Cetti's.

Also on the opposite side of the road there is a high sandy knoll with steps leading to the top. A bird hide used to be situated here but it was burnt down (arson) in early 2005. However, the platform at the top still provides a good elevated viewpoint for looking out over a stretch of reedy marshes. Hopefully, the hide will be re-built at some time in the future.

Another bird hide overlooks the lagoon and the entrance to this can be found by walking 40 some metres along the road to the west and passing through a gate.

Laguna de Primera de Palos

This is the largest of the three accessible lagoons and to reach it from the previous lagoon you should continue towards Huelva for 800 metres until you see a turn-off onto a dirt track, on the right. Turn off the road here and park about 15 metres from the road and the lagoon should be visible. There is a disused railway track that gives good elevated views of the southern end of the lagoon where Purple Swamp-hens, Squacco Herons, Water Rails, Red-knobbed Coots, ducks, grebes and waders are often found feeding. Both Ospreys and Caspian Terns are regular visitors to this lagoon and are often seen hunting over the water.

By following the railway lines to the right, or by walking uphill, along the dirt track you can reach the eastern edge and the top end of the lagoon. Views of this part of the site are somewhat reduced by vegetation, but you can find areas where the open water and the reedbeds are visible. Once again, I would suggest that you also pay attention to the stone pine forest and the agricultural land for warblers, larks, finches, wagtails and wheatears.

General Information

The Laguna de Palos is on private land and is fenced-off to the public. There are two bird-hides at the site, within the fenced-off area, but these are for private use only. As frustrating as it may be not to have the excellent views that the hides offer, please respect the rights of the owners and do not trespass onto their land.

The first and third lagoons are accessed by sandy tracks and are not really suitable for wheelchair users. The second lagoon is fairly accessible by wheelchair, but the tall vegetation around the area may prevent any worthwhile viewing of the site.

Much of the surrounding area is agricultural land and the tracks are in constant use by farm vehicles. Please ensure you park sensibly so as not to obstruct the tracks.

There is a fourth lagoon, the Laguna de las Madres, that is much larger and can be seen from the main road, before you reach the other three, but decent access is not possible by car. This lagoon can be partially viewed by parking off-road and walking up small sand dunes, but I have always found this to be an unsatisfactory experience.

When To Visit

The three lagoons and the surrounding seasonal marsh areas are of interest throughout the year. In the spring and summer you can find the summer visitors, such as Bee-eaters, Melodious, Subalpine and Olivaceous Warblers, Golden Orioles, Great Spotted Cuckoos, Black-eared Wheatears, Woodchat Shrikes, Little Bitterns, Whiskered and Black Terns and Collared Pratincoles. In the autumn and winter there are many species of ducks, grebes, egrets and waders to be found and, possibly, small numbers of White-headed Ducks.

Although the sites can be viewed at any time of the day, I have always found that morning or evening visits produce the best birding.

Estero De Domingo Rubio
West 5

The Estero de Domingo Rubio is an area of two lagoons, comprised of 480 hectares of wetlands and reedbeds which is a part of a large inlet of the Río Tinto, close to the town of Palos de la Frontera. It was designated as a Paraje Natural in 1989 and comes under the protective umbrella of the AMA. The accessible areas are in two parts, separated by the A-494 main road between Mazagón and Moguer. It is a regular breeding ground for Purple Swamp-hens, Squacco, Purple and Black-crowned Night Herons, Marbled Ducks, Little Bitterns, Red-knobbed Coots, ducks, herons, egrets and many other bird species. White Storks, Spoonbills and Ospreys are regular visitors to the site and Marsh Harriers are often seen hunting over the reedbeds.

The muddy margins of the lagoons hold numerous wader species, amongst which, Black-winged Stilts, Snipe, Common and Green Sandpipers, Ringed and Kentish Plovers and Dunlin are the most numerous, although Black-tailed Godwits, Sanderlings, Redshanks, Greenshanks, Ruff and Curlew Sandpipers are also occasional visitors. In the summer, Whiskered, Black and Little Terns are regularly seen at this site.

The reedbeds hold resident Sardinian and Cetti's Warblers, Zitting Cisticolas and Common Waxbills. These may be joined in the breeding season by Savi's, Reed and Great Reed Warblers.

Much of the southern side of the site is vegetated with eucalyptus trees, some pines and a great number of tamarisk trees and scrub. These provide winter roosting sites for Cormorants, Little and Cattle Egrets and Grey Herons.

To the north, which is the main viewing area, there is open scrubland and strawberry plantations where Meadow Pipits, Crested Larks, Black Redstarts, Woodchat and Southern Grey Shrikes, Stonechats, Wheatears, Hoopoes, Serins and other finches and wagtails are common.

The whole length of the site is walkable and although fenced-off, access to within 5 metres of the water's edge is possible in some places. A bird hide, which should offer views of the open water, has been constructed, but the windows face directly into a line of tamarisk trees, so this is not a suitable viewing point.

Access

From the east (El Rocío, Villamanrique, etc.) you should take the A-494 from Matalascañas to Huelva. At the main roundabout at Mazagón you should take the first exit and continue along the A-494 towards Moguer, which leads first through stone pine forests and then strawberry plantations. Just after passing the km 18 marker there is a junction. You can go straight ahead to reach the site, but I have always found it better to turn left, towards Palos de la Frontera, and proceed until the first lagoon opens up on the right. As you reach the end of the lagoon there is a green and cream sign that states "*Sendero, 50 mts*". Just beyond this there is a turning that cuts back sharply to the right. Turn here and the continue straight ahead to reach a car park and the bird hide.

Alternatively, you can go straight across the roundabout at Mazagón and proceed until you reach a set of traffic lights at the start of the large oil refineries. This is just beyond the Lagunas de Palos. Turn right and continue for approximately 3 kms until you reach a T-junction. Turn left and you will then reach the entrance to the lagoons, as described above.

Estero de Domingo Rubio (W-5)

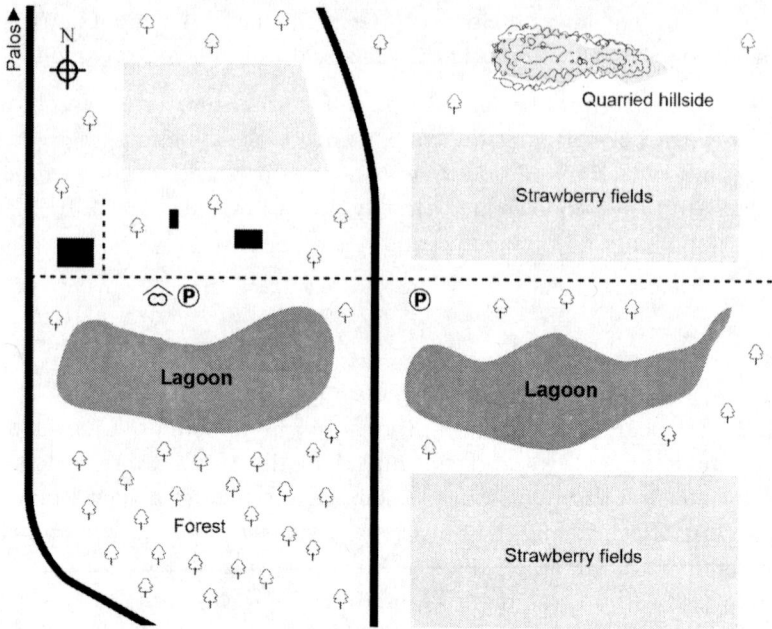

You can walk along the road, getting good views of the open water, small islands and reedbeds until the road turns left, away from the lagoon. By continuing further, you reach the main road to Moguer. Cross directly over the road to reach the second lagoon. I would suggest that, for the sake of security, you drive your car to the second lagoon, where you can keep it in your view.

The second lagoon is smaller, with more tamarisk scrub growing in the water and less reedbeds. However, it produces all of the species that can be found at the larger lagoon.

If you are driving from Huelva, towards Mazagón on the coast road, you have the same two choices of routes, ie. turning left at the traffic lights at the oil refineries or continuing on for another 7 kms and then turning left at the roundabout at Mazagón .

If you are travelling from Isla Canela, Ayamonte or from Portugal, it would be best to drive along the main A-49 road towards Sevilla and take the exit signed for San Juan del Puerto and then following the A-494, which is signed for Moguer and Palos de la Frontera. Continue along the road, ignoring all turn-offs, until you reach the km 16 marker. You should now slow down and look for a green and cream sign with *"Sendero, 100 mts"*. Just beyond this, at km 16.4, there is a turning to the right. This is the entrance to the first lagoon. The entry point to the other lagoon is directly opposite, on the other side of the road.

General Information

The site was originally part of a large tidal inlet of the Río Tinto, but it has now been isolated and is not influenced by the tide. The water level is now fairly constant, but can be affected by rainfall and by water running into the lagoons from the nearby strawberry plantations. At the times when the water level is high there will be few waders to be seen, as they prefer the lower levels when the muddy margins are exposed and feeding opportunities exist.

The first part of the site can be viewed from a tarmacked road that runs alongside the lagoon. The second part is accessed by a dirt track that can become a minor problem in wet weather. However, the area is completely flat and the height of the reeds is fairly low, so I would class this site as being suitable to wheelchair birders.

When To Visit

The lagoons hold reasonable levels of water throughout the year and are always of interest, although bird activity is at its lowest during July and August.

Sunlight can play an important factor when viewing this site. In the morning the eastern end will be affected by sunlight reflecting off the water and the same problem affects the western end in the evenings.

The best times for viewing are very early in the morning or between 11.00 - 16.00hrs. On days when there is no sunshine, all day viewing is possible.

The Río Tinto At La Rábida
West 6

This site consists of an area alongside the east bank of the Río Tinto (the red river) near the city of Huelva. It is famous for being the site that Christopher Columbus set sail from in 1492 on his journey of discovery to the Americas. Here you will find various monuments to that voyage and there is also a tourist site, the *Muelles de las Carabelas* (the wharf of the Caravels), where full-scale replicas of his three ships, La Santa Maria, La Pinta and La Niña are on display.

Varying habitats exist here, including the river, the mudbanks, salt-marsh, a small reed-fringed lagoon and several water scrapes. Waders and seabirds are the most prominent birds, especially at low tide, when the muddy banks and marshes are exposed, offering good feeding. Several gull species, including Audouin's, Mediterranean and Slender-billed are occasionally recorded, along with Sandwich, Little and Caspian Terns. The wader numbers can be high and on good days you can find Curlews, Whimbrels, Turnstones, Red and Greenshanks, Ringed, Little-ringed, Kentish and Grey Plovers, Snipe, Sanderlings, Dunlins, Common, Green, Wood and Curlew Sandpipers, Oystercatchers and both Black and Bar-tailed Godwits. During the winter months there may also be Black-necked Grebes, Red-breasted Mergansers and Razorbills present on the river.

The reedy lagoon in front of the *Muelles de las Carabelas* is home to a few pairs of Purple Swamp-hens and is also a reliable spot for Reed Warblers, Willow Warblers, Chiffchaffs, White, Yellow and Grey Wag-tails, Kingfishers and several duck and grebe species at the appropriate times of the year. Across the pedestrianized promenade there is a rather scruffy waterscape where Black-winged Stilts, Moorhens, Common Coots and various waders breed each year.

The site is not noted for raptors but Kestrels, Marsh Harriers and Ospreys are regularly seen here.

Access

The easiest way to access this site is from the main Matalascañas - Huelva road. However, this can be confusing as the first part of the road, up to the town of Mazagon, is the A-494. Once beyond Mazagón the road becomes the N-442. Continue until you reach a roundabout at km 7 and turn right, where signed for La Rábida. You then pass over a river, the Estero de Domingo Rubio and just beyond the bridge you turn left. Follow the road for 500 metres and at the roundabout go straight across. This will lead you to a large open car-parking area in front of the *Muelles de las Carabelas*. The Lagoon and waterscape are in front of and at each side of the entrance to the Caravel site. To reach the best viewing point of the river, walk to the left alongside the lagoon until you reach a road that leads right. Here you will find a large statue *(Monumento Plus Ultra)* and a public pier that leads out into the water, allowing views of passing gulls and terns

La Rábida (W-6)

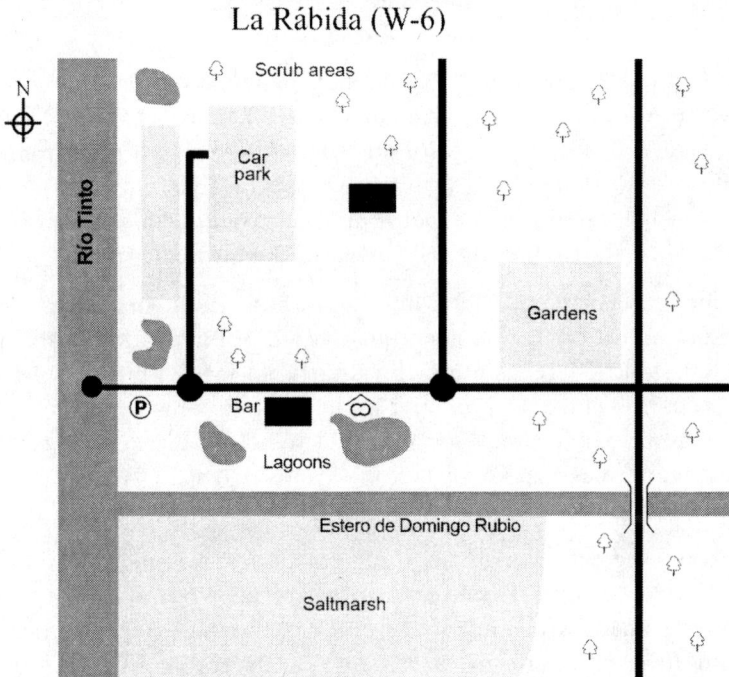

Map showing La Rábida area with: Río Tinto, Scrub areas, Car park, Gardens, Bar, Lagoons, Estero de Domingo Rubio, Saltmarsh, and parking (P).

General Information

There is a bar/restaurant very close to the parking area and several other tourist attractions in the immediate vicinity. At weekends the area can sometimes get busy as it is a stopping point for touring coach excursions. The whole of this site is completely flat and well surfaced and will present no problems for wheelchair birders.

When To Visit

The site is of interest throughout the year, but as with most tidal river sites it is always more productive to visit this area at low tide, as there will be far more birds feeding on the exposed mudbanks. At high tide, some of the waders move to the waterscape to continue feeding, although the vast majority will fly the short distance over to the Marismas del Odiel to either feed or use the high water roosts.

Laguna El Portil
West 7

The Laguna El Portil is a 15.5 hectare expanse of fresh water set in a *Reserva Natural*, which covers some 1,300 hectares of varied habitats. The lagoon is situated right beside the main HV-4113 road from Punta Umbria to El Rompido, just to the east of the coastal resort town of El Portil. An elevated viewing platform beside the road looks out over most of the open water, offering good views of the birds.

The lagoon is permanent, although water levels vary from season to season, and it holds a resident population of Purple Swamp-hens, Water Rails, Little Grebes and several duck species. A public nature trail encircles the entire lagoon, and leads through forests of pine, oak and eucalyptus, where Great Spotted and Green Woodpeckers, Crested Tits, Short-toed Treecreepers, Jays and various warblers, finches and larks can be found.

Other vegetation includes junipers, tamerisk, broom, cistus, rosemary, lavender and thyme. At the western edge of the lagoon there are dense reedbeds which attract Penduline Tits and Reed Buntings in the winter and Little Bitterns, Savi's, Reed and Great Reed Warblers in the summer.

Resident non-waterbirds include Sardinian, Dartford and Cetti's Warblers, Zitting Cisticolas, Common Waxbills, Iberian Magpies, Hoopoes and Common Buzzards. The summer visitors include Subalpine and Melodious Warblers, Woodchat Shrikes, Golden Orioles, Common Redstarts, Spotted Flycatchers, Whiskered and Black Terns, Red-rumped Swallows, Pallid Swifts and Red-necked Nightjars.

Laguna El Portil (W-7)

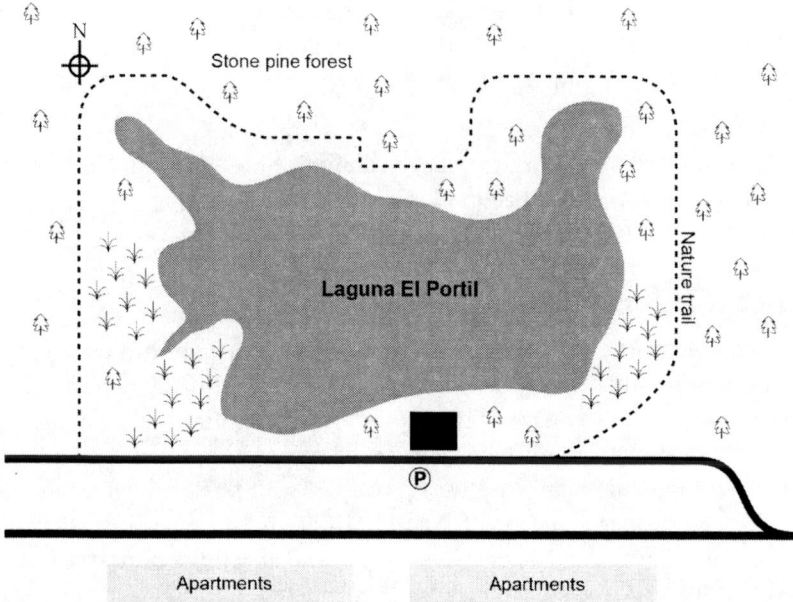

The lagoon is probably best noted as a wintering site for large numbers of ducks, mainly Common Pochards, Shovelers, Wigeon, Gadwalls, Mallard and Teal, but smaller numbers of Great Crested and Black-necked Grebes, Red-crested Pochards and Ferruginous and White-headed Ducks are also regularly found here.

Numerous other forms of wildlife live within the reserve area and you may be fortunate enough to see otters, mongooses, tortoises, foxes, chameleons, lizards and snakes.

Access

The Laguna El Portil is on the Atlantic coast, some 15 kilometres beyond the Marismas del Odiel, and could be included as an extension to a visit to that site. Follow the directions to the bridge over the Río Odiel, but instead of turning off to the Marismas, continue towards Punta Umbria on the A-497 until you reach the junction at km 9, which is signed for El Portil, El Rompido and Cartaya. Turn off here and once on the slip-road take the left-hand option where the road forks. Continue until you reach a roundabout, where you should go straight across. You now approach the sea and at the junction you should turn right, toward El

171

Portil. After 1.5 kms there is a set of traffic lights. Take the slip road to the right, just before the traffic lights, and continue for 150 metres until you reach the viewing platform on the right. You can park your car on the road beside the viewing platform. The start of the nature trail will be found near the traffic lights.

The lagoon can be visited after the Marismas del Odiel by following the Punta Umbria signs as you leave the marshes. This will lead you to the A-497 and you should then follow the directions above.

General Information

The lagoon is at the very edge of the town of El Portil, within easy reach of bars, restaurants and toilet facilities. The wide Atlantic beach is less than 150 metres away and Cormorants and gulls often use the lagoon, especially in stormy conditions. The beach can also be visited to look for waders and passing seabirds. There are plenty of parking places alongside the road to the east of El Portil. Although the nature trail holds several interesting bird species, I do not feel it would be particularly beneficial for you to take this route. It is time consuming and the birds are usually seen better at other forested sites.

The reedbeds to the left of the lagoon are worth visiting for the warblers and for better chances of seeing Purple Swamp-hens and Little Bitterns. You can reach this area by car by driving along the road and taking the first turning on the right. You can park about 150 metres down and then walk across open scrubland to the lagoon. A track leads alongside a fence and will lead you to the reedbeds.

The viewing platform is ideal for wheelchair users but the access to the reedbeds, over scrubland, may prove a problem. The nature trail is not suitable for wheelchairs.

When To Visit

Although there are good numbers of birds present throughout the year, the period between September and April are the most productive for the Penduline Tits, Reed Buntings and the scarcer duck species. April, May and June are the best months for seeing Reed and Great Reed Warblers and marsh terns. In July and August the water level is usually lower and the bird numbers are less.

Apart from the early mornings, when the eastern corner can be affected, sunlight does not affect this site as it does at many other lagoons as the sun is either behind you or directly overhead, this makes all day viewing possible.

El Rompido And The Marismas De Río Piedras West 8

The town of El Rompido is about six kilometres west of the Laguna El Portil and can be reached by continuing along the coast road from that site. The Río Piedras flows along the western side of the town and then runs eastward for 7 kms towards the Atlantic, channelled by a long sand spit known as *"La Flecha del Rompido"* (the Arrow of Rompido). The sand spit creates a natural breakwater and is used mainly as a safe mooring area for boats. The river is tidal and at low tides there are exposed mudflats and sandbars that attract waders, gulls and terns.

Once in the town, there are numerous access roads that lead to the public beaches *(Acceso Playas)*, where easy parking is always available. At the western end of the town there is a small port which offers the opportunity to view a large part of the river and the sand spit on the opposite bank. At low tide, when the mudflats are exposed, many waders and seabirds can be seen feeding or resting on the mud. These regularly include Curlews, Whimbrels, Sanderlings, Ringed, Grey and Kentish Plovers, Dunlins, Turnstones, Curlew Sandpipers, Red Knots, Oystercatchers, Black-tailed Godwits, Red-breasted Mergansers, Common Scoters, Sandwich, Little and Caspian Terns and Audouin's Gulls.

A new marina and a golf course have recently been built alongside the river which has led to the destruction of some excellent marshland, but other areas have been protected and are classed as the *"Paraje Natural Marismas del Río Piedras y Flecha del Rompido"*. This protected site covers an area of over 2,500 hectares and includes tidal inlets, salt marshes, salinas, scrubland and stone pine forests, where Stone Curlews, Purple Swamp-hens, Spoonbills, Red-legged Partridges, Iberian Magpies, Great Spotted Cuckoos, Southern Grey and Woodchat Shrikes, Sardinian and Dartford Warblers, Hen and Montagu's Harriers, Booted Eagles and storks, herons and egrets are usually found.

Access

From the Laguna El Portil, follow the coast road westwards for approximately 6 kms until you reach El Rompido. As you drive through the town there are many small roads that will lead you to the river and beaches, where at low tide you should see waders, terns and gulls. However, the best place for viewing is at a small port area at the far end of the town. To reach this site, continue through El Rompido until you reach a roundabout, where you should turn left (3rd exit) and drive downhill to the port. Here you will find a car park and a small pier that often produces good viewing.

Marismas de Río Piedras (W-8)

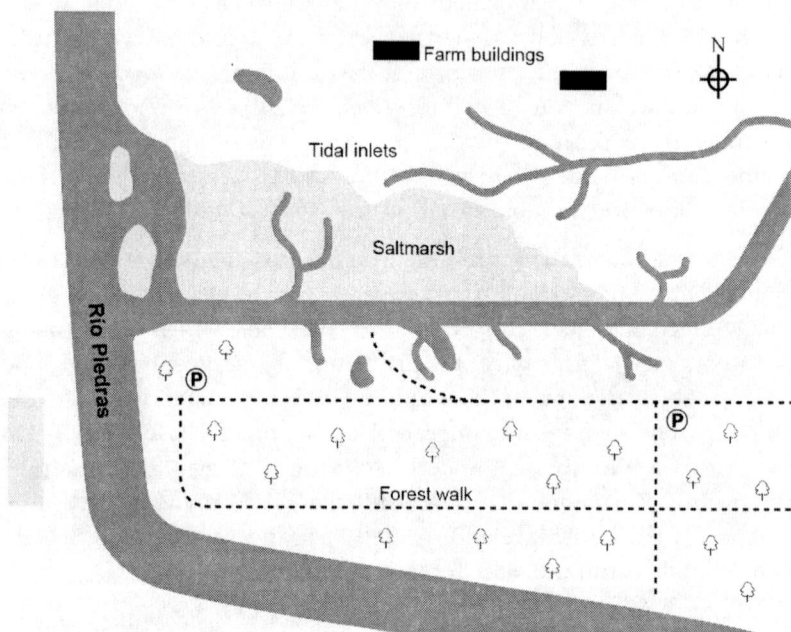

To reach the *Paraje Natural* you should return to the roundabout and then take the second exit. Proceed for one kilometre, passing the entrance to the new marina, until you reach a roundabout beside a petrol station. Take the third exit (left) and continue to the roundabout at the entrance to the El Rompido golf course. Go straight ahead, onto a dirt road and keep going to the very end of the track, about 2.8 kms, until you reach the Río Piedras. You can park here and view the river, the salt marsh and a few inlets. At low tide, some areas upstream become exposed and are popular feeding sites for many species of waders, which include Ruddy Turnstones, Kentish Plovers, Little Stints, Sanderlings, Common and Spotted Redshanks and both Black and Bar-tailed Godwits. During the winter there are usually good numbers of Red-breasted Mergansers, Black-necked Grebes and Razorbills to be seen on the water. Gulls and terns are often seen resting on the exposed mud and this is one of the best areas I know for seeing Caspian Terns throughout the year.

There is a nature trail in the stone pine forest to the left which can be visited in search of woodland birds that include Short-toed Treecreepers, Green and Great Spotted Woodpeckers, Golden Orioles and Tree Sparrows. There are Red-necked Nightjars present during the spring and summer, but these will only be seen during the day if they are accidentally flushed.

The open scrubland and salt marshes hold sizeable populations of Stone Curlews, Red-legged Partridges and Dartford Warblers and the small tidal inlets can often produce Kingfishers and many wader species.

All three harrier species can be seen here at the appropriate times of the year. The resident Marsh Harriers are joined by Hen Harriers in the winter and Montagu's in the summer. Ospreys occasionally hunt along the river and have been known to perch on the small boats moored in mid-stream.

General Information

As you drive along the track from the roundabout at the golf club entrance there are several areas of interest that can be viewed. The first is after 1 km where there is a seasonal lagoon and the start of a 4 km walk. The lagoon often holds Purple Swamp-hens, Black-winged Stilts, Little and Cattle Egrets and several duck species.

After a further 300 metres there is an entrance that leads into the pine forest. Another walk begins from this point.

The next point of interest is after another 650 metres, where a dirt track leads off to the right. It would be worth driving, or walking, this track to the end, about 400 metres, as it passes close to several tidal inlets and ends right beside a tributary of the main river.

This is a rather isolated site without any facilities and I would suggest that you carry an adequate supply of drinks with you. The site is generally flat and I cannot see any areas that would cause problems for wheelchair birders.

When To Visit

Most of the sites described in this area are tidally influenced and as such are best viewed at low tide when waders are feeding. As with all similar sites there can be problems with heat haze and sunlight reflecting off the water at certain times of the day.

La Ribera
West 9

La Ribera, meaning "the riverbank", is situated at the upper reaches of the Río Piedras, close to the town of Cartaya. The site is classified as a Paraje Natural and consists of the river, tidal inlets, sandbars, mudbanks, pools, saltmarsh and open scrubland. It is an important winter feeding site for numerous wader species and also attracts many gulls, terns, storks and Spoonbills. It is also a regular breeding ground for Black-winged Stilts, Kentish and Little-ringed Plovers, Little and Cattle Egrets, White Storks and Marsh Harriers.

The area is usually very quiet, being non-residential, apart from a few nearby houses, but there is a small beach alongside a part of the river that is sometimes used for picnics and bathing at weekends and during the summer school holidays.

An attractive wooden pier with several canopies offers the chance to look out over much of the top end of the site. The canopies supply shade in hot weather and shelter from the rain, so you can concentrate on your birding in relative comfort.

Access

From the previous site you should return to the main road and turn left at the roundabout, heading toward Cartaya on the A-5053. After 3.8 kms you pass a waterpark and a go-kart track on the left-hand side. From here, continue for 2 kms until you reach a small turning on the left. The turning is not easily seen coming from this direction, but you should slow down and look for the turning once the floodlight stanchions of the local football ground come into view. If you are approaching from Cartaya you need to take the A-5053 road to El Rompido and turn right 150 metres beyond the football ground.

After 500 metres there is a sharp right-hand bend in the road. At this point you will find an area where you can park. A small track will lead you out into the top end of the marshes where feeding/breeding birds can be found.

Continue for another 700 metres and you reach a T-junction where you need to turn left. A further 500 metres along the road there is another junction, where you should turn left again. Now proceed for 200 metres, passing through a large set of gates, until you reach a parking area just beyond a large building. The wooden pier can be reached by way of a boardwalk. The birds that are regularly found here include Curlews, Whimbrels, Dunlins, Ruddy Turnstones, Common and Spotted Redshanks, Greenshanks, Green, Common, Wood and Curlew Sandpipers, Little Stints, Oystercatchers, Ringed and Grey Plovers, Kingfishers and various herons and egrets.

To the left, close to the pier, there is a large private house on a hill, with well vegetated gardens and a number of trees where Iberian Magpies, Golden Orioles, Great Spotted Cuckoos, Serins, Bee-eaters and numerous warbler species can be found at the appropriate times of the year.

La Ribera (W-9)

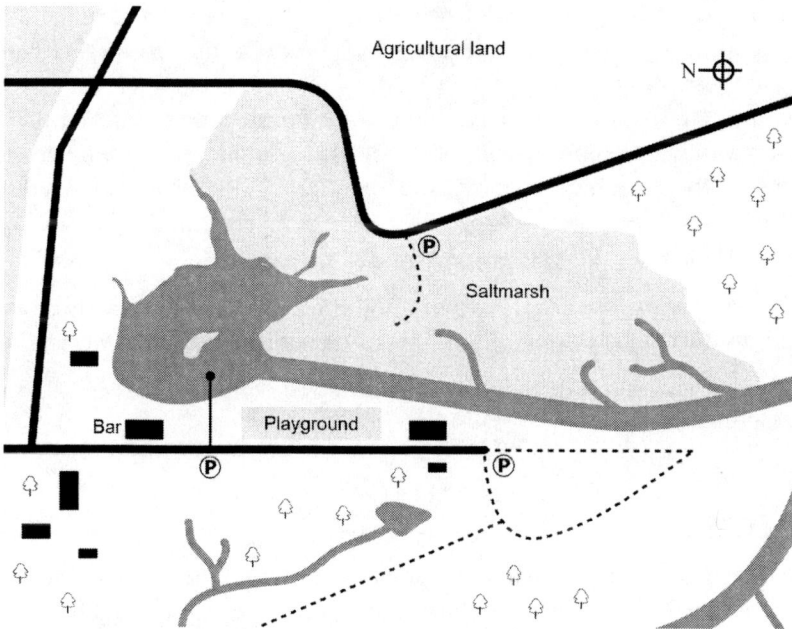

Agricultural land

N

Saltmarsh

Bar

Playground

Beyond the car park there are two houses. A track leads between these and gives access to the lower end of the marshes. Once past the houses the track degenerates into a poor condition and I would suggest you park here and walk 150 metres to a small hill that offers good elevated views of the whole area. Resident Marsh Harriers and summer visiting Montagu's Harriers may be seen quartering the area and both Woodchat and Southern Grey Shrikes are fairly common. Ospreys are regularly sighted in the winter and occasionally one or two may be seen in the summer, along with Booted Eagles and Black Kites. The vantage point also gives the best views of Red-breasted Mergansers, gulls and terns as they hunt along the river, with Sandwich, Little and Whiskered Terns being the most prominent, although I have recorded Caspian Terns here on several occasions.

The dry open scrubland should be checked for such species as Stone Curlews, Red-legged Partridges, Common Quail, Stonechats, Whinchats, Yellow Wagtails, Crested and Greater Short-toed Larks, Dartford and Sardinian Warblers, Hoopoes and Zitting Cisticolas. Overhead you may find Pallid and Common Swifts, Barn and Red-rumped Swallows, House and Sand Martins and raptors.

General Information

This site is usually very quiet, with minimal human interference and should produce a couple of hours of pleasurable birding and a good bird list, especially if visited on weekdays. At weekends, you can expect more human activity from local picnicking families and children using a nearby playgound. A number of small fishing boats are moored on the river and the craft owners may cause temporary disturbance to feeding flocks of birds at times as they travel along the river and leave and return to their mooring places.

There is a bar/cafe here, although it is often closed, but a small village just 300 metres away offers the chance of finding refreshments.

Most of this site, although rather bumpy in places, is accessible to wheelchair birders.

When To Visit

The site holds the greatest number of birds during the winter period, when large flocks of waders, terns and gulls are present. The spring period is also very good for breeding birds and passage migrants, such as Northern and Black-eared Wheatears, Whinchats, Subalpine, Olivaceous and Orphean Warblers, Rufous-tailed Scrub Robins and several raptor species.

The river and water levels of the marshes are affected by the tide and, as with most such sites, are of greater interest at low tide, when sand and mudbanks are exposed and large wader flocks form to feed.

Sunlight reflecting off the water can be a problem at certain times of the day as the sun moves across the sky, but the site is such that there are always large parts of the area that will be unaffected, allowing good viewing conditions.

Other Sites of Interest

Throughout the region there are sites that although not described fully in this book, may be of interest to birders. I have visited each of these sites on many occasions and have had success, but they may not always hold the wide diversity of bird species as those sites that form the main part of this book.

The Centro de Visitantes del Guadiamar.

As the name suggests, this is a visitors centre, but within the grounds are a botanical garden *(El Jardín Botánico)* and a public recreational area *(Área Recreativo de Buitrago)*. It forms a part of the Corredor Verde and is situated beside the Río Guadiamar, close to the town of Aznalcázar. The office in the centre has very erratic opening times but the gates to the site are generally open throughout the day. There is a boardwalked trail of about 700 metres that leads through the gardens and across the lagoon.

Entry is free and the grounds include a reed-fringed lagoon where Cetti's Warblers, Moorhens, Coots, finches, larks and various duck species can be found throughout the year. Seasonal visitors include Penduline Tits, Golden Orioles, Reed Buntings, Common and Black Redstarts, Nightingales, Bee-eaters, Melodious, Reed and Great Reed Warblers and Spotted Flycatchers.

There are various access points to the river, both inside the site and from the car parking area. The birds that are often seen along the river include Grey and Black-crowned Night Herons, Kingfishers and small numbers of waders.

The site can be easily found beside the river near to the town of Aznalcázar, at the km 22 marker on the A-474 road between Pilas and Aznalcázar. A gravel pit beside the park is being turned into another lagoon and a bird observatory is planned for the future.

Centro de Naturaleza La Juliana.

This is a small nature park and wildlife education centre located near to the town of Bollullos de la Mitación where a good selection of habitats attract numerous passerine species. The grounds cover about 4.5 hectares and a nature path leads through a forest of assorted trees and shrubs, which include stone pines, various oak and wild olive trees, lavender, thyme, rosemary, Spanish broom and lentiscus.

The resident birds that are commonly found here are Hoopoes, Great Spotted Woodpeckers, Short-toed Treecreepers, Little and Tawny Owls, Collared Doves, Iberian Magpies, Crested Larks, Tree Sparrows, Spotless Starlings Crested Tits, Sardinian Warblers, Zitting Cisticolas, Southern Grey Shrikes, Serins and other finch and tit species. These may be joined in the summer by Common Quail, Bee-eaters, Woodchat Shrikes, Common Redstarts, Golden Orioles, Spotted Flycatchers, various raptors, such as Black Kites, Booted and Short-toed Eagles, Montagu's Harriers and swifts, swallows and martins.

The centre is free to visit and is open all year. The opening times are from 09.00 - 21.00hrs in April to October and 10.00 - 18.00hrs in November to March. There is a bar/restaurant on site that opens in winter from 20.00 - 24.00hrs on Tuesdays - Fridays, 12.00 - 24.00hrs on Saturdays and 12.00 - 18.00hrs on Sundays. The summer hours are the same for weekdays but it is open from 12.00 - 24.00hrs on both Saturday and Sunday. Outside of these hours there is a cold drinks machine available.

The centre is situated at km 12.5 on the A-474 road between Aznalcázar and Bollullos de la Mitación.

Las Doblas.

This is a very large nature park situated 2 kms outside of the town of Sanlúcar la Mayor. It forms part of the Corredor Verde de Guadiamar and offers many kilometres of walking trails in an excellent birding environment. The Río Guadiamar runs along the western edge of the site and there are many small pools, streams and waterscapes that are of interest. The centre piece of the site is a large reed-fringed lagoon that attracts waterfowl and waders in good numbers.

The reedbeds and surrounding stone-pine and eucalyptus trees hold resident Cetti's and Sardinian Warblers, Short-toed Treecreepers, Zitting Cisticolas, Stonechats, Iberian Magpies, Great Spotted and Green Woodpeckers, Little Grebes and Purple Swamp-hens. These are joined in the breeding season by Little Bitterns, Purple Herons, Whinchats, Hoopoes, Bee-eaters, Common Redstarts, Golden Orioles, Spotted Flycatchers, Sedge, Melodious, Savi's and both Reed and Great Reed Warblers. Winter visitors include Reed Buntings, Woodlarks, Penduline Tits (some breed here), Robins, Blackcaps and Black Redstarts.

The surrounding scrubland holds Red-legged Partridges, Northern Wheatears, Yellow and White Wagtails, Dartford Warblers, Crested Larks, Woodchat and Southern Grey Shrikes and Common Quail.

Raptor species are usually evident over the site and these include Booted and Short-toed Eagles, Lesser Kestrels, Black-shouldered Kites and Common Buzzards.

A raised boardwalk leads across the main lagoon, offering opportunities to scan the reedbeds from an elevated position. At the end of the boardwalk there is a small island with a building on it. This was planned as a cafeteria, but as yet it has not opened. There is an open-air roof terrace above the building that allows more elevated views of the site. Access to the roof is via a ramp which begins behind the building. Although rather steep, it should prove suitable for a wheelchair birder, especially if there is an enabler to help them.

In the spring of 2007, access to this small island was closed off due to the building being vandalized and it is not known when, or if, it will be re-opened.

To the southern end of the site there are two bridges where the river flows under the road. This can be an interesting spot for Red-rumped Swallows, House and Sand Martins, waders and wagtails

The best way to reach this site from the west, ie. the Doñana area, Huelva or Portugal, is by taking the A-49 toward Sevilla, turning off at Junction 34 and then turning left towards Chucena. Pass through the town and after 2 kms turn right towards Sanlúcar la Mayor on the A-472. The entrance to the Las Doblas site is on the left, just after the km 5 marker. Keep your eyes peeled on the way for both Great and Little Bustards in the fields to the left.

If you are approaching from the Sevilla direction, you should follow the main Huelva road (the A-49) until you reach junction 16, which is signed for Benacazon and Sanlúcar la Mayor. At the end of the slip-road, turn right toward Sanlúcar and continue for about 3 kms until you reach a roundabout. Turn left here and follow the main road through the town until you reach the other side. Continue for another 3 kms and at the bottom of a long hill you will find the site on the right-hand side of the road, just before you reach the km 5 marker.

The Bustard trail.
Whilst in the area of Las Doblas, you could consider driving up to Aznalcóllar and from there to Gerena and then Olivares. This is a large area of vast rolling plains where both Great and Little Bustards and Pin-tailed Sandgrouse can sometimes be found, although only in small numbers. At one point along the route, between Gerena and Olivares, there is a large tower, the "Torre de San Antonio", that is worth a few minutes of

your time in the spring and summer, searching for Black Redstarts, Lesser Kestrels, Black-eared Wheatears and Rollers, which live and breed in, or near the tower.

To enter this area you should take the A-477 road to Aznalcóllar, which can be found about 500 metres to the west of the Las Doblas site. After about 5 kms there is a series of ponds on the right, which are fenced off, but can be viewed from the road. Ducks, grebes, herons and egrets are usually present and Marsh Harriers, Buzzards and Kestrels are often seen.

Just after entering Aznalcóllar, look out for the road on the right that is signed for Gerena. A few kms outside the town there is a huge and ugly mining concern, but just beyond this you cross over the Río Agipo, where there is a part of the Corredor Verde that can be visited. The river often holds some interesting birds and the surrounding scrubland should produce Zitting Cisticolas, Stonechats, Serins, Hoopoes, Song Thrushes, Red-legged Partridges and finches, wagtails and warblers. Scanning the mountainous waste heaps behind the mine may produce Blue Rock Thrushes and Black Wheatears.

As you approach Gerena there is a road to the right that is signed for Olivares. This road offers the best chance of seeing bustards and sandgrouse, although many stops and much scanning of the fields may be required to achieve any success. It is estimated that as few as 60 Little Bustards and a smaller population of Great Bustards, perhaps no more than 20, reside in this vast region. You will, perhaps, have better chances of finding Little Owls, Marsh, Hen and Montagu's Harriers, Booted and Short-toed Eagles and Calandra Larks.

Approximately 300 metres after turning onto the Olivares road you will reach a turning (dirt road) on the right. This leads for 500 metres and ends at a small pool, set in a rocky outcrop with grassed surroundings and a few bench seats. This is the local "duck pond" and numerous domestic and hybrid duck and goose varieties reside here. These are regularly fed by the locals and their presence helps to attract genuine passing wildfowl and some interesting resident and migratory species, such as Southern Grey and Woodchat Shrikes, Black Redstarts, Hoopoes, Grey Wagtails, Blue Rock Thrushes and Black-eared Wheatears. The surrounding agricultural land holds Red-legged Partridges, Common Quail, Zitting Cisticolas and Thekla and Calandra Larks.

Return to the main road and continue towards Olivares. And after about 6 kms you will come to the *"Torre de San Antonio"* There is a convenient parking space just in front of the gates, which may, or may not, be open. At Olivares you have the choice of returning back the way you came or you can pass through the town and continue to either Sevilla or Sanlúcar la Mayor.

Cañada de los Pájaros.

This is a privately owned site which is located on the road between the Isla Mayor rice fields and the town of Puebla del Río. It has a surface area of about 15 hectares, of which, 6 are open to the public and contains some caged birds and pinioned species but things are not as bad as they may seem as many of these birds belong to a captive breeding programme which is operated here, especially for some of the more scarce and endangered species, such as Red-knobbed Coots, White-headed and Marbled Ducks and Purple Swamp-hens. The ultimate aim is to release the captive-bred birds into the wild in an attempt to support the low numbers of the natural populations. The captive breeding programme for the coots has been so successful that about 500 young birds have been released into the wild in the last 15 years.

The centre-piece of the site is a large lagoon where the majority of the birds are free-flying wild birds that come to feed during the day and roost at night. Amongst these are Greater Flamingos, Spoonbills, White Storks, Red-knobbed Coots, Ferruginous and Marbled Ducks, Ruddy Shelducks, Black-crowned Night Herons and many other wildfowl and waders. The trees and gardens within the centre offer the chance of finding many passerine species and raptors are also often present.

This site is a business venture and there is an admission fee of about 6 euros per person, part of which goes towards the costs of running the captive breeding programme. By supporting this centre you will be helping to fund a very important preservation initiative. The centre is open throughout the year, from 10.00 until dusk and there is a bar/cafeteria on site where food and drinks are available.

From Thursday to Sunday, entry is via the ticket office beside the cafeteria, near the road. On Mondays, Tuesdays and Wednesdays, you should drive up a track to the back of the site and ring the bell at the gate.

To reach this site you should drive past the Dehesa de Abajo and continue until you reach the roundabout beside the Venta el Cruce. Go straight across the roundabout on the A-8050 road and the Cañada de los Pájaros is 2 kms along on the left-hand side of the road, just before you reach the km 7 marker.

PLEASE NOTE. If it is your intention to photograph the birds and you are carrying large camera equipment, you will be asked to pay an extra fee of about 15 euros. However, you will not be charged for a small compact or pocket digital camera.

Further Afield

I am aware of the growing number of people that are either buying holiday homes, or are now spending holidays, at the new developments to the west of Huelva, along the Portuguese border in the towns of Ayamonte, Isla Cristina, Lepe, Islantilla or at the Isla Canela. For the sake of completeness and to help any birders that may be staying in these areas, I have included a few sites that may be of interest to them. Although these sites are somewhat outside of my normal area for bird tours, I have conducted tours here in the past and have visited each of the sites on a number of occasions, finding them all to be very good for birding.

Isla Canela (the Cinnamon island).
A large development programme has been taking place here for a number of years and work is still in progress, building hotels, apartments and holiday homes. An international airport is planned nearby which will make the area more interesting and available for foreign property buyers and holidaymakers. A golf course, marina and beaches are also attractions here.

The Isla Canela is situated almost at the estuary of the Río Guadiana, the river which forms the border between Spain and Portugal. The island itself is cut off from the mainland by the Río Guadiana, the Atlantic ocean and the Río Carreras. It was once a vast tidal saltmarsh before the developers moved in, but now only about a third of the island remains as a protected "*Reserva Natural*". Many species of waterbirds are to be found in the marshes, tidal inlets, abandoned saltpans, on small sandbars and along the bank of the river. The open scrubland holds many interesting species, such as Sardinian and Dartford Warblers, Zitting Cisticolas, Hoopoes, Southern Grey Shrikes, Crested Larks, Common Quail and Stone Curlews.

There is a fair amount of raptor activity, as you would imagine at such a site, with Marsh, Hen and Montagu´s Harriers, Kestrels, Buzzards, Booted Eagles, Peregrine Falcons and Ospreys being present at most times of the year.

At the southernmost end of the island is the beach holiday resort of Punta del Moral where seawatching for gulls, terns, shearwaters, gannets and waders is possible, especially outside of the peak holidaying periods. The eastern end of the town offers the best area for viewing.

Just a few hundred metres from Punta del Moral, on the road to Isla Canela, there is a track on the right-hand side of the road that leads to a small bird hide. This looks out over several old salinas and a saltmarsh, where waders, gulls, terns and birds of prey can often be seen.

The Isla Canela is just a short drive to the south of the town of Ayamonte and is well signposted.

Paraje Natural de Isla Cristina.
This is a 2,145 hectare site of rivers, streams, saltmarsh, disused salinas, tidal inlets and small islands, which is situated on both sides of the road a kilometre to the west of the town of Isla Cristina. It holds several interesting species throughout the year and should always produce a good bird list. Being a coastal site, it is subject to tidal variations and as such, is better visited at times of low tide. The area is better known for waterbirds, such as Greater Flamingos, White Storks, Spoonbills, Black-winged Stilts, Avocets, Dunlins, Redshanks, Ringed, Kentish and Grey Plovers, Little and Cattle Egrets and other waders, but good numbers of seabirds can often be found, amongst which, you may see Yellow-legged, Lesser Black-backed, Black-headed, Mediterranean and Audouin's Gulls and Sandwich, Little, Black, Whiskered and Caspian Terns.

The surrounding scrubland holds an impressive number of larks, warblers, chats, wagtails, finches, wheatears and other passerines and is exceptionally good in the spring migration period, when large numbers of birds stop over to feed before continuing on their way north.

The dry marshland holds sizeable populations of resident Stone Curlews, Dartford and Sardinian Warblers and Southern Grey Shrikes. These are joined in the summer by Collared Pratincoles, Woodchat Shrikes, Common Quail and Hoopoes. Birds of prey are often present and can include Buzzards, Kestrels, Ospreys and kites, harriers and eagles.

To reach this site from the Isla Canela area you should drive through Ayamonte until you reach the N-431 road to Huelva. Continue until you reach a turning onto the A-5150, which is signed for Isla Cristina, just beyond km 128. Proceed for about 2.5 kms until you reach a village called Pozo del Camino. Pass through the village until you reach a turning on the right which is signed for a petrol station (Gasolinera). Turn here and park. On the other side (inland) of the main road there is a walking route, (La Via Verde), which will lead you for over 4 kms through the marshlands. Crude bench seats are to be found every 100 metres or so along the route and excellent close-up views of the birds can be obtained.

To visit the seaward side of the marshes you can drive beyond the petrol station and park near the *"Molino Mareal de Pozo del Camino"*, where there is a convenient parking place. From here, a dirt track will lead you alongside the marshes.

It is possible to drive from the Molino back to Ayamonte by following the tarmacked road, which will then become a dirt track leading beside the old salinas. As you travel along this track you will also be passing small wooded areas, scrubland, salt marsh and tidal flood plains. The track needs to be driven with care, especially after wet weather, but it can produce some excellent birding. It will eventually join the N-431 road about one kilometre west of Ayamonte.

These marshes can also be accessed from the A-49 road by turning off where it is signed for Isla Cristina, at Junction 122, and then following the road signs.

Reserva Natural do Sapal de Castro Marim (Portugal).

Just across the Portuguese border, almost directly opposite Ayamonte, is the 2,154 hectare nature reserve of Sapal de Castro Marim. The site has several types of habitats which include saltmarsh, tidal inlets, saltpans (used and disused), the river bank, open scrubland and small forested areas. Access is relatively easy. Simply cross the border bridge and once across take the first exit road, which is signed for the town of Castro Marim and then follow the brown road signs for "Reserva Natural Castro Marim".

The entry road is a dirt track that ends at a car park beside a large visitors centre, which has a small shop and offers various information leaflets, but you will be lucky to find any in English. At the rear of the centre there is an indoor observation area where you can look out over areas of saltmarsh, tidal inlets and the Río Guadiana. This is very handy on cold, wet or windy days, when birding would otherwise be uncomfortable.

A short circular nature trail of about 600 metres starts from beside the car park and leads up to a house on a small knoll, which gives excellent elevated views of a large part of the reserve. Most of the birds that can be found here, ie. Greater Flamingos, Spoonbills, White Storks, waders, ducks, gulls, terns, passerines, etc. can also be found at many other sites with similar habitats, but this site offers the bonus of the chance of also finding Little Bustards, which are regularly recorded here.

There is also a track that leads to the left, alongside the river, as you approach the visitors centre. This track can be walked or driven, depending on weather conditions and the state of the track. It leads for over a kilometre, passing under the border bridge and ends beside the river, close to a small house.

As you walk/drive along the track, you should check the scrubland and waterscapes for waders, warblers, larks, chats and shrikes. The riverbank offers you the chance to see passing gulls and terns.

Raptors are usually present and these can, depending on the time of year, include Marsh, Montagu's and Hen Harriers, Buzzards, Kestrels, Booted and Short-toed Eagles, Ospreys, Merlins and Peregrine Falcons.

The Doñana Bird List

It must be stressed that this is not a comprehensive list of Spanish birds. It only contains those species which are regularly recorded in the Doñana region. The status shown for each bird (ie. common, scarce or rare) relates only to Doñana and not to Spain as a whole.

Although many of the species are considered to be migratory and supposedly return to Africa for the winter, significant numbers of some of the species will, in fact, remain throughout the year. Therefore, there will be some instances in this section where the information I give will conflict with that which may be contained within your own bird books and field guides.

The English names that I have listed are those that are currently used in the official British birds list that is compiled by the British Ornithologists' Union. I have also included the Spanish names that are currently recommended by the Sociedad Española de Ornitología (SEO).

Great Crested Grebe *(Podiceps cristatus)* Somormujo Lavanco
A fairly common resident species of about 250 pairs that breed on large lagoons and in favourable sites in the marshes.

Black-necked Grebe *(Podiceps nigricollis)* Zampullín Cuellinegro
A fairly common resident, with up to 2,000 pairs breeding in the area. Far more numerous in the winter, when more than 6,000 individuals may be present, especially around the Marismas del Odiel area.

Little Grebe *(Tachybaptus ruficollis)* Zampullín Común
A common resident that can be found at any lagoon, river or marsh area. Perhaps as many as 2,000 pairs breed in the area.

Cory's Shearwater *(Calonectris diomedea)* Pardela Cenicienta
Present offshore throughout the year but not in great numbers. Best seen from Matalascañas or from the Espigón near Huelva. More numerous in the summer months.

Sooty Shearwater *(Puffinus griseus)* Pardela Sombria
A scarce but regular visitor to the Atlantic coast, usually in the winter months, but seldom seen from the shore.

Mediterranean Shearwater   *(Puffinus Yelkouan)*   Pardela Yelkouan
Present offshore throughout the year but more commonly seen in the
summer. Best seen from Matalascañas or the Espigón near Huelva.

Northern Gannet   *(Morus bassanus)*   Alcatraz Atlántico
Fairly common offshore all year but more numerous from September to
March.

Great Cormorant   *(Phalacrocorax carbo)*   Cormorán Grande
A very common winter visitor, usually from September to March, although a small number remain through the summer. The usual subspecies is *P.c.sinensis*.

Great Bittern   *(Botaurus stellaris)*   Avetoro Común
A scarce but regular winter visitor to suitable habitats. In January 2005,
an influx of birds from Scandinavia resulted in up to 15 individuals being present in the Entremuros and along the Brazo de la Torre. Breeding
has been recorded in Doñana in recent years..

Little Bittern   *(Ixobrychus minutus)*   Avetorillo Común
A fairly common summer visitor, with up to 3,000 pairs breeding in
dense reedbeds. A very small number regularly remain throughout the
winter.

Squacco Heron   *(Ardeola ralloides)*   Garcilla Cangrejera
A fairly common breeding species with up to 300 pairs being present
most years. A species that nests communally with other herons and
egrets. It is usually a migratory species, but a reasonable number remain in the region throughout the winter.

Black-crowned Night Heron   *(Nyticorax nycticorax)*   Martinete
A fairly common resident and abundant summer visitor, often breeding
in mixed heron/egret colonies. Significant numbers remain throughout
the winter, when they form large flocks, with up to 1,000 birds regularly
roosting in a 1km stretch of the Río Guadiamar in the Corredor Verde
area.

Cattle Egret   *(Bubulcus ibis)*   Garcilla Bueyera
A very common resident with up to 10,000 breeding pairs. They roost
and breed communally in trees and reedbeds, often in mixed colonies
with other herons and egrets.

Little Egret   *(Egretta garzetta)*   Garceta Común
A very common resident. Found on coasts, marshes, rivers, lagoons and most other wetlands. It is often found nesting in mixed egret/heron colonies and it is estimated that up to 15,000 individuals may be present in the winter.

Great Egret   *(Egretta alba)*   Garceta Grande
A fairly scarce resident species. Winter visitors increase the numbers but they are still not numerous, with perhaps a maximum of 50 birds being present. A pair bred here in 1998 and it is hoped that this species may soon breed regularly in the Doñana area.

Grey Heron   *(Ardea cinerea)*   Garza Real
A very common resident species with up to 1,000 breeding pairs. Northern migrants greatly increase the numbers in the winter.

Purple Heron   *(Ardea purpurea)*   Garza Imperial
A fairly common summer visitor with over 1,000 pairs breeding in mixed colonies with other herons/egrets. Usually present from March to October, but a few individuals regularly remain throughout the winter.

Eurasian Spoonbill   *(Platalea leucordia)*   Espátula Común
A fairly common resident species. It is estimated that about 30% (400 pairs) of the European population breed in the region. Large flocks are often seen outside of the breeding season.

White Stork   *(Ciconia ciconia)*   Cigüeña Blanca
A very common resident species with an estimated 1,500 pairs nesting throughout the region. Up to 500 pairs breed at the Dehesa de Abajo (one of the largest breeding colonies in Europe) and they can also be found nesting on any village church and on telegraph poles beside roads and railway lines. Although many thousands of birds will migrate to Africa, wintering numbers in Doñana can be as high as 5,000 birds.

Black Stork   *(Ciconia nigra)*   Cigüeña Negra
Fairly common during passage periods. A significant number, perhaps as many as 150, overwinter in the ricefields and marsh areas between September and March. A small number, mainly juveniles and a few non-breeders remain throughout the summer.

Glossy Ibis   *(Plegadis falcinellus)*   Morito Común
The ibis first arrived in Doñana in the early 1990's as a winter visitor
and bred for the first time in 1996. They have since become a common
resident species with a population of up to 3,500 birds. They nest communally in reedbeds, often amongst herons and egrets. Numbers are
increasing annually and they are now expanding their range to other
parts of Spain and Portugal.

Greater Flamingo   *(Phoenicopterus ruber)*   Flamenco Común
A very common resident. Liable to turn up on any lake, river, estuary
or marsh. Up to 1,000 pairs breed in Doñana in favourable years and
winter flocks of up to 30,000 birds have been recorded.

Greylag Goose   *(Anser anser)*   Ansar Común
A very common winter visitor. As many as 100,000 arrive from the
north, usually from October onwards. The majority leave by mid-April,
but a small number remain in the summer.

White-fronted Goose   *(Anser albifrons)*   Ansar Careto
A very scarce winter visitor. Usually seen in small numbers amongst
Greylag flocks from October to March.

Common Shelduck   *(Tadorna tadorna)*   Tarro Blanco
A very scarce breeding species but regular visitor to the region during
the winter months, when as many as 1,000 may be present.

Mallard   *(Anas platyrhynchos)*   Ánade Azulón
A very common resident species with up to 40,000 being present in the
winter.

Gadwall   *(Anas strepera)*   Ánade Friso
A reasonable resident population of perhaps 1,000 breeding pairs. In
the winter months there may be up to 15,000 birds present.

Eurasian Wigeon   *(Anas penelope)*   Silbón Europeo
A fairly common winter visitor and passage migrant. Numbers, which
can reach 50,000, rely upon suitable water levels.

Eurasian Teal   *(Anas crecca)*   Cerceta Común
A common winter visitor. It is estimated that numbers can be as high
as 60 - 70,000 in some years. There are occasional reports of a small
number of pairs breeding in the region.

Garganey *(Anas querquerdula)* Cerceta Carretona
A fairly scarce breeding species but is a quite common on passage during March, April and May. A few may overwinter in the region.

Northern Pintail *(Anas acuta)* Ánade Rabudo
A very common winter visitor to the region with up to 50,000 birds being present most years. There are occasional reports of breeding in the region.

Northern Shoveler *(Anas clypeata)* Cuchara Común
Possibly as many as 70,000 spend the winter in the Doñana region. There are a few records of birds breeding in the area in favourable years.

Marbled Duck *(Marmaronetta angustirostris)* Cerceta Pardilla
A scarce resident species. Numbers increase in the spring with up to 50 pairs breeding in the Doñana region. Large flocks sometimes form in the summer, after the breeding season.

Red-crested Pochard *(Netta rufina)* Pato Colorado
A fairly common resident species with up to 700 breeding pairs throughout the region. During the winter, numbers can be as high as 5,000 individuals.

Tufted Duck *(Aythya fuligula)* Porrón Moñudo
A fairly scarce but regular winter visitor to Doñana, when up to 300 individuals may be present. They are mainly to be found on the larger, deeper lagoons.

Common Pochard *(Aythya farina)* Porrón Europeo
A very common winter visitor, when up to 10,000 birds may be present. Significant numbers, perhaps 1,000 pairs, breed in the region each year.

Ferruginous Duck *(Aythya nyroca)* Porrón Pardo
A scarce winter/spring visitor and passage migrant. There are regular reports of small numbers from the Laguna El Portil and from Brazo del Este.

Common Scoter *(Melanitta nigra)* Negrón Común
Fairly scarce winter visitors which are sometimes seen offshore at such sites as Matalascañas and the Espigón near Huelva.

Red-breasted Merganser *(Mergus serrator)* Sereta Mediana
A fairly scarce winter visitor. Regularly recorded at the Marismas del Odiel and the Marismas del Río Piedras.

White-headed Duck *(Oxyura leucocephala)* Malvasia Cabeciblanca
A fairly scarce species overall but they are regularly recorded from suitable locations, such as the Laguna Tarelo, Isla de los Olivillos, Laguna El Portil and the Laguna Primera de Palos. At least two pairs bred at the Cañada de Rianzuela in the spring of 2006.

Osprey *(Pandion haliaetus)* Águila Pescadora
A fairly common winter visitor with up to 50 individuals being present in the region, usually arriving from September onwards and returning north by May. A few non-breeders regularly remain throughout the summer.

Black Kite *(Milvus migrans)* Milano Negro
A very common summer visitor with up to 800 pairs breeding in the region. They are early migrants, with the first birds arriving from late February onwards, but the vast majority leave by the end of September. However, a small number regularly remain throughout winter.

Red Kite *(Milvus milvus)* Milano Real
A fairly common winter visitor to the region, when up to 200 may be present. A very small number will remain in summer and there are recent reports of successful breeding.

Black-shouldered Kite *(Elaneus caeruleus)* Elanio Común
In the past, these were fairly scarce but regular winter visitors from central Spain. However, recent successful breeding attempts in the last five years have been made in the Corredor Verde and a few other locations, with the families remaining throughout the summer. This now appears to have resulted in the formation of a resident population and I now class them as locally common. During my tours, we regularly see up to 15 individuals in a day, making Doñana one of the easiest and most reliable places in Spain to see this species.

Short-toed Eagle *(Circaetus gallicus)* Culebrera Europeo
Fairly common summer visitor with perhaps 100 pairs breeding. They are usually present from March to October, but a few individuals regularly remain throughout the winter. Often referred to as the Snake Eagle.

Egyptian Vulture   *(Neophron percnopterus)*   Alimoche Común
A fairly scarce species in the region. Usually recorded during the passage periods and throughout the summer, although a few individuals regularly spend the winter here.

Cinereous Vulture   *(Aegypius monachus)*   Buitre Negro
A scarce species in the Doñana region, although they are occasionally seen during passage periods, feeding on carrion in the marshes with flocks of Griffon Vultures. Also known as the Black or Monk Vulture.

Griffon Vulture   *(Gyps fulvus)*   Buitre Leonardo
A fairly common resident species in the surrounding hills. Often seen at carrion sites in the marshes.

Eurasian Marsh Harrier *(Circus aeruginosus)*   Aguilucho Lagunero
A fairly common resident species with up to 100 breeding pairs throughout the region. Numbers greatly increase with northern visitors in the winter, when up to 1,000 individuals may be present.

Hen Harrier   *(Circus cyaneus)*   Aguilucho Pálido
A fairly common winter visitor between October and March, when up to 200 individuals are present. Very scarce in the summer, although occasional sightings are made.

Montagu's Harrier   *(Circus pygargus)*   Aguilucho Cenizo
A fairly common summer visitor with up to 300 pairs breeding throughout the region. It is usually present from March to October and its arrival/departure times often overlap with the wintering Hen Harriers

Eurasian Sparrowhawk   *(Accipiter nisus)*   Gavilán Común
A fairly scarce resident species. Numbers increase during the migration periods and in the winter, when many birds from northern Europe arrive to spend the winter here.

Northern Goshawk   *(Accipiter gentilis)*   Azor Común
A scarce resident species of forest habitats, with probably no more than about 20 breeding pairs.

Common Buzzard   *(Buteo buteo)*   Busardo Ratonero
A fairly common resident species with up to 200 breeding pairs. Winter visitors from the north greatly increase the numbers. The resident birds are subspecies *B.b.vulpinus*.

European Honey Buzzard   *(Pernis apivorus)*   Abejero Europeo
A scarce passage migrant. Occasional sightings are recorded in late April-early May and in late August to mid-September, but usually only of single birds or small passing flocks.

Bonelli's Eagle   *(Aquila fasciatus)*   Águila-azor Perdicera
Extremely scarce in the Doñana region, being a hill/mountain bird, although there are occasional sightings of mainly juvenile birds as they disperse from their breeding areas.

Booted Eagle   *(Aquila pennata)*   Aguililla Calzada
A common summer visitor with up to 250 breeding pairs. Present from March to October, but significant numbers remain throughout the winter. Both light and dark morph birds are usually present.

Golden Eagle   *(Aquila chrysaetos)*   Águila Real
A very scarce resident species. There are occasional reported sightings in the area. The local birds are of the subspecies *A.c.homeyeri*.

Spanish Imperial Eagle   *(Aquila adalberti)*   Águila Imperial Ibérica
A scarce resident species of about 8 breeding pairs, all but one of which, nest within the National Park boundaries. It features high on most birders' lists, but they can be hard to find as they seldom stray outside the boundaries of the park.

Peregrine Falcon   *(Falco peregrinus)*   Halcón Peregrino
A fairly scarce resident population of the subspecies *F p brookei*. Migrants from the north increase the numbers in the winter.

Eurasian Hobby   *(Falco subbuteo)*   Alcotán Europeo
A very scarce summer visitor, usually between April and October. It is estimated that up to 15 pairs may breed in the region.

Merlin   *(Falco columbarius)*   Esmerejón
Usually present in small numbers in marshland habitats between October and March. Most are of subspecies *F.c.aesalon or F.c.subaesalon*.

Common Kestrel   *(Falco tinnunculus)*   Cernícalo Vulgar
A very common resident species throughout the region. Migrants from the north greatly increase the numbers in the winter.

Lesser Kestrel   *(Falco naumanni)*   Cernícalo Primilla
A fairly common summer visitor. They are communal breeders, usually using old buildings in cities, towns and villages, such as the castle at Niebla and the cathedral in Sevilla, where over 30 nesting pairs can be found at each location. The overall numbers throughout the region could be as high as 700 breeding pairs. The largest numbers are present from late February to September, although a small number regularly remain throughout the winter.

Red-legged Partridge   *(Alectoris rufa)*   Perdiz Roja
A very common resident species that can be found in suitable dry areas throughout the region. As a "game" bird, it suffers greatly from hunting and therefore is rather shy in its behaviour.

Common Quail   *(Coturnix coturnix)*   Codorniz Común
A very common passage migrant and summer visitor but, as ever, hard to see unless flushed from cover.

Corn Crake   *(Crex crex)*   Guion de Codornices
A very scarce passage migrant. Occasional reported sightings during the passage periods.

Spotted Crake   *(Porzana porzana)*   Polluela Pintoja
A fairly scarce passage migrant and summer visitor. Small numbers breed in the Doñana marshes. A few remain throughout winter.

Little Crake   *(Porzano parva)*   Polluela Bastarda
There is thought to be a small resident breeding population existing in the Doñana region, although they are more often seen on passage during February - May and October/November.

Water Rail   *(Rallus aquaticus)*   Rascón Europeo
An elusive resident species that is probably more common than it seems. The breeding population could be as high as 500 pairs.

Common Moorhen   *(Gallinula chloropus)*   Gallineta Común
A very common resident with as many as 10,000 breeding pairs.

Purple Swamp-hen   *(Porphyrio porphyrio)*   Calamón Común
A very common resident species with up to 5,000 pairs that breed in reedbeds and ricefields. They are sometimes observed in 100's, feeding in the recently harvested ricefields of Isla Mayor and the Brazo del Este

regions. It is estimated that the winter population could be as high as 15,000 birds.

Common Coot *(Fulica atra)* Focha Común
A very common resident species. Numbers greatly increase during the winter, sometimes with congregations of thousands of individuals.

Red-knobbed Coot *(Fulica cristata)* Focha Moruna
There is a very small resident population whose numbers increase during the breeding season, when as many as 50 pairs may be present. They are far more approachable than Common Coots which, in the past, resulted in them being slaughtered by local hunters in this region, who, until recently, still shot and ate coots. Many captive-bred birds have been released into the wild as part of a re-populating programme. These birds have been fitted with numbered white PVC neck-collars as a means of deterring hunters from shooting them and for identifying and monitoring the individuals.

Common Crane *(Grus grus)* Grulla Común
A common winter visitor to the region, usually between October and March, with up to 3,500 individuals being present in favourable years.

Little Bustard *(Tetrax tetrax)* Sisón Común
A fairly scarce resident population. Occasionally, small groups of up to 20 birds are reported from around the region, especially during the spring and autumn migration periods.

Great Bustard *(Otis tarda)* Avutarda Común
Very scarce (rare) in the region but occasional sightings are reported from the Cádiz side of the Río Guadalquivir, from the Andévalo plains to the north of Huelva and from the plains to the west of Sevilla. A single male was recorded by four clients and I near the Bar La Pará (Villamanrique) in October 2005.

Oystercatcher *(Haematopus ostralagus)* Ostrero Euroasiático
A fairly common wintering species seen along most coasts. Small numbers remain throughout the year at the Marismas del Odiel and at the Salinas de Bonanza.

Black-winged Stilt *(Himantopus himantopus)* Cigüeñuela
A very common resident species with up to 5,000 breeding pairs through-

out the region. Large flocks, sometimes of 1,000's, can be observed in the winter.

Pied Avocet　　　　　*(Recurvirostra avosetta)*　　　　Avoceta Común
A common resident species with up to 2,000 breeding pairs in favorable years. Numbers increase during winter periods, when up to 8,000 birds may be present.

Stone Curlew　　　　　*(Burhinus oedicnemus)*　　　　Alcaraván Común
A common resident species with up to 1,000 breeding pairs. Large concentrations of up to 300 birds can be found in the winter.

Collared Pratincole　　　　*(Glareola pratincola)*　　　Canastera Común
A very common summer visitor with up to 3,500 pairs breeding in the marsh areas and on agricultural land. They are usually present from April to October and are often found in large flocks, especially once the young have flown.

Ringed Plover　　　　　*(Charadrius hiaticula)*　　　Chorlitejo Grande
Very common during the winter and passage periods with up to 15,000 birds being present throughout the region. Some remain throughout the summer.

Little Plover　　　　　*(Charadrius dubius)*　　　Chorlitejo Chico
Formerly known as the Little-ringed Plover, it is a fairly common resident with perhaps 200 - 300 breeding pairs throughout the region. It is more common as a winter visitor and passage migrant. The resident subspecies is *C.d.curonicus.*

Kentish Plover　　　*(Charadrius alexandrinus)*　　Chorlitejo Patinegro
A fairly common resident species with up to 1,000 breeding pairs. Winter visitors and passage migrants increase the numbers, when up to 5,000 birds may be present.

Grey Plover　　　　　*(Pluvialis squatarola)*　　　Chorlito Gris
Very common at coastal sites between autumn and spring. Often also found in the Doñana marsh areas. Some non-breeding birds will remain throughout the summer.

European Golden Plover　*(Pluvialis apricaria)*　　Chorlito Dorado
A common winter visitor to the region. Flocks of thousands of birds are often seen in the marshes, on agricultural land areas and the harvested

rice fields. Usually present between October and April.

Northern Lapwing *(Vanellus vanellus)* Avefría Europeo
Very common in the winter when up to 10,000 birds arrive from the north. A small number of breeding pairs, perhaps 100 or so, remain in the summer.

Dunlin *(Calidris alpina)* Correlimos Común
Very common in winter and during passage periods when up to 50,000 birds may be present, both at coastal and inland sites. Small numbers are regularly recorded during the summer.

Curlew Sandpiper *(Calidris ferruginea)* Correlimos Zarapitín
Very common during the spring and autumn passage periods. Small numbers remain throughout the winter, both on the marshes and at coastal sites.

Red Knot *(Calidris canutus)* Correlimos Gordo
A fairly scarce passage migrant with a very small number overwintering at coastal sites and on the inland marshes.

Sanderling *(Calidris alba)* Correlimos Tridáctilo
A very common winter visitor and passage migrant to coastal areas, although it is often recorded in the marshes and ricefields during the winter. A significant number remain in the region during the summer.

Temminck's Stint *(Calidris temminckii)* Correlimos de Temminck
A fairly scarce species, usually seen during the main passage periods between March to May and July to August, although varying numbers regularly overwinter in the region. There are probably many more than is realised as they are easily overlooked amongst the masses of other waders.

Little Stint *(Calidris minuta)* Correlimos Menudo
Very common between September and March, when flocks of thousands of birds can be found in the marshes, in rice fields and at coastal sites.

Purple Sandpiper *(Calidris maritima)* Correlimos Oscuro
A very scarce winter visitor to coastal sites. Prefers rocky shores but occasional individuals are sometimes seen along the espigón at the Marismas del Odiel.

Ruff *(Philomachus pugnax)* Combatiente
Very common on passage and during the winter when up to 40,000 birds may be present. Due to the different migratory times of males, females and juveniles it is possible to find reasonable numbers throughout the year.

Common Snipe *(Gallinago gallinago)* Agachadiza Común
Fairly common during migration periods and in the winter (September - March) when 1,000's may be present. Small numbers have been recorded during the summer and, with the exception of June and July, there are usually some birds present.

Jack Snipe *(Lymnocryptes minimus)* Agachadiza Chica
A scarce passage migrant and winter visitor. It could be that up to 1,000 birds spend the winter here but their secretive behaviour makes a realistic estimate impossible.

Eurasian Woodcock *(Scolopax rusticola)* Chocha Perdiz
A fairly scarce inhabitant of some of the forested areas in the region. Present from October until February/March.

Black-tailed Godwit *(Limosa limosa)* Aguja Colinegra
A very common passage migrant and winter visitor with up to 50,000 birds being present at favourable times. Some remain throughout the year at suitable sites, such as the marshes of the Río Piedras and the Río Odiel.

Bar-tailed Godwit *(Limosa lapponica)* Aguja Colipinta
A fairly common migrant, passing through the region in April/May and August/September. A very small number may remain throughout the winter, especially at the marshes of the Río Odiel and the Río Piedras.

Eurasian Curlew *(Numenius arquata)* Zarapito Real
A fairly common passage migrant during April/May and July/August. Significant numbers will spend the winter here.

Whimbrel *(Numenius phaeopus)* Zarapito Trinador
A fairly common passage migrant during April/May and August/September. Wintering flocks of 500 birds are not unusual, especially at the Marismas del Odiel and the Marismas del Río Piedras. There also appears to be a small resident population of maybe 100 birds.

Spotted Redshank *(Tringa erythropus)* Archibebe Oscuro
A very common passage migrant and winter visitor to both coastal sites and inland marshes. It is estimated that as many as 10,000 individuals may be present during the winter

Common Redshank *(Tringa totanus)* Archibebe Común
A fairly common resident breeding species of perhaps 1,500 pairs. Much more abundant in the winter, when up to 20,000 individuals are present and flocks of up to 200 birds are recorded.

Common Greenshank *(Tringa nebularia)* Archibebe Claro
There is a small resident population but they are very common during the passage periods of April/May and August/September. Up to 5,000 birds overwinter in the Doñana region.

Marsh Sandpiper *(Tringa stagnatillis)* Archibebe Fino
A scarce migrant during March/April and August/September. A few regularly overwinter in the region. Usually seen singularly or in small groups of up to five or six birds.

Wood Sandpiper *(Tringa glareola)* Andarríos Bastardo
A common passage migrant during March/April and August/September, when up to 10,000 could pass through the region. Significant numbers, perhaps as many as 2,000, spend the winter in the region.

Green Sandpiper *(Tringa ochropus)* Andarríos Grande
A common passage migrant and winter visitor, but small numbers remain throughout the year. Wintering numbers are estimated to be as many as 1,000 and although they may be found at coastal sites, they prefer the fresh-water marshes, rice fields and irrigation ditches.

Common Sandpiper *(Actitis hypoleucos)* Andarríos Chico
There is a fairly scarce resident population existing in the region. It is far more common in the winter and during the migration periods in April/May and in August/September.

Ruddy Turnstone *(Arenaria interpres)* Vuelvapiedras Común
A very common passage migrant and winter visitor to many coastal sites, but occasionally seen at inland locations. A small number usually remain during the summer, especially at the Marismas del Odiel and the Marismas del Río Piedras.

Arctic Skua   *(Stercorarius parasiticus)*   Págalo Párasito
Very scarce but may be seen offshore from suitable locations. The Espigón at the Marismas del Odiel offers one of the best viewing points.

Great Skua   *(Stercorarius skua)*   Págalo Grande
Very scarce, but may be seen offshore at any time. although the vast majority of sightings occur between September and March. The Espigón is probably the most appropriate viewing site for this species.

Audouin's Gull   *(Larus audouinii)*   Gaviota de Audouin
Fairly common at coastal sites such as the Marismas del Odiel, Salinas de Bonanza and Salinas de Monte Algaida, where they gather in large flocks. Occasional visitors to inland sites and in 2002 over 250 were seen together in the Isla Cristina (Sevilla) area, some 25 kms from the sea.

Slender-billed Gull   *(Larus genei)*   Gaviota Picofina
A fairly scarce resident with breeding populations at the Marismas del Odiel, Salinas de Monte Algaida, Salinas de Bonanza and Veta la Palma, a large, private fish-farming concern at the southern end of the Isla Mayor that is inaccessible to the public. Small numbers are regularly recorded at sites such as the Lucio del Lobo and in the Isla Mayor rice fields.

Black-headed Gull   *(Larus ridibundus)*   Gaviota Reidora
A fairly common resident species of both coastal and inland sites. During the winter, the numbers can increase to up to 10,000 individuals.

Little Gull   *(Larus minutus)*   Gaviota Enana
A fairly scarce passage migrant and infrequent winter visitor. Usually coastal, but can sometimes be seen inland near some of the larger wet areas of the Doñana marshes.

Mediterrranean Gull *(Larus melanocephalus)*   Gaviota Cabecinegra
A scarce but regular winter visitor to suitable coastal sites such as the Marismas del Odiel. More commonly seen during passage periods in March/April and October/November.

Yellow-legged Gull   *(Larus cachinnans)*   Gaviota Patiamarilla
A very common resident species found at both coastal and inland locations. The usual species found here are *L.c.michahellis* and *L.c.atlantis*.

Lesser Black-backed Gull   *(Larus fuscus)*   Gaviota Sombría
A very common passage migrant and winter visitor. Flocks of thousands can often be found, both at coastal and inland sites. A small number of non-breeders remain in the summer. The two subspecies that are commonly seen are *L.f.graellsii* and *L.f.intercedes*.

Kittiwake   *(Rissa Tridactyla)*   Gaviota Tridáctila
A scarce winter visitor to suitable coastal locations. Occasionally recorded further inland. An even scarcer "red-billed" variety of Kittiwake was recorded by a group of eight clients and I at the Marismas del Odiel on the 24/9/2005.

Caspian Tern   *(Hydroprogne caspia)*   Pagaza Piquiroja
A fairly scarce passage migrant and winter visitor, usually to coastal sites such as the Marismas del Odiel, Marismas de Río Piedras and Salinas de Bonanza.
Small numbers are regularly present at the Marismas del Río Piedras in the winter and occasional summer sightings are reported.

Common Tern   *(Sterna hirundo)*   Charrán Común
A fairly scarce but regular passage migrant and winter visitor along the coast, especially at the Marismas del Odiel.

Little Tern   *(Sterna albifrons)*   Charrancito Común
A very common summer visitor, breeding at both coastal and inland sites. Usually present from April to September, but occasional winter sightings occur. Over 300 pairs nest on open land at the Marismas del Odiel.

Sandwich Tern   *(Sterna sandvicensis)*   Charrán Patinegro
Very common along the coastal strip during the passage periods. Large flocks form at the Marismas del Odiel in winter. Small numbers remain throughout the year.

Gull-billed Tern   *(Sterna nilotica)*   Pagaza Piconegra
A fairly common summer visitor, with up to 1,000 pairs breeding in colonies in suitable marsh habitats. They are usually present from early April until the end of September.

Black Tern   *(Childonias niger)*   Fumarel Común
A fairly common passage migrant and summer visitor. Small numbers breed in the region. They are usually present between April and Sep-

tember, with small numbers regularly recorded as overwintering in the region.

Whiskered Tern   *(Childonias hybridus)*   Fumarel Cariblanco
A very common summer visitor with up to 1,500 pairs breeding throughout the region. Usually present from March until October, although small numbers regularly remain throughout the year.

Razorbill   *(Alca torda)*   Alca Común
Fairly common along any stretch of the coastline and offshore at the Marismas del Odiel during passage periods and in the winter.

Pin-tailed Sandgrouse   *(Pterocles alchata)*   Ganga Ibérica
A fairly common but elusive resident population of perhaps 1,000 birds, living mainly in the drier marsh and agricultural areas. They often form large winter flocks, but they can be difficult to find unless seen flying to or from drinking stations.

Rock Pigeon   *(Columba livia)*   Paloma Bravía
Fairly common throughout the region.

Stock Pigeon   *(Columba oenas)*   Paloma Zurita
A scarce winter visitor that can turn up at almost any type of habitat throughout the region.

Common Wood Pigeon   *(Columba palumbus)*   Paloma Torcaz
A common resident species. Northern visitors increase the numbers in winter, when flocks of thousands can be seen.

Eurasian Collared Dove*(Streptopelia decaocto)*   Tórtola Turca
A common and rapidly increasing resident species. Thousands of birds can be found at La Rábida and the large industrial area to the east of Huelva.

European Turtle Dove   *(Sreptopelia turtur)*   Tórtola Europea
Very common during the passage periods of March/April and August/September. Significant numbers breed in the forested areas of the region. Occasional reports of overwintering birds are recorded.

Rose-ringed Parakeet   *(Psittacula krameri)*   Cotorra de Kramer
A small resident population exists within the region, mainly on the eastern side of the Río Guadalquivir and in the city of Sevilla.

Monk Parakeet   *(Myiopsitta monachus)*   Cotorra Argentina
A small resident population breeding in colonies, very often in cities, such as Sevilla. More widespread than the previous species. Evidence from other areas of Spain show that this species will quickly expand in numbers and will colonize much of the area.

Great Spotted Cuckoo   *(Clamator glandarius)*   Críalo Europeo
A fairly common but seldom seen migratory species that parasitizes both Iberian and Black-billed Magpies. Usually present between January and September. A small number regularly overwinter.

Common Cuckoo   *(Cuculus canorus)*   Cuco Común
A fairly common passage migrant and summer visitor, with up to 500 pairs breeding throughout the region. Usually present from late February until September, but are much more difficult to find after the breeding season, when they stop calling.

Little Owl   *(Athene noctua)*   Mochuelo Europeo
A common resident species which is easily seen during the daytime. Breeds in holes in old trees, especially olives, also in walls and derelict buildings. The local birds are subspecies *A.n.Vidalli.*

Eurasian Scops Owl   *(Otus scops)*   Autillo Europeo
A fairly common but hard to see summer visitor with up to 70 pairs breeding. They are usually present from March to October/November. It is mainly nocturnal and is best detected by its tree frog-like call.

Eagle Owl   *(Bubo bubo)*   Búho Real
A fairly scarce but increasing resident population, estimated at about 30 pairs throughout the region. However, they prefer dense pine forests in hilly areas on the surrounds of the marshland, where they breed. They can occasionally be seen during the daytime, especially if they have young to feed. The local subspecies is *B.b.hispanus.*

Long-eared Owl   *(Asio otus)*   Búho Chico
A fairly scarce resident population of perhaps 40 pairs that breed in mature pine forests, often taking over the old nests of Black Kites. They often form small groups of up to 10 birds in the winter.

Short-eared Owl   *(Asio flammeus)*   Búho Campestre
Fairly common passage migrants and winter visitors. Usually present

from October to March. They are often active during the daytime and may be seen sitting on fence posts or in open fields. In the past, I have had exceptional views of groups of up to 24 birds in one field between the Casa de Huerta Tejada and the Finca los Caracoles.

Tawny Owl *(Strix aluco)* Cárabo Común
A common resident species with up to 300 breeding pairs. They nest in both deciduous and pine forests throughout the region and can also be found in parks and large gardens. The local subspecies is *S.a.sylvatica*.

Barn Owl *(Tyto alba)* Lechuza Común
A common resident species of over 1,000 pairs, nesting in old buildings and forests. Northern visitors of the subspecies *T.a.guttata* increase the numbers in winter, when they can often be found roosting in tamarisk trees.

European Nightjar *(Caprimulgus europaeus)* Chotocabras Europeo
A fairly common migrant, passing through the region in April/May and returning south between September and November. It is highly probable that a few pairs may breed in suitable areas.

Red-necked Nightjar *(Caprimulgus ruficollis)* Chotocabras Cuellirrojo
A common summer visitor throughout most of the region. Can usually be seen flying just before nightfall and in the early morning. They are not normally active during the daytime, unless flushed from roosting places. They are usually present in suitable habitats from March to October. There are a few records of overwintering birds

Alpine Swift *(Apus melba)* Vencejo Real
A fairly scarce passage migrant that passes through the region in March/April and September/October.

Common Swift *(Apus apus)* Vencejo Común
A common passage migrant and summer visitor. Usually present from March to October.

Pallid Swift *(Apus pallidus)* Vencejo Pálido
A very common summer visitor to much of the region. Usually present from March to September.

Common Kingfisher *(Alcedo atthis)* Martín Pescador
A fairly common resident species with up to 200 breeding pairs. Can

be found at almost any wetland area. Northern birds of the *A.a.ispida* subspecies increase the numbers in the winter.

Hoopoe   *(Upupa epops)*   Abubilla
A fairly common resident and an abundant summer visitor. They can often be located by their far carrying "hoop, hoop, hoop" call. Several hundred pairs breed in the Doñana region.

European Bee-eater   *(Merops apiaster)*   Abejaruco Común
A very common summer visitor. Usually present in large flocks from late March until mid-September.

European Roller   *(Coracias garrulous)*   Carraca
A fairly scarce passage migrant and summer visitor. Small numbers pass through the region in April and September, but very few remain in the area, preferring to move further north, especially to the Extremadura region. At least one or two pairs regularly breed at the ancient *"Torre de San Antonio"* near Gerena.

Green Woodpecker   *(Picus viridis)*   Pito Real
A locally common resident species with up to 200 pairs. They can be found in almost any forested area. The birds are of subspecies *P.v.sharpei.*

Great Spotted Woodpecker   *(Dendrocopus major)*   Pico Picapinos
A fairly common resident species of perhaps 300 breeding pairs. Can be found in forests, olive plantations, parks and gardens, but are very difficult to see. The local birds are of the subspecies *D.m.hispanicus.*

Lesser Spotted Woodpecker   *(Dendrocopus minor)*   Pico Menor
A very scarce resident with isolated populations scattered around the region. The birds are of the subspecies *D.m.buturlini.*

Eurasian Wryneck   *(Jynx torquilla)*   Torcecuello
A fairly scarce but regular passage migrant and even scarcer summer visitor, with just a few pairs breeding in the region. Small numbers remain throughout the winter.

Woodlark   *(Lullula arborea)*   Totovía
There is a small resident population of this species, but they are much more abundant in the passage periods and during the winter, when they form into sizeable flocks.

Eurasian Skylark   *(Alauda arvensis)*   Alondra Común
A scarce resident species but very common winter visitor. Usually present in large numbers from September to April, when large flocks often form in the marshes and on agricultural land.

Crested Lark   *(Galerida cristata)*   Cogujada Común
A very common resident species that can be found in any type of habitat throughout the region, although they are more abundant in the drier areas of the marshes. The resident birds are of the *G.c.pallida* subspecies.

Thekla Lark   *(Galerida theklae)*   Cogujada Montesina
A fairly common species that prefer the areas of higher ground in the hills that surround the region. Small numbers can be seen in the marshlands during the winter months, where the temperature is milder and there is a more abundant food supply at lower levels.

Greater Short-toed Lark   *(Calandrella brachydactyla)*   Terrera Común
A very common passage migrant and summer visitor. Present mainly from late March to October. Small numbers have been known to remain in the marsh areas throughout the winter.

Lesser Short-toed Lark   *(Calandrella rufescens)*   Terrera Marismeña
A common resident species that are confined mainly to agricultural land and the drier marsh areas. The subspecies usually present is *C.r.apetzii*, of which there could be up to 10,000 birds.

Calandra Lark   *(Melanocorypha calandra)*   Calandria Común
A very common resident species numbering many thousands of individuals. They prefer agricultural land and the dried edges of the marshes, often forming large flocks during the winter.

Sand Martin   *(Riparia riparia)*   Avión Zapador
A very common passage migrant, summer visitor and breeding species. They are usually present from March to September and a small number regularly remain throughout the winter. Very large flocks form in the Isla Mayor area in August and September (with some flocks being estimated at 30,000 birds) prior to migrating back to Africa.

Eurasian Crag Martin   *(Ptyonoprogne rupestris)*   Avión Roquero
A fairly scarce resident that spends the summer in the hills surrounding the region. They are more commonly seen during the winter when they are to be found at lower levels where food is more plentiful.

Northern House Martin   *(Delichon urbica)*   Avión Común
A very common breeding species and passage migrant. Usually present
in large numbers (perhaps 100,000 individuals) from March to September but a small number regularly overwinter, especially in coastal areas
and around the marsh at El Rocío.

Red-rumped Swallow   *(Hirundo daurica)*   Golondrina Dáurica
A fairly common passage migrant and summer visitor. As many as 1,000
pairs may breed in the region and they are often found near bridges, under which they build their nests. Usually present from February/March
until October. A significant number regularly remain throughout the
winter. The local birds are usually of subspecies *H.d.rufala*.

Barn Swallow   *(Hirundo rustica)*   Golondrina Común
This is a very common summer visitor throughout the region. They are
usually present from February to October, although a few will remain
throughout the winter period.

Tree Pipit   *(Anthus trivialis)*   Bisbita Arbóreo
A fairly common passage migrant, passing through the region between
March and May and returning from August to October when they are often seen in small groups. Some birds will remain throughout the winter
and small numbers may also be seen during the summer.

Meadow Pipit   *(Anthus pratensis)*   Bisbita Común
A very common passage migrant and winter visitor. Usually present from
October to April and can be found throughout the region, sometimes in
flocks numbering several hundred birds.

Water Pipit   *(Anthus spinoletta)*   Bisbita Alpino
A fairly scarce winter visitor that may be present from October until
March. Regularly reported from the northern marsh area and from the
agricultural land of the Isla Mayor.

Tawny Pipit   *(Anthus campestris)*   Bisbita Campestre
A fairly common passage migrant that passes through the region from
March to May and returns from August to mid-October. Usually report-
ed from the dry, open areas of the marshlands.

White Wagtail   *(Motacilla alba)*   Lavandera Blanca
Fairly scarce in the summer but are present in large numbers (up to

30,000) between October and April when they are often seen in very large groups. They are not to be confused with the northern Pied Wagtail, *M.a.yarrellii*, which is a very rare winter visitor.

Grey Wagtail   *(Motacilla cinerea)*   Lavandera Cascadeña
A fairly scarce species, preferring hillier terrain with faster flowing water than is to be found in the flat, open lands of the Doñana region. More often recorded from the marsh areas during the passage periods in March and October.

Yellow Wagtail   *(Motacilla flava)*   Lavandera Boyera
A very common passage migrant and summer visitor. Usually present from February/March to October but small numbers regularly overwinter. Large flocks of 1,000's can sometimes be observed in September, prior to their migration. The common subspecies is *M.f.iberiae* but there are also regular reports of *M.f.thungbergi*, *M.f.flavissima* and *M.f.flava*.

Hedge Accentor   *(Prunella modularis)*   Acentor Común
A scarce winter visitor to the Donana region. Very seldom recorded.

Common Nightingale *(Luscinia megarhynchos)*   Ruiseñor Común
A common passage migrant and summer visitor. Usually present from mid-March to mid-October. During the spring, birds are usually easily seen as they perch and sing to proclaim their territories and to attract a partner. At other times they can be quite secretive and are best detected by their song.

Rufous-tailed Scrub Robin *(Cercotrichas galactotes)*   Alzacola
A fairly scarce summer visitor. Usually present from April to October in their preferred habitats, which include orchards, olive groves, vineyards and prickly pear hedges.

European Robin   *(Erithacus rubecola)*   Petirrojo
A fairly scarce resident population. Common on passage and during the winter, with maximum numbers present between October and March.

Bluethroat   *(Luscinia svecica)*   Pechiazul
A fairly common migrant and winter visitor that is usually present from September to April. The preferred habitat is damp, muddy areas with nearby vegetation for cover. The common subspecies to this region is *L.s.cyanecula*, with the white spot on the throat.

Black Redstart *(Phoenicurus ochrurus)* Colirrojo Tizón
Very scarce in the summer months, preferring the hills and mountainous areas, but are very common on passage and in the winter, when they descend to lower levels where food is more abundant. The resident birds are *P.o.aterrimus* whilst the passage migrants are mostly *P.o.gibraltariensis*.

Common Redstart *(Phoenicurus phoenicurus)* Colirrojo Real
A fairly common passage migrant, usually between March and April and returning south from August to November. Small numbers remain throughout the summer and occasional sightings are recorded during the winter months.

Stonechat *(Saxicola torquata)* Tarabilla Común
A fairly scarce resident breeding population *(S.t.rubicola)* but very common on passage and in the winter when northern birds *(S.t. hibernans)* arrive. Maximum numbers are present from September to March.

Whinchat *(Saxicola rubetra)* Tarabilla Norteña
A fairly common passage migrant, passing through the region from late March to early June and usually returning in September and October, when large numbers are usually observed. Small numbers regularly remain throughout the summer.

Northern Wheatear *(Oenanthe oenanthe)* Collalba Gris
A common passage migrant which passes through the region between March and May and returns from August to October. There are occasional records of birds being seen both in summer and winter.

Black-eared Wheatear *(Oenanthe hispanica)* Collalba Rubia
A fairly common summer visitor but more abundant in the Doñana region during the passage periods. Normally present between March and September.

Black Wheatear *(Oenanthe leucura)* Collalba Negra
A very scarce resident species. Usually found in hilly areas on the edges of the Doñana region.

Rufous-tailed Rock Thrush *(Monticola saxatilis)* Roquero Rojo
A very scarce summer visitor and passage migrant. Occasionally seen on migration during April/May and in September/October.

Blue Rock Thrush   *(Monticola solitarius)*   Roquero Solitario
Very scarce resident in the hilly areas surrounding Doñana, but occasional winter sightings occur at a disused quarry near the Dehesa de Abajo.

Common Blackbird   *(Turdus merula)*   Mirlo Común
A very common resident that can be found throughout the region. Migrants from the north increase the numbers during the winter.

Ring Ouzel   *(Turdus torquatus)*   Mirlo Capiblanco
A scarce passage migrant that is usually recorded in March/April and October/November. There are occasional reports of birds being seen in mid-winter.

Fieldfare   *(Turdus pilaris)*   Zorzal Real
A very scarce irregular winter visitor. Occasional sightings occur between October and February.

Redwing   *(Turdus iliacus)*   Zorzal Alirrojo
A scarce migrant and winter visitor to the region. Occasional sightings occur between October and March.

Song Thrush   *(Turdus philomelos)*   Zorzal Común
A fairly scarce resident species but a common winter visitor, when the largest numbers are present from late September to March.

Mistle Thrush   *(Turdus viscivorus)*   Zorzal Charlo
A fairly scarce resident population. Numbers increase slightly with the arrival of northern birds in the winter.

Grasshopper Warbler   *(Locustella naevia)*   Buscarla Pintoja
A fairly scarce and elusive passage migrant that is occasionally recorded in the marsh areas. The passage periods are from April/May and August to mid-October.

Savi's Warbler   *(Locustella luscinioides)*   Buscarla Unicolor
A fairly common summer visitor that is easily overlooked. Best detected by listening for the monotonous reeling song, often performed from a prominent perch. Up to 1,000 pairs breed in reedbeds throughout the region and are normally present from early April until October.

Eurasian Reed Warbler *(Acrocephalus scirpaceus)*   Carricero Común
A very common summer visitor to suitable sites throughout the region.
Usually arrives from mid-March and departs by mid-October.

Great Reed Warbler *(Acrocephalus arundinaceus)*   Carricero Tordal
A fairly common summer visitor to suitable breeding habitats, usually in large reedbeds in the marsh areas. Easily detected by its loud,
deep, froglike call. Normally present from mid March until mid-October.

Moustached Warbler *(Acrocephalus melanopogon)*   Carricerín Real
 Small numbers of migratory birds pass through the region in April/May
and return in September/October. Occasional reports of both summer
and winter sightings which may point to a very small resident population.

Aquatic Warbler   *(Acrocephalus paludicola)*   Carricerín Cejudo
A very scarce but regular passage migrant. Occasionally recorded during passage periods in April/May and September/October.

Sedge Warbler *(Acrocephalus schoenobaenus)*   Carricerín Común
A common passage migrant that passes through the region in March to
May and returns from August to October.

Cetti's Warbler   *(Cettia cetti)*   Ruiseñor Bastardo
A common resident species throughout the region. Numbers are increased from September to March by migrant birds, when small numbers of birds often join together. Nearly always found along the densely
vegetated margins of streams and rivers.

Zitting Cisticola   *(Cisticola juncidis)*   Buitrón
A fairly common resident species, although a variable number may migrate to and from Africa each winter. The exceptionally cold winter/
spring of 2005 killed off up to 90% of the local resident population,
although the breeding seasons of 2005 and 2006 has helped to restore
their numbers.

Eastern Olivaceous Warbler *(Hippolais pallida)*   Zarcero Pálido
A fairly common passage migrant and summer visitor. The local subspecies is *H.p.opaca* and is usually present from April until late September.

Melodious Warbler (*Hippolais polyglotta*) Zarcero Común
A fairly common passage migrant and summer visitor which is usually present from April to early October. Perches openly and sings continuously from the tops of small trees.

Icterine Warbler (*Hippolais icterina*) Zarcero Icterino
A scarce migrant to the Doñana region, usually seen during the passage period in April and May.

Garden Warbler (*Sylvia borin*) Curruca Mosquitera
A fairly common passage migrant that crosses the region in March to May and returns from August to late October.

Common Whitethroat (*Sylvia communis*) Curruca Zarcera
A fairly scarce passage migrant and even scarcer summer visitor, although there are breeding records from the region. Passage occurs between April and May with the return journey to Africa taking place between August and October.

Blackcap (*Sylvia atricapilla*) Curruca Capirotada
A fairly common resident population, mainly of subspecies *S.a.heineken*. Numbers increase greatly during the passage periods and in the winter.

Sardinian Warbler (*Sylvia melanocephala*) Curruca Cabecinegra
A fairly common resident species which can be found throughout the region in all types of habitat. Best detected by the distinct chattering call. Along with the Zitting Cisticola, numbers of this species were badly depleted by the cold winter of 2005.

Orphean Warbler (*Sylvia hortensis*) Curruca Mirlona
A scarce summer visitor to open woodlands in the region. Usually present between April and September.

Dartford Warbler (*Sylvia undata*) Curruca Rabilarga
A fairly common resident of heathland and gorse areas. Migrant birds increase the numbers in the breeding season. Passage periods are normally in March and October.

Spectacled Warbler (*Sylvia conspicillata*) Curruca Tomillera
A fairly scarce resident population exists in the northern marshes and perhaps in a few other areas. They are often to be found in salicornia along the sides of the sparsely vegetated tracks in the marsh areas.

Numbers increase slightly with the arrival of passage migrants and summer visitors. Passage occurs in March/April and from August to October.

Subalpine Warbler　　　*(Sylvia cantillans)*　Curruca Carrasqueña
A fairly scarce summer breeding visitor but abundant during the passage period of March/April and September/October.

Western Bonelli's Warbler *(Phylloscopus bonelli)* Mosquitero Papialbo
Very scarce breeding species in Doñana but fairly common in the surrounding forested hills and mountains. Passage occurs during March to May and the birds return to Africa from July to September.

Wood Warbler　　　*(Phylloscopus sibilatrix)*　Mosquitero Silbador
A fairly scarce passage migrant that is occasionally recorded during the spring migration, usually during April and May.

Common Chiffchaff　*(Phylloscopus collybita)*　Mosquitero Común
A very common passage migrant and winter visitor to the region. Usually present from September to April, with the maximum numbers present between October and February.

Iberian Chiffchaff　　*(Phylloscopus ibericus)*　Mosquitero Ibérico
A fairly scarce resident population that may be found in the surrounding forests. Best detected by their monotonous, monosyllabic "chiff, chiff, chiff" call.

Willow Warbler　　　*(Phylloscopus trochilus)*　Mosquitero Musical
Very common on migration, passing through the area from March to May and returning from July to October. Small numbers remain throughout the year.

Firecrest　　　　　*(Regulus ignicapillus)*　Reyezuelo Listado
A fairly scarce resident of both deciduous and pine forests throughout the region, although it is more common as a passage migrant winter visitor.

Spotted Flycatcher　　*(Muscicapa striata)*　Papamoscas Gris
A fairly common passage migrant and summer visitor. Usually present in a wide variety of habitats throughout the region from April until October.

Pied Flycatcher *(Ficedula hypoleuca)* Papamoscas Cerrojillo
A fairly common passage migrant that passes through the region in April and May and returns from August to October.

Long-tailed Tit *(Aegithalos caudatus)* Mito
A resident species that is locally common in broadleaved forested areas, very often close to water. They are usually seen in small groups and are of the Spanish race *A.c.irbii.*

Eurasian Penduline Tit *(Remiz pendulinus)* Pájaro Moscón
A fairly scarce resident population almost exclusively associated with dense reedbeds. Migrant birds increase the numbers in the winter when they are often seen in small flocks.

Crested Tit *(Parus cristatus)* Herrerillo Capuchino
A fairly common resident species that is often seen in small groups, usually feeding in the canopies of pine and cork-oak forests.

Coal Tit *(Parus ater)* Carbonero Garrapinos
A very scarce resident that is almost exclusively found in pine forests. A small number of winter visitors helps to increase the numbers between October and March.

Great Tit *(Parus major)* Carbonero Común
A fairly common resident species. Mainly to be found in mixed forests, orchards and olive groves.

Blue Tit *(Parus caeruleus)* Herrerillo Común
A fairly common resident. Winter migrants increase the numbers from October to March.

European Nuthatch *(Sitta europea)* Trepador Azul
A very scarce resident in the Doñana region. Occasional sightings occur, usually in forests at the fringes of the region. The subspecies present is *S.e.hispaniensis.*

Short-toed Treecreeper *(Certhia brachydactyla)* Agateador Común
A fairly common resident of mixed forests throughout the region. Best detected by their distinct call and their feeding habit of climbing one tree and then flying down to the base of the next.

Winter Wren *(Troglodytes troglodytes)* Chochín
A fairly common resident of the *T.t.kabyloram* subspecies. Often found in forests with dense undergrowth and in reedbeds on the edges of lagoons and marshes.

Southern Grey Shrike *(Lanius meridionalis)* Alcaudón Real
A fairly common resident species and an abundant winter visitor throughout the region. Prefers dry, open areas with scattered vegetation. Often seen perched openly on fence posts and telegraph wires . The pinkish coloured breast, the small wing bars and the small white line above the eye mask separate it from the Great Grey Shrike, which is a very scarce bird here.

Woodchat Shrike *(Lanius senator)* Alcaudón Común
A common passage migrant and summer visitor throughout the region. Usually present from March to October. Prefers open habitats but can also be found in forests, orchards and olive groves. Occasional winter sightings are recorded.

Eurasian Jay *(Garrulus glandarius)* Arrendajo Común
A fairly common resident species that is almost exclusively confined to forested areas.

Black-billed Magpie *(Pica pica)* Urraca
Very common in certain areas of the region but scarce in others. Often found in fairly large flocks during the winter.

Iberian Azure-winged Magpie *(Cyanopica cooki)* Rabilargo
Referred to in this book as the Iberian Magpie. It is a very common resident found throughout the region and is more often seen in large family groups of up to 100 birds. Until recently it was referred to as the Azure-winged Magpie (*Cyanopica cyana*) but has now been split from the only other population in SE Asia, which retains the nominate name.

Eurasian Jackdaw *(Corvus monedula)* Grajilla
A locally common resident usually found in large flocks. Up to 200 birds inhabit the area around the Dehesa de Abajo.

Common Raven *(Corvus corax)* Cuervo
A fairly common resident species throughout the region. Large flocks of up to 150 individuals often form during the winter, roosting communally in forests. They can usually be seen at carrion sites, where vultures,

eagles and kites may be feeding.

Eurasian Golden Oriole   *(Oriolus oriolus)*   Oropéndola
A fairly common summer visitor to the region. Usually present from April until September. Prefers broadleaved wooded areas close to rivers or other water. Although brightly coloured, they can sometimes be very hard to see as they tend to perch deep inside the foliage of trees.

Common Starling   *(Sturnus vulgaris)*   Estornino Pinto
A fairly common winter visitor from central and northern Europe. Often found in large mixed flocks with Spotless Starlings in the open areas of the marshes and on agricultural land.

Spotless Starling   *(Sturnus unicolor)*   Estornino Negro
A very common resident throughout the region. Flocks of thousands of birds may be seen during the winter, often joining with the wintering Common Starlings.

Rock Sparrow   *(Petronia petronia)*   Gorrión Chillón
Although a resident species in areas surrounding Doñana, it is an infrequent breeder here. However, a few birds are occasionally found along the Corredor Verde and in the northern marshes during the winter.

Spanish Sparrow   *(Passer hispaniolensis)*   Gorrión Moruno
A fairly common but localized resident that breeds in colonies in selected areas. A copse of eucalyptus trees at the Dehesa de Pilas is a favoured site, with up to 250 pairs breeding there each year. They are often seen in large flocks in the marshes and on agricultural land during the winter.

House Sparrow   *(Passer domesticus)*   Gorrión Común
A very common resident species found in all types of habitat throughout the region. They often form large winter flocks, sometimes mixing with Tree and Spanish Sparrows.

Eurasian Tree Sparrow   *(Passer montanus)*   Gorrión Molinero
A common resident species. Often found in both broadleaved and pine forests, where nest boxes have been sited to encourage their breeding.

Golden Bishop   *(Euplectes afer)*   Tejedor Dorado
Also known as Yellow-crowned Bishop. There are numerous resident colonies of this exotic species throughout the region, mainly in reedbeds

and the rice producing areas of Isla Mayor and Brazo del Este. They breed between August and October. It is a possibility that the numbers exceed 1,000 birds altogether. At the present time this is a category E bird.

Red Bishop   *(Euplectes orix)*   Tejedor Rojo
There are regular reports of a resident colony of up to 25 pairs of this exotic species breeding in rice fields and reedbeds near the Río Guadaira, close to the Brazo del Este. Also a category E bird.

Common Waxbill   *(Estrilda astrild)*   Pico de Coral Senegales
Numerous resident breeding colonies of this exotic species can be found at certain locations, such as the rice fields and reedbeds of Isla Mayor, Brazo del Este, Isla de los Olivillos and perhaps other sites. The number could be as many as 1,000 birds overall.

Black-rumped Waxbill   *(Estrilda trogloditas)* Pico de Coral Culinegro
Another exotic species with numerous resident breeding colonies within the region. Habitats and locations are similar to those reported above. Overall numbers could be in the 100's. Classed as category E by the SEO.

Avadavat   *(Amandava amandava)*   Bengali Rojo
Very small resident population exists near the Isla de los Olivillos/Brazo del Este area and at the site I refer to as "the reedbeds". Probably no more than 30 birds in all. Also known as the Red Munia.

Brambling   *(Fringilla montifringilla)*   Pinzón Real
A very scarce irregular winter visitor to the region, usually found in forested areas between October and March.

Chaffinch   *(Fringilla coelebs)*   Pinzón Vulgar
A very common resident and passage migrant. Usually found in most forested areas.

European Serin   *(Serinus serinus)*   Verdicillo
A fairly common resident species and very common migrant and winter visitor. Maximum numbers are present from October to March, when large flocks are often seen. Frequently found in mixed flocks with other finches.

Common Linnet   *(Carduelis cannabina)*   Pardillo Común
A fairly common resident species throughout the region. Numbers in-

crease greatly with the arrival of northern visitors during the winter, when they are often seen in quite large flocks.

Eurasian Siskin *(Carduelis spinus)* Lúgano
A fairly scarce but regular winter visitor to the region. Usually present from October until April and the numbers vary greatly from year to year, depending on climatic conditions in the north of Europe.

European Goldfinch *(Carduelis carduelis)* Jilguero
A very common resident throughout the region. The resident subspecies is *C.c.Parva*, but this is joined by large numbers of the nominate species which migrate from northern and eastern Europe in the winter.

European Greenfinch *(Carduelis chloris)* Verderón Común
A very common resident species and, as with the Goldfinch, the winter numbers are greatly increased by migrant visitors. The resident population is of the subspecies *C.c.aurantiiventris*.

Common Bullfinch *(Pyrrhula pyrrhula)* Camachuelo Común
A very scarce winter visitor to the region. Occasionally recorded between October and April.

Hawfinch *(Coccothraustes coccothraustes)* Picogordo
A scarce resident species which is regularly joined by small numbers of migrants from northern Europe in the winter. Most commonly found in or near fruit orchards or in forests.

Common Crossbill *(Loxia curvirostra)* Piquituerto Común
A scarce resident of the hills and mountains surrounding Doñana. Occasionally seen in pine forests in the area during the winter.

Corn Bunting *(Miliaria calandra)* Triguero
A fairly common resident species but very common between October and April when very large wintering flocks, sometimes of several thousand, form in the marshes and on agricultural land.

Rock Bunting *(Emberiza cia)* Escribano Montesino
A fairly common resident species in the hills and mountins outside the Doñana region. Occasional sightings do occur during the migration periods and in the winter.

Cirl Bunting *(Emberiza cirlus)* Escribano Soteño
A fairly scarce resident and migrant species. Can be found in most types of habitat but prefers dry agricultural land and open areas with scattered trees.

Ortolan Bunting *(Emberiza hortulana)* Escribano Hortelano
A scarce passage migrant that is usually recorded during passage periods in April/May and September/October.

Reed Bunting *(Emberiza schoeniclus)* Escribano Palustre
A fairly common winter visitor from northern Europe. Usually present between September and April when they can be found at many of the reedbeds throughout the region.

Following changes announced by the by the British Ornithologists' Union, the Latin name of some birds have been updated. As these changes may not be in your current field guides, which will probably not be updated for a few years, I have kept the original Latin names above, but, for completeness, I have added the new names below.

Little Tern *(Sternula albifrons)*
Gull-billed Tern *(Gelochelidon nilotica)*
Caspian Tern *(Hydroprogne caspia)*
Whiskered Tern *(Childonias hybrida)*
House Martin *(Delichon urbicum)*
Red-rumped Swallow *(Cecropis daurica)*
Blue Tit *(Cyanistes caeruleus)*
Crested Tit *(Lophophranes cristatus)*
Coal Tit *(Periparus ater)*

Rare Birds List

This section deals with the rare birds that have been recorded in the Doñana region since 1990. All of these records have been ratified by the Spanish Rarities Committee, or are currently under consideration by them.

The geographical location of Doñana and its close proximity to the Atlantic Ocean, the African continent and the main migration routes between Africa and Europe means that the region is perfectly placed to receive both overshooting migrants and storm-blown vagrants and new birds are being added to the Spanish bird list every year.

Birdwatching in Spain is still very much in its infancy compared to some countries and many birders here tend not to report their sightings with the same enthusiasm that birders in Britain and some other European countries do. However, things are changing and there is an excellent website, "Rare Birds in Spain, run by Ricard Gutierrez, who is currently a member of the Spanish Rarities Committee (RC/SEO), which gives all the latest reports and sightings. His website is www.rarebirdspain.com

There is no doubt that many Spanish rarities have gone unreported in the past. This may be due to the fact that rarities have been seen by people on holiday in Spain and they have not known who to report their sightings to, so have returned home taking that knowledge with them. If you should be fortunate enough to discover a rare bird in this region, or indeed, anywhere else in Spain, I strongly advise you to submit a report to the Spanish Rarities Committee.

Any reports can be made in English and should give as full a description of the bird as possible. A sketch of the bird would be of assistance as would a size comparison with another species. The time, date, location, habitat, and any weather conditions will all help the committee in their deliberations. The use of any field aids, such as binoculars, telescopes, books etc, should also be stated. In all cases your reports should be sent to:

Dr. Eduardo de Juanar.
Comité de Rarezas de SEO.
Dept. de Biologia, Animal 1.
Univ. Complutense.
E-28040 Madrid.

You can now also submit rarity reports by e-mail to www.rarezas@ seo.org.

Obviously there are many earlier records than those listed below, but I do not think they are relevant in the context of this book.

Red-throated Diver   *(Gavia stellata)*   Colimbo Chico
A single bird was discovered and positively identified by 3 clients and I at the Marismas de Río Piedras on the 15/2/07.

Great Northern Diver   *(Gavia immer)*   Colimbo Grande
There is a record of a single bird being recorded at the Marismas del Odiel on 24/12/2000.

Slavonian Grebe   *(Podiceps auritis)*   Zampullín Cuellirrojo
One record from an unspecified location from 15/1/1990. A group of three birds was recorded at the Estero de Domingo Rubio on 15/9/98.

Bulwer's Petrel   *(Bulweria bulwerii)*   Petrel de Bulwer
A single bird was recorded at the Marismas del Odiel on 7/6/2000. This was the first record for Spain.

Leach's Storm Petrel *(Oceanodroma leucorrhoea)*   Paíno Boreal
Five birds were reported from the Marismas del Odiel area on the 24/12/2002. Two others, probably from the same group, were reported from nearby Punta Umbría six days later.

Great White Pelican   *(Pelecanus onocrotalus)*   Pelícano Común
At least three birds have been resident in the Doñana region since 1999. They are regularly recorded in the northern marshes area and at Veta la Palma and the latest number is estimated at seven.

Pink-backed Pelican   *(Pelecanus rufescens)*   Pelícano Rosado
One was recorded in the Doñana region in December 1997 and another was sighted at the Embalse de Celamín (Cádiz) on the 3rd of April 2001.

Western Reef Heron   *(Egretta gularis)*   Garceta Dimorfa
There have been countless records of individual birds over the last few years, mainly from the northern marshes area, the Brazo del Este and the Isla Mayor.
I have personally recorded 5 different individuals of the *E.g.gularis* sub-species in Doñana. There are also a number of hybrid birds *(E.g.garzetta)* in the region. They all now appear to be resident and are most likely breeding.

African Spoonbill   *(Platalea alba)*   Espátula Africana
Recorded at Brazo de la Torre on 1/8/1997 and the Marismas del Odiel and Doñana marshes in 1999. Another bird, which was first recorded by two clients and I, was present at the Cortijo de los Olivillos for four days from the 6/10/2002 and at Brazo del Este on the 14/12/2002 and 8/3/2003. This bird has been ratified and accepted as the 7th record for Spain. It is still being recorded in the region, the latest sightings being in June and July 2005 and in June 2006.

Sacred Ibis   *(Threskiornis aethiopicus)*   Ibis Sagrado
There are numerous reports of a single bird being in the Doñana region in the summer of 1995. A bird was seen on the 8/8/1997 and 15/8/1997 at Brazo del Este. There are also two reports, of probably the same bird, from Brazo del Este and the Isla de los Olivillos on the 8-9/7/1999. Another bird was seen at the Los Olivillos area from 21-27/8/2003.

Yellow-billed Stork   *(Mycteria ibis)*   Tántalo Africano
There are only two accepted records for this species in Doñana. Both were originally discovered by me and have since been ratified by the Iberian Rarities Committee as only the 3rd and 4th Spanish records. The first of these was found at Brazo del Este on 22/10/2002. The second was recorded near the Casa de Bombas on 7/5/2003. Since then there have been many other sightings of these birds. A group of 6 clients and I had the pleasure of seeing both birds in one day.

Marabou   *(Leptoptilos crumeniferus)*   Marabú Africano
Confirmed records from Veta la Palma on the 24/10/2000, Brazo del Este in Feb/March 2001, El Rocío on 3/5/2001, Lucio del Lobo on 22/6/2001 and the Dos Hermanas area on 21/08/2002. A bird discovered by two clients and I remained at the Caño de Guadiamar between 5-29/6/2004.

Saddle-billed Stork *(Ephippiorhynchus senegalensis)* Jabirú Africano
A single bird, of unknown origin but suspected of being an escape, was seen many times and photographed in the Doñana region between September 2003 and January 2004.

Lesser Flamingo *(Phoenicopterus minor)* Flamenco Enano
Single birds have been recorded at Veta la Palma on 15/5/1994, the "JAV" in the winter of 2001, Laguna de Calderón Grande, La Lantijuela on 1/12/2002, the Caño de Guadiamar on the 12/6/2004, La Rocina on the 19/01/2006 and at the Marismas del Odiel on the 18/02/2006.

Mute Swan *(Cygnus olor)* Cisne Vulgar
There are numerous winter records of this species from around the region, although two birds were regularly recorded by numerous groups of clients and I at the Cañada de Rianzuela for almost six weeks in May and June 2005. Another bird was discovered by two clients and I in the Isla Mayor ricefields on the 16th of September 2006.

Black Swan *(Cygnus atratus)* Cisne Negro
A single bird was recorded at Veta la Palma on the 25/10/2001. A more recent sighting was recorded by two clients and I at the Lucio del Lobo in February 2004.

Bean Goose *(Anser fabalis)* Ansar Campestre
Records of single birds exist from Hato Ratón on 24/11/1994 , the Marismas de Hinojos on 4/2/2000, the Entremuros on 15/1/2002 , Isla Mayor on 13/1/2002 and from the northern marsh area on the 7/1/2006.

Pink-footed Goose *(Anser brachyrhynchus)* Ansar Piquicorto
Suspected of being a regular winter visitor to the region, but so far there has only been one confirmed record, from near the JAV on 2/12/1996.

Lesser White-fronted Goose *(Anser erythropus)* Ansar Chico
Numerous winter records exist for this species, mostly from the northern marsh areas. It is estimated that as many as 20 birds may be present each winter, usually amongst very large numbers of Greylags, making them very hard to find and identify.

Bar-headed Goose *(Anser indicus)* Ansar Indio
Records exist of single birds at El Rocío marshes on 23/10/1993, at Hato Ratón on 24/11/1994, at Veta la Palma on 11/11/1999 and at the Entremuros on 5/12/2001.

Snow Goose   *(Anser caerulescens)*   Ansar Nival
Two birds were recorded at the Entremuros on 16-17/2/1992 and two others near the JAV on 14/4/1993.

Canadian Goose   *(Branta canadensis)*   Barnacla Canadiense
There are numerous reports of this species, usually from the marshes area and all during the winter period.

Barnacle Goose   *(Branta leucopsis)*   Barnacla Cariblanca
There are numerous reported sightings of this species. They are generally recorded as being present in very small numbers each winter.

Brent Goose   *(Branta bernicla)*   Barnacla Carinegra
Regular winter sightings of this species are recorded. The latest was of three birds seen by two Finnish clients and I at the Marismas de Río Piedras on the 20/02/2006.

Red-breasted Goose   *(Branta ruficollis)*   Barnacla Cuellirroja
There is an accepted record of a single bird being present at Veta la Palma during the winter of 1995/96.

Egyptian Goose   *(Alopochen aegyptiacus)*   Ganso del Nilo
There was a single bird present at Veta la Palma on 11/11/1999. Two were regularly recorded at Laguna El Portil by numerous other birders and I during May, June, July and September 2005.

Ruddy Shelduck   *(Tadorna ferruginea)*   Tarro Canelo
A regular winter visitor to the Marismas and ricefields, usually found amongst flocks of Greylags, but only in very small numbers.

American Wigeon   *(Anas americana)*   Silbón Americano
One record of a single bird at the Entremuros on 25/3/1997.

Blue-winged Teal   *(Anas discors)*   Cerceta Aliazul
Records of single birds from the Brazo del Este on 2/4/1994, from Veta la Palma on 20/2/2002 and from the Caño de Guadiamar on 11/6/2003.

Ring-necked Duck   *(Aythya collaris)*   Porrón de Collar
A single bird was present at Veta la Palma during the winter of 1999/2000. This could be the same bird that was at Laguna Tarelo for over two weeks between late March/April 2000. A single male was

discovered by two clients and I on the 4/5/2003 at the José Antonio Valverde Centre.

Greater Scaup   *(Aythya marila)*   Porrón Bastardo
A single bird (male) was recorded at the Laguna El Portil on 26/1/1999 and 16/2/1999.

Long-tailed Duck   *(Clangula hyemalis)*   Pato Havelda
One was recorded at the Marismas del Río Piedras in October/November 1993. A winter-plumaged female was present on the El Acebuche lagoon in December 2005 and January 2006.

Goosander   *(Mergus merganser)*   Serreta Grande
A group of three birds were recorded from the Espigón, Marismas del Odiel on 16/2/2001.

Rüppell's Vulture   *(Gyps rüpellii)*   Buitre Moteado
A single bird was recorded at Veta la Palma on 3-4/11/1999.

Rough-legged Buzzard   *(Buteo lagopus)*   Busardo Calzado
One was positively identified by a Finnish client and I as it flew over the Entremuros and the Corredor Verde on the 3/11/2005. If this record is accepted by the Rarities Committee it will be the first for Doñana and only the sixth for Spain.

Long-legged Buzzard   *(Buteo rufinus)*   Busardo Moro
Recent records include two birds at the Isla Menor on 2/3/2000 and single birds at La Lantejuela on the 7/1/2001 and 25/12/2001. A single bird was seen at El Rocío on 7/5/2001 and another was identified by several other birders and I at the Lucio del Lobo during February 2005. More recently, a juvenile bird was recorded by two clients and I at the Entremuros on the 14/3/2007.

Spotted Eagle   *(Aquila clanga)*   Águila Moteado
Records exist of single birds being seen over the Coto del Rey on 2/12/1996, at Hato Ratón on 4/2/1997, over Doñana park on 24/2/1999, at the Lucio del Lobo on 25/11/2000, Entremuros on 8/12/2001 and 10/1/2002, over the national park on 7/12/2002 and near the "JAV" on 31/12/2002. More recently, I recorded one that was at El Rocío marshes for several days during February 2005 and another in the Isla Mayor ricefields on the 13th and 15th of October 2005.

Lesser Spotted Eagle   *(Aquila pomarina)*   Águila Pomerana
There are regular sightings recorded of single birds during the migration periods, usually from the El Rocío marshes. I regularly recorded one that was present at El Rocío between September and December 2004.

Lanner Falcon   *(Falco biarmicus)*   Halcón Borni
A bird was reported from the José Antonio Valverde centre on 15/4/2003 and another was recorded in December 2004, at the Corredor Verde.

Red-footed Falcon   *(Falco vespertinus)*   Cernícalo Patirrojo
There is a fairly recent record of a single bird being seen at an unspecified location in the Guadalquivir marshes on 28/1/2003.

Baillon's Crake   *(Porzana pusilla)*   Polluela Chica
Two birds were reported from Veta la Palma in November 2002. At least three birds were regularly recorded by other birders and I at the "JAV" centre during March, April and May 2005.

Allen´s Gallinule   *(Porphyrio alleni)*   Calamoncillo Africano
One was present at El Rocío marshes during December 2006 and January 2007. It was seen by four clients and I, but later reports suggest it may have been an "escape".

Cream-coloured Courser   *(Cursorius cursor)*   Corredor Sahariano
I can find only one record for this species, that of a single bird being seen at La Algaida on 13/12/1999.

Dotterel   *(Charadrius morinellus)*   Chorlito Carambolo
Records exist of single birds near the "JAV" on 3/6/1996 and 20/3/2000. A group of 7 birds was reported from an unspecified location in the region on 22/4/2003 and a group of 5 was recorded at the Dehesa de Pilas in November 2005.

Sociable Lapwing   *(Vanellus gregarius)*   Chorlito Social
One was found in the Isla Mayor ricefields on the 25/1/2003. The most recent records are of individual birds being seen at the Boca del Lobo, El Rocío, between the 6th and 9th of March 2006, another in the same area between the 4th and 7th of January 2007 and one at the Marismas de Hinojos between the 5th and 19th of April 2007.

Red-necked Stint   *(Calidris ruficollis)*   Playerito de Cuello Rojo
One was recorded amongst a flock of Little Stints by a group of four cli-

ents and I at the Caño de Guadiamar on 21/9/2004. Although the bird was positively identified by all concerned, the Spanish rarities committee decided not to ratify this sighting.

Baird's Sandpiper *(Calidris bairdii)* Correlimos de Baird
A single bird was reported from an unspecified location, probably within the national park, on 22/4/2002.

Pectoral Sandpiper *(Calidris melanotos)* Correlimos Pectoral
One was recorded in the Isla Mayor ricefields on the 4/10/2003 and two more were seen by groups of clients and I at the Entremuros in February 2005 and at the Cantarita ricefields in September 2006.

Broad-billed Sandpiper *(Limicola falcinellus)* Correlimos Falcinelo
There is one accepted record of a bird found by one of my clients, Steve Lister, and seen by other clients and I at the Marismas del Odiel on 6/5/2003.

Short-billed Dowitcher *(Limnodromus griseus)* Agujeta Gris
A single bird was discovered by two clients and I in the Brazo del Este area on the 16/9/2006.

Long-billed Dowitcher *(Limnodromus scolopaceus)* Agujeta Escolopácea
Several sightings of this species have been recorded in the Doñana area, the latest being of a single bird that was regularly recorded by numerous clients and I at the El Rocío marshes over a three-week period in April/May 2005.

Greater Yellowlegs *(Tringa melanoleuca)* Archibebe Patigualdo Grande
There are records from the Entremuros on 15/12/2000 and in the Isla Mayor on the 19/12/2000. Taking into consideration the closeness of the two areas and the dates concerned, it should be assumed that this was probably the same bird.

Lesser Yellowlegs *(Tringa flavipes)* Archibebe Patigualdo Chico
A positive sighting of a single bird was recorded by a client and I at the Caño de Guadiamar on 15/3/2003. Sadly, this record was not accepted by the RC/SEO.

Solitary Sandpiper *(Tringa ochropus)* Andarríos Grande
There is one accepted record from Aznalcázar in September and two

other unconfirmed sightings in the northern marsh area in December 2002 and February 2003.

Terek Sandpiper *(Xenus cinereous)* Andarríos de Terek
One record from Veta la Palma in October 1995 and another from the Entremuros on 23/4/2001.

Grey Phalarope *(Phalaropus fulicarius)* Falaropo Picogrueso
Occasional sightings of this species have been recorded, both from coastal and inland locations, the latest being on the 22nd of December 2006, when two clients and I found one in the Isla Mayor ricefields.

Red-necked Phalarope *(Phalaropus lobatus)* Falaropo Picofino
A group of three birds were seen at the Espigón, Marismas del Odiel, on the 30/12/2000. Two birds were seen at the Salinas de Bonanza on 6/9/2003 and another was reported from there on the 20/5/2004. Single birds were seen at the José Antonio Valverde centre on the 20/5/2004 and at El Rocío on the 27/7/2004. The most recent sighting was by a group of 8 clients and I of a single bird at La Calatilla, Marismas de Odiel on the 3/5/2005.

Wilson's Phalarope *(Phalaropus tricolor)* Falaropo de Wilson
A single bird was recorded at the Marismas del Odiel on the 23/5/1999.

Sabine's Gull *(Larus sabini)* Gaviota de Sabine
A single bird was recorded at Punta Umbría, near Huelva, on 30/12/2000.

Grey-headed Gull *(Larus cirrocephalus)* Gaviota Cabecigris
A single bird was reported from an unspecified location in the region in June 1997.

Laughing Gull *(Larus atricilla)* Gaviota Guanaguanare
One record exists of a single bird seen at the Playa de Doñana on 28/9/2000.

Ring-billed Gull *(Larus delawarensis)* Gaviota de Delaware
There are records from the Marismas del Odiel on 24/12/2000 and the 8/5/2003. Another was recorded by a group of 8 clients and I near the La Calatilla visitors centre, also at the Odiel marshes, on the 23/9/2005.

Great Black-backed Gull   *(Larus marinus)*   Gavion Atlantico
Only one record of a bird being found at the Entremuros in February 1996.

Royal Tern   *(Sterna maxima)*   Charrán Real
There are two records from the Doñana region. The first was off Playa de Doñana in August 1992 and the second was at Marismas del Odiel on 23/7/2000.

Lesser Crested Tern   *(Sterna bengalensis)*   Charrán Bengales
There have been several sightings in recent years. A group of three were recorded at the Marismas del Odiel on 7/7/2005 and a single bird was recorded by 8 clients and I on the 24th of September 2005 on Matalas-cañas beach.

Elegant Tern   *(Sterna elegans)*   Charrán Elegante
Only one record of a bird being seen at the Marismas del Odiel on the 30/10/2006.

Roseate Tern   *(Sterna dougallii)*   Charrán Rosado
A dying bird was found at the Marismas del Odiel on 19/4/2003. One was recorded by Dr Philip Jones and I on 13/10/2003 and another by me in March 2004, both at the Marismas del Odiel. These were only the 4th and 5th records for Spain. A more recent sighting involved two birds at the Marismas del Odiel in July 2005. The latest sighting was made by four clients and I at the Marismas del Odiel on the 15/3/2007.

Forster's Tern   *(Sterna forsteri)*   Charrán de Forster
A bird which was recorded by Dr Philip Jones and I at the Marismas del Odiel on the 13/10/2003 was only the second accepted record of this species in Spain.

White-winged Black Tern *(Childonias leucopterus)* Fumarel Aliblanco
Recorded at Brazo del Este on 29/4/2000, Laguna El Portil on 17/8/2001 and Salinas de Monte Algaida on 6/5/2002. The most recent sighting was at El Rocío marshes on 14/5/2007. Several other unconfirmed sightings exist.

White-winged Lark   *(Melanocorypha yeltoniensi)*   Calandria Aliblanco
There is a record of a single bird being seen at Hato Ratón in December 1995.

Dupont's Lark *(Chersophilus Dupont)* Alondra de Dupont
A single bird was recorded at the Brazo del Este on 26/4/2002.

Little Swift *(Apus affinis)* Vencejo Moro
One was recorded at El Acebuche visitors centre on 18/4/1995 and a second bird was reported at nearby Matalascañas on 13/5/1995. There is a strong possibility that both sightings were of the same bird. A bird was seen by several clients and I at the Laguna de Mancho Zurillo on the 20/3/2006 and another was recorded by me at the Casa de Bombas on the 15/6/2006.

Rock Pipit *(Anthus petrosus)* Bisbita Costero
A single bird was recorded at El Rocío in March 1991.

Richard's Pipit *(Anthus richardi)* Bisbita de Richard
There are two records of single birds from Aznalcázar in February 2000. Two birds were recorded together in the northern marshes on 30/12/2001, another record exists from an unspecified location in the Doñana region on 14/12/2002 and two birds were recorded in the Isla Mayor ricefields in January 2003.

Red-throated Pipit *(Anthus cervinus)* Bisbita Gorgirrojo
I can find only one record for this species, that being of a single bird reported from El Rocío on 6/5/2001.

Desert Wheatear *(Oenanthe deserti)* Collalba Desertica
There is only one accepted record of this species for this region, that being of a male that was discovered by two clients and I at the Caño de Guadiamar on 31/8/2002.

Paddyfield Warbler *(Acrocephalus agricola)* Carricero Agricola
Two birds were recorded in the Brazo del Este area on 6/11/1996 and another was seen at La Marmoleja on 25/1/1997.

Lesser Whitethroat *(Sylvia curruca)* Curruca Zarcerilla
A single bird matching the ssp *minula* was recorded by two clients and I at the Dehesa de Abajo on the 22/9/2003. Another of the same ssp was also recorded by me at the Marismas del Odiel on the 30/10/2003.

Pallas´s Leaf Warbler *(Phylloscopus proregulus)* Mosquitero de Pallas
A single bird was recorded by a group of Finnish birders at the El Acebuche visitors centre on the 21/4/2005.

Yellow-browed Warbler *(Phylloscopus inornatus)* Mosquitero Bilistado
Two records from the Doñana region on 1/11/1999 and 5/11/2003.

Red-breasted Flycatcher *(Fidecula parva)* Papamoscas Papirrojo
A single record from Manecorro, El Rocío, on 1/10/1999.

Great Grey Shrike *(Lanius excubitor)* Alcaudón Norteño
Single birds have been recorded at El Acebuche visitors centre on 18/1/2000, the Dehesa de Abajo in April 2004 and again at Dehesa de Abajo in February 2005.

Rosy Starling *(Sturnus roseus)* Estornino Rosado
Two records of this species, from the Vuelta de Arenas near the Casa de Bombas on 8/12/2000 and from the Brazo del Este on 27/7/2002.

Black-headed Weaver *(Ploceus melanocephalus)* Tejedor de Cabeza Negra
A very small breeding population has been recorded at various locations around the Brazo del Este area.

Black-headed Bunting *(Emberiza melanocephala)* Escribano Cabecinegro
There is an accepted record of a single bird that was discovered at the Brazo del Este on 16/5/1999.

ISBN 142512192-6